A BLOOD-BACKED
AGREEMENT
IS THE MOST
POWERFUL DOCUMENT
KNOWN TO MANKIND.

NATIVE PEOPLE HAVE
ALWAYS KNOWN THIS.

IT IS SO ANCIENT,
THEY STILL PRACTICE IT
IN ONE FORM OR ANOTHER.

THE HOLY BIBLE
IS A BOOK OF
BLOOD COVENANTS
RATIFIED IN THE
SINLESS BLOOD OF JESUS.

—KENNETH COPELAND

GOD

THE
COVENANT
AND THE
CONTRADICTION

Kenneth Copeland *and* Greg Stephens

KENNETH COPELAND
PUBLICATIONS

God, the Covenant, and the Contradiction
Accessing God's Promises of Healing, Peace and Provision

ISBN 978-1-60463-508-9   30-0086

28 27 26 25 24 23   6 5 4 3 2 1

© 2023 Kenneth Copeland, Greg Stephens

Kenneth Copeland Publications
Fort Worth, TX 76192-0001

For more information about Kenneth Copeland Ministries, visit kcm.org or call 1-800-600-7395 (U.S. only) or +1-817-852-6000.

DEDICATION

FROM KENNETH...

First, to my wife, Gloria Jean Copeland. On the thirteenth of April 1962, I entered into marriage covenant with her. Her selfless, precious, unconditional love changed my life forever! Her goodness and sweetness to me softened my heart to the place where, on the second day of November 1962, I accepted Jesus as my LORD and Savior.

Second, to Kenneth E. Hagin. The title of the book was inspired by the title of a message he preached that changed our lives forever: *God, a Covenant, and a Contradiction.*

FROM GREG...

First, I must recognize my mother and father (now in heaven), who, when I was a child, always included me in their late-night discussions with guest ministers visiting our home. This fostered a passion in me to discover truth.

Second, to my spiritual fathers, all of whom have directly imparted divine and natural wisdom in different seasons of my life— for which I am humbled and grateful. Thank you, Kenneth Copeland, Kenneth W. Hagin and Kenneth E Hagin. Thank you, Rabbi Joel, for our at-times "fierce discussions," which caused the Word to make sense in a new way as we reasoned together.

Third, to my wife Michelle, who "saw potential" in me and has never wavered in her support.

And finally, to the Greatest Rabbi, the One who is the Covenant Personified, of whom I am Your grateful disciple...Jesus *(Yeshua),* my Savior.

...YOU LIVED IN THIS WORLD
WITHOUT GOD
AND WITHOUT HOPE.

BUT NOW YOU
HAVE BEEN UNITED
WITH CHRIST JESUS.

ONCE YOU WERE
FAR AWAY FROM GOD,

BUT NOW YOU HAVE BEEN
BROUGHT NEAR TO HIM
THROUGH THE BLOOD OF CHRIST.

EPHESIANS 2:12-13,
New Living Translation

TABLE OF CONTENTS

A NOTE TO
THE READER

Throughout this book, you will notice several unconventional upper and lowercase words. These are the result of instruction over the years Brother Copeland has received from The LORD. Words consistently in all capital letters include *BLESS* in any form *(BLESSING, THE BLESSING, BLESSED)*. Also capitalized are *The LORD, The WORD, God's WORD, His WORD.*

Other uppercase words include *Friend,* as in "Friend of God." It is a covenant term also capitalized in the *King James* and *New King James Versions* of the Bible, specifically in James 2:23. *Covenant* is also capitalized where it refers to the nature of God's absolute holy and eternal Covenant with His people.

Finally, *satan* is lowercased throughout the book and in anything Brother Copeland writes. He refuses to capitalize the name, first, because in Hebrew it merely means "an adversary" and is not the actual name given to that fallen being. Second, in awful combat in the pit of hell, Jesus paralyzed and completely brought him to nought, taking from him the keys of hell and death (Colossians 2:15; Revelation 1:18).

INTRODUCTION

Wherefore remember, that ye being in time past Gentiles in the flesh, who are called Uncircumcision by that which is called the Circumcision in the flesh made by hands; that at that time ye were without Christ, being aliens from the commonwealth of Israel, and *strangers from the covenants of promise,* having no hope, and without God in the world: but now in Christ Jesus ye who sometimes were far off are made nigh by the blood of Christ.

Ephesians 2:11-13

LET THE RIVERS OF REVELATION RISE

King Solomon, the wisest man to ever live, once said, "All the rivers run into the sea; yet the sea is not full; unto the place from whence the rivers come, thither they return again" (Ecclesiastes 1:7). Rivers of truth flow through the Bible, from Genesis to Revelation. Yet, for all the knowledge Solomon had obtained, none of it could help him resolve how a holy God could have a relationship with broken men and women in a broken world. Since the beginning of time as we know it, mankind has made whole religions in an effort to restore what was lost back in the Garden of Eden— relationship with God.

Is there a God-given way back to that place Adam and Eve once had? Yes! Knowledge of God's covenants open a whole new dimension of understanding of the breadth, length, depth and height of His Love for you. The magnitude of His promises and scope of partnership with Him in the earth can become an exciting adventure as the truth of who He really is and what He has done for you begins to change your thinking about yourself and your relationship with Him.

Understanding covenant will increase your faith and stir in you a boldness like you've never known before. You'll find that you cannot but reach out with confidence to receive all your heavenly Father has planned for your life (Jeremiah 1:5, 29:11; Psalm 139:15). The fear that once dogged your every step will melt away as the confidence in your Blood Covenant Partner, Jesus, begins to flood your being.

Overdue bills and living paycheck to paycheck will be a thing of the past as the Architect of your Covenant agreement has made a way of abundance for you. Maybe it's sickness you can't seem to shake. Not anymore, as you determine to remain in the presence of your Covenant Healer, who has paid the price for your complete healing...spirit, soul, and body, financially and spiritually (Exodus 23:26; Isaiah 53:4-5; 1 Peter 2:24).

As we start down the path of studying these individual covenants, you will begin to see how you will never have to work another day in your life trying to earn your Father's favor, work your way into His good graces, or be good enough to earn His great Love and mercy toward you. He loves you with an everlasting Love (Jeremiah 31:3), and you can reach that place Adam and Eve once had—a place of grace, glory, BLESSING and covenant FRIEND-SHIP with God.

PART 1

WHEN

COVENANT PROMISES

WERE

MADE

THE
FIRST STEPS
TO
UNDERSTANDING
COVENANT

CHAPTER ONE

THE FIRST STEPS TO UNDERSTANDING COVENANT

"How will I know when I'm in love?"

I don't remember exactly how old I was when I asked my mother this all-too-important question, but I remember her answer to this day: "You'll know," she said, "you'll know."

At first, I didn't know what to make of her answer. I mean, what kind of answer is, "You'll know"? But years later when I met Gloria Jean Neece, LORD, did I know!

The first time I laid eyes on her was the first weekend of October 1961. Texas Christian University was playing the University of Arkansas in the Southwest Conference Championship in Little Rock, and I was flying co-pilot on a charter plane headed there. An extra seat was available on the plane so, with my boss' permission, I invited my dad to come along. He worked for National Old Line Insurance Company in Little Rock. He was quite successful. When he asked for access to the company's fifth-floor penthouse suite, they readily agreed.

That evening, I was invited to an after-game party at a country club. Now, this was before Jesus, mind you, so I went. It was there that I met Gloria's father, Wallace (Babe) Neece. The first thing he said to me was, "My daughter is the best-looking girl in the state of Arkansas."

I said, "Is that right?"

"That's right," he said.

A little while later, he came back and said it again.

"Oh, you don't believe me, do you? My daughter is the best-looking girl in the state of Arkansas."

Then he asked, "Where are you staying? I'm going to prove it to you."

I told him we were staying in the penthouse of the National Old Line Insurance Company, and explained that access to the elevator was on the outside of the building.

"I know where that is," he said.

The next morning, when that elevator opened, I said, "Man, he wasn't kidding! That's the best-looking girl I've ever seen."

After being introduced by her father, and after everyone had met my dad, I invited Gloria out onto the balcony.

"Would you like to see the city of Little Rock this morning?" I asked.

"I'd like that," she said.

She and I went out onto the balcony overlooking the city. We talked like we'd known each other for years. The moment she put her arm around me and patted me on the back, I was gone!

I *knew*, just like my mother said I would.

I had never heard the term "root of bitterness." However, instantly all of the bitterness and hardheartedness and anger that I had lived with for so long left me.

For several weeks, I couldn't think of anything or anyone else but the "prettiest girl in Arkansas."

During that time, my boss had taken over the airport Fixed Based Operation in a town forty miles from where Gloria lived. When he asked me to go there, I was all about it. I had her number, and I couldn't wait to call her.

We had our first date at a restaurant called The Rocket Room, which was in a hotel in downtown Camden. They had a Wurlitzer "One More Time" jukebox and a little dance floor. I couldn't take my eyes off Gloria. She had such class! We ate supper and just talked about music and the big songs of the day.

Although I could sing, I couldn't dance—and I swore I'd never dance and sing to a woman at the same time. But that was all before I met Gloria. When that jukebox started playing Johnny Mathis singing "Misty," I completely forgot what I'd sworn never to do. I couldn't pass up the opportunity, so I asked Gloria, "Would you like to dance?"

I don't know what I did to Gloria's toes, but I attempted to dance—and sing...

Look at me/
I'm as helpless as a kitten up a tree...
Never knowing my right foot from my left/
My hat from my glove/
I'm too misty, and too much in love.[1]

I have no remembrance of the drive home. But when we got back to Gloria's house, I walked her up the front walk and onto the porch. Then, right out of the blue I said, "Gloria, will you marry me?"

Her response shocked me.

"OK," she said.

Then she turned and went inside the house, leaving me out on the porch...*stunned!*

I didn't find out until later that right after she shut the door, she thought, *What have I done? I don't even know this guy. Oh well, I'll get out of it later.*

At the time of this writing, we have been married sixty-one years, and she's not out of it yet.

Little did I know, and little did Gloria know, that God was preparing a covenant. He knew what He had planned. At the time I was

---

1   "Misty," written by Erroll Garner and Johnny Burke, 1954.

flying airplanes as a commercial pilot, and I planned to stay in that line of work. But God had something else in mind.

THE BEST DECISIONS I'VE EVER MADE

On April 13, 1962, six months after our first date, Gloria and I entered into a covenant agreement that would change our lives forever. The moment I looked intently into Gloria Jean Neece's beautiful blue eyes and said, "I do," life for me only got better. That's because on that day I chose to commit to love, and I chose to do it at all costs. And I can say this: It was absolutely the second-best decision I ever made.

From that day I have loved her more than my own life.

The first-best decision I ever made also came in the form of a covenant. It was when I received Jesus as my Savior and LORD. Gloria had already received Him as her LORD a week earlier but hadn't told me about it. After being married for six months, we both made that decision one week apart from each other, with neither of us knowing the other had made the decision. But oh, when we found out! We were two young newlyweds who, having fallen in love and gotten married, then fell in love and got married all over again. Only this time to Jesus.

That's when life started really getting good, as we say in Texas.

Quite simply, that is what covenant is all about. It's what covenant is designed to do. That's why it exists. Covenant was established by God to take us up to a better place through relationship with Him and with others.

Covenant is just that simple, yet it's also profound and life-changing—which is why I want to teach you everything Greg and I have learned about it, and everything Gloria and I have learned about it from each other over the years.

In our sixty-one years of being married, we've learned a lot! Yet we've made it through all our years together without having an argument, without fussing, or in any way allowing the devil to get between us. Of course, that's more because of Gloria than because of me. She absolutely refused to argue. One day, after abruptly walking out of the room, she said to me: "I started to get mad, but I decided I wouldn't." Then she came over and hugged me and that was it. I call that pretty good for sixty-one years.

Something else I call good is how our little family has blossomed over the years. What started out as just Gloria and me and Jesus now includes children, grandchildren, and great-grandchildren. Add in the Covenant Partners who've joined us during the fifty-six years Gloria and I have been ministering together—and we've become quite a bunch!

We've grown into a great big Covenant family, which from the start is exactly what God had in mind.

GOD'S DREAM COME TRUE

Family has always been precious to God. Long before the beginning of time, He fell in love with the idea of having one of His own. He loved the thought of being surrounded by sons and daughters made in His own likeness. His heart yearned for a family of people He could love and BLESS.

All the magnificent splendor of creation we see around us today came out of that divine desire. God made it all for one purpose only—to BLESS His family. He created the earth and everything in it for *us!* We were in His heart and mind long before we ever showed up on the planet. His dream before the foundation of the world was to prosper you and me and all the rest of His family in every way imaginable as we spend eternity building our lives and world together with Him.

If you know the story of Creation, then you know that God's dream first sprang to life with Adam and Eve, the great-great-grandparents of us all. You also know that things didn't go well for them, nor for God pretty much from the beginning. In the Garden of Eden Adam committed high treason. He bowed his knee to the devil, a spiritual outlaw and thief who at one time had been an archangel created by God. When Adam surrendered his authority to him, the devil became the god of this world (2 Corinthians 4:4). As a result, from then on, many times throughout the course of history, God would be faced with situations that threatened to destroy His dream forever.

So, in His endless wisdom and foresight, God put into motion the truth and power of blood-backed agreement—or COVENANT! You could say that covenant became God's way of holding on to His family for dear life.

The word *covenant* comes from the Latin phrase that means "a coming together." In a general sense, it's simply an agreement between two or more people or parties. It brings those parties into relationship through a formal commitment made binding by arrangement, a testament or will, or a legal contract.

In the Bible, whenever a covenant is made between God and man, it's always God who initiates it. In each case, He sets the conditions and standards of the agreement. He determines how the people with whom He is making covenant gain access to the benefits of the arrangement.

If that makes God sound controlling, like He's trying to back people into a corner by setting all the demands, it's because HE IS! God has done and is doing everything He possibly can to squeeze every one of us as tightly as He can into a place of BLESSING— once and for all. It's the reason He wants you in Covenant with Him.

His motive has always been relationship. He desires more than anything to be in constant fellowship with you and shower you with His goodness. When you enter into Covenant agreement with Him, as Gloria and I did fresh into our marriage, you are obligating yourself by Faith to a relationship with Him. You're binding yourself to Almighty God. Once you make that connection and commitment, He can release His purpose and desire for you, your life, and all creation, through the promises and BLESSINGS of the Covenant.

DO YOU SPEAK COVENANT?

One problem we as believers have today however is we don't have a covenant mindset. We live in a world that's lost touch with the value and significance of covenant. A world where it's often said that covenants (or "contracts") are made to be broken. A world that has little to no clue about what it means to be in a covenant relationship—whether those relationships are with spouses, family, business partners, or with God.

Because of this, the concept of covenant as God has revealed it for us throughout Scripture often escapes us. We don't listen to the Bible with covenant ears. We hear Bible stories at church, but without understanding the covenant context we can find it difficult to apply them to our lives.

The remedy, of course, is for us to renew our minds so that we do start thinking about covenant like God does. Granted, for us Americans, that will require some study. But I promise you, it will be worth the effort. Understanding covenant will make a world of difference in your life and take you to places in God you never imagined!

It certainly took Sir Henry Morton Stanley to some unimaginable places. If you've read about him, you may remember his story. A nineteenth century Welsh-American explorer and journalist, Stanley was sent to Africa by the *New York Herald* newspaper to find the famous Dr. David Livingstone. Livingstone, a Scottish physician, missionary, explorer, and overall hero to the British public, had been missing about six years.

Stanley's search for Dr. Livingstone soon turned treacherous. He lost nearly all his 100-plus-member expedition team to desertion and disease. He also encountered hostile African tribes that further slowed his efforts. Desperate, Stanley finally heeded the advice of his young African interpreter—to consider entering a *covenant* with the chieftain of one particularly powerful, warring tribe.

At first, Stanley was hesitant to commit to some foreign idea of a peace treaty or agreement. He felt vulnerable and uncertain about how it would play out. He almost called the whole thing off when he found out that this "covenant rite" would require him and the chief to drink some of each other's blood. The very thought was revolting.

Stanley's attitude changed though when his interpreter explained to him the covenant benefits. "Everything the chieftain has will be yours if you need it!" he said.[2]

At that, Stanley agreed to start the "covenant" process, and negotiations between the two parties began.

First, the tribal chief wanted to know what Stanley's motives for the agreement were. What was he hoping to get out of their arrangement?

Next, the chief began asking Stanley about his resources and ability to keep his end of the agreement. The chief was old and experienced and not about to cut a blood covenant with just anyone. He wanted to know if Stanley was someone he could trust; someone who had significant benefits to offer him in return.

Finally, it came down to the moment of exchanging gifts—an important step in covenant-making. Stanley was confident that with all the precious trinkets, bales of cotton cloth, and other valuable items he and his men brought on their expedition, the chief surely would be impressed with something they had. And he was. He set his eyes on Stanley's little, white goat.

The goat was one of Stanley's most prized possessions. He suffered from poor health at the time and the goat produced milk that seemed to help him. The thought of parting with it was particularly challenging. Yet, of all his possessions, it was the only thing the chief would accept as a gift. So, Stanley finally agreed and handed over the goat.

What did he receive in exchange?

The chief gave Stanley a spear, seven feet long and wound with copper wire. The reason it was that long was that chief was nearly that tall. The fact that he was such a big man was one reason he was chief.

Stanley's first thought was that he had been cheated by the old

2 E.W. Kenyon, *The Blood Covenant* (New Kensington, Penn: Whitaker House, 2019) p. 21.

chief. *This* was what his (obviously naïve) interpreter had meant by *everything the chieftain has will be yours if you need it?*

Stanley's problem at that moment, much like ours today, was he didn't speak *covenant*. So, initially the true value and significance of the chief's spear eluded him. It didn't take Stanley long however to figure out the spear's covenant meaning. When he took to the trail and reentered the bush, he found he held in his hand a scepter of power. He had in his possession something that gave him the authority and brought him respect equal to that of a king.

From that day on, in the eyes of all the people he encountered, *he* was now seven feet tall and wrapped in royalty. Everywhere he went the people acknowledged it by bowing to him.

Why?

When they saw the spear, they understood that he had a covenant with someone far more powerful. He had the backing of a king.

That revelation of the value of covenant changed Stanley's destiny. A revelation of our Covenant BOOK—The holy Bible—will change ours too.

JESUS WAS ALWAYS THE PLAN

God is the King of the universe. Through Covenant, He puts in our hand His scepter of power. He backs us and says to us, "Everything I have is yours." He gives us the right to exercise His authority and BLESSES us with the same BLESSING He originally gave to Adam. (See Genesis 1:28.)

God's perfect plan for mankind was for that original BLESSING to continue uninterrupted. His perfect will would have been for Adam to never sin and to be an eternal man. But because He knew in advance that Adam would fall, God's plan for mankind's redemption was already in place.

From before the foundation of the world, Jesus was that Plan.

All the covenants we will study in this book point to Him. He's there in what God said after Adam and Eve broke relationship with their Creator. He's the One God was talking about when He told the devil that Eve's Seed "shall bruise thy head, and thou shalt bruise his heel" (Genesis 3:15). All through the Old Covenant, every Old Testament sacrifice represented Jesus.

Like many believers, you may have thought of the Old Testament and the New Testament as two separate Covenants. But as you're about to discover, the two are *very* connected. As it's been said: The Old Covenant is the New *concealed,* while the New Covenant is the Old *revealed.*

Even in the life of Jesus, we see both of those Covenants. As Professor Stephens will show you in the following pages, during His earthly ministry, one moment Jesus would step out and advance the cause of the New Covenant. The next moment He would reach back to fulfill a remaining detail of the Old Covenant. "Think not that I am come to destroy the law, or the prophets:" He told His followers, "I am not come to destroy, but to fulfil" (Matthew 5:17).

What you're about to read in the following pages will help you better understand what that means. You'll get a clear picture, as we walk together through all the covenants in the Bible, of how intricately this string of agreements forged by God with mankind over thousands of years are intertwined. You'll get a deeper revelation of these covenants, what they mean to your relationship with God, and how they impact our world.

STEP ONE OF THE THREE-STEP PROCESS

Before we dig into the covenants themselves, though, there are some basics you need to know. Getting them established in your thinking is important. They'll help make the seeming complexity of the covenant process and elements make sense.

The process of entering into a covenant always involves three steps. To God, three is a significant number. Throughout Scripture, He often works with groupings of *three,* a number that conveys *completeness.* The Bible tells us for example:

- There are three members of the Godhead—God the *Father,* God the *Son* (Jesus), and God the *Holy Spirit*— which makes the Trinity.
- There are three facets of God's existence throughout time—God who *was,* who *is,* and who *is to come* (Revelation 1:4).
- God created us to be triune beings made up of *spirit, soul* and *body.*

This pattern of threes emerges repeatedly in all God-initiated covenants because it's a reflection of His divine nature. It also signifies the fact that all three Persons of the Godhead are actively involved in His covenants. Each member of the Trinity plays a unique part in the process of fulfilling the Father's plan to redeem mankind and restore us back to Himself.

The first step in the covenant process is the *calling* to covenant. God, the Father, takes this step by graciously inviting us to join ourselves to Him. Then, He in turn can join Himself to us, bringing all of who He is and all of what He has into our lives.

Nehemiah 9 tells us it was God who *chose* Abraham. It wasn't Abraham who initiated their covenant relationship. God approached him first. He brought Abraham up from his homeland, and gave him a new identity. He even promised to give him all the land as far as his eyes could see (verses 7-8), an offer seemingly too good to be true.

God has essentially done the same for us as believers today. He has called us just as He called Abraham and made us an astounding offer. He's offered us the opportunity to enter into a relationship with Him for all eternity. He's promised to BLESS us and assured us, as Romans 8:28 says, that "all things work together for good to them that love God, to them who are *the called* according to *his* purpose."

Do you see it? As believers we are "the called"! That means God has already taken the first step in the process of establishing Covenant with us. He has extended to us a personal invitation to join ourselves to Him.

STEP TWO: ENTERING COVENANT

The second step in establishing a covenant is the actual *entering* into the covenant. This is where the terms of the covenant are agreed upon by both parties, and the agreement is executed or acted upon. In Hebrews 11:8 and 9, we see Abraham taking this step. We see that "by faith Abraham, when he was called to go out into a place which he should after receive for an inheritance, obeyed; and he went out, not knowing whither he went. By faith he sojourned in the land of promise, as in a strange country, dwelling in tabernacles with Isaac and Jacob, the heirs with him of the same promise."

Imagine how much trust it took for Abraham to say yes to God's call without knowing where that call would take him. Imagine how much Faith it took for him to leave everything behind without having any idea of exactly what lay ahead.

That's like what Gloria did when she said yes to marrying me. Talk about an offer that seemed too good to be true! My lightning-fast mind figured out quickly that I was getting the better end of that deal. So, I did everything I could to get her to the altar before she could change her mind.

It took a lot of trust for her to marry me. She had to be willing to leave what was familiar to her and step out into a territory she was destined to inherit which, at the time, was nothing more than all my debts. I know for a fact she was in the dark about where her destiny with me was going to take her, because I didn't have a clue myself. Yet, even so, she headed out with me into the great unknown.

She started a new life with me based only on a *promise*—a promise I made to her in our wedding vows the day we were married. She took the second step in the covenant process, committed to love and joined herself to me.

That's what Abraham did. When he acted on God's promise in Faith, he entered into covenant. He accepted God's invitation and joined himself to Him.

Hundreds of years later when God gave the people of Israel the opportunity to enter into a covenant relationship with Him, He added to this second step. He required the Israelites to agree *verbally* with His covenant conditions. He had them declare out loud together all the BLESSINGS and the curses of the Law. Like the reading and signing of a contractual agreement, this formalized their agreement to *enter* covenant with Him (Deuteronomy 27-30:19).

"But Brother Copeland," you might say, "How does what Abraham and the people of Israel did in the Old Testament apply to us today? God hasn't called us to go to a physical place called the Promised Land or asked us to declare out loud all the requirements of the Old Covenant Law. So, how do we take the second step of entering into Covenant with God?"

We do it by believing on God's Son, Jesus, the *second* Person of the Trinity, and receiving Him by Faith as our Savior and LORD!

As Jesus declared, "I am the way, the truth, and the life: no man cometh unto the Father, but by me," (John 14:6). In other words, He told us, "The only way you can enter into Covenant with the Father is through Me. Yes, He has called and invited you, but I'm your way in!"

Jesus did for us what we couldn't. He did what mankind had tried and failed to do for thousands of years. By living a sinless life and perfectly keeping God's law, He fulfilled all God's Covenant requirements. Then He became the ultimate Covenant sacrifice, paid the price for the sin of all mankind forever, and shed His blood to ratify a second Covenant, a New Covenant.

The New Covenant cannot be broken. It is between the eternal, Almighty God, and the resurrected, glorified man, Jesus Christ—and we get in on it by Faith in Him. One of the articles of this precious Covenant is recorded in 1 John 1:9: It says that when we sin, "If we confess our sins, he is faithful and just to forgive us our sins, and to cleanse us from all unrighteousness."

That means we can't mess up this Covenant! As The BOOK says, "Jesus Christ [is] the same yesterday, and today, and for ever" (Hebrews 13:8). Because He is always the same, so is His Covenant with God, therefore ours is, too.

STEP THREE: KEEPING COVENANT

The third and final step of the covenant process is *keeping* or *maintaining* the agreement. A covenant relationship, like any relationship—whether it's in a marriage, in parenting, business or simply a friendship—requires maintenance. Relationships need nurturing. For them to remain healthy and vital, you can't just forget about them. You must remember and attend to them.

Jesus spoke about this to His disciples just before He left them to go to the cross. During their last Passover meal together, He took the bread, "and when he had given thanks, he brake it, and said, Take, eat: this is my body, which is broken for you: this do in remembrance of me. After the same manner also he took the cup, when he had supped, saying, this cup is the new testament in my blood: this do ye, as oft as ye drink it, in remembrance of me" (1 Corinthians 11:24-25).

When Jesus instructed His disciples to do this "in remembrance of Me," He was pointing back to what their Hebrew forefathers had done for thousands of years. When they ate the Passover meal, they remembered how God had delivered them from the bondage of Egypt (Exodus 13:3; Deuteronomy 4:9). This *remembering* kept their minds focused on their covenant with Him.

This is why Jesus established under the New Covenant what we today call "Communion." By telling us to eat and drink the Covenant meal, He provided us with a simple action step we can take to remind us that we're in Covenant with God through Him. He gave us a powerful way to release our Faith in that Covenant. A way to nurture our connection with Him and keep it not only intact but healthy, active, strong, thriving—alive!

Right after that last Covenant meal Jesus shared with His disciples, He also told them about another way He was going to help them remember and maintain their connection with Him. He was going to send them the *third* member of the Trinity, the Holy Spirit, to help with this third Covenant step. He said:

> If ye love me, keep my commandments. And I will pray the Father, and he shall give you another Comforter, that he

may abide with you for ever; even the Spirit of truth; whom the world cannot receive, because it seeth him not, neither knoweth him: but ye know him; for he dwelleth with you, and shall be in you.... he shall teach you all things, and bring all things to your remembrance, whatsoever I have said unto you (John 14:15-17, 26).

Notice a major role of the Holy Spirit is to help us *remember* our Covenant and keep our relationship with our heavenly Father dynamic. He also helps us by empowering us to be faithful to the conditions of the Covenant agreement and to obtain its benefits. But as we will see, under the New Covenant, this doesn't involve following an overwhelming list of rules and regulations, as was required under the First Covenant.

No, as born-again believers, our focus is to be on the One who went before us and fulfilled for us the terms of the Covenant. We take step three by giving attention to Jesus, to His Love for us, and to our place in Him. And we do that with the ever-present help— and continual prompting—of the Holy Spirit.

IF IT LOOKS LIKE A WEDDING...

In fifty-six years of ministry, I cannot tell you how many times I have officiated at weddings. There have been many. But I can recall and tell you precisely what I said to each of those couples in each of those ceremonies. I told them about *covenant*—and I have always done so in great detail—because that's what marriage is about. From start to finish, marriage is covenant through and through— even in ceremony.

This is why most all marriage ceremonies contain three major covenant elements. Like the three covenant steps we just discussed, each one is revealed in the Bible. And each one in its own way re-flects a major aspect of our ultimate union with Jesus Christ—our Savior, LORD, and soon-coming King.

First, most traditional wedding vows exchanged at the altar be-gin with the words: "I promise." God-initiated covenants begin the same way. Each of the Biblical covenants we're about to study starts with a *promise*. The promise is made by God the Father—the first Person of the Godhead—when He initially lays out the conditions, standards, and BLESSINGS of the agreement.

Second, there is the *cutting* of the covenant. In weddings, this cutting is signified by the bride and groom proceeding down the center aisle with her family sitting on one side and his on the other. This symbolizes the fact that two families are being joined here. Two families are coming together in covenant and becoming one (Genesis 2:23).

When God cut Covenant with us, the same thing happened. Two became one. Only in the cutting of God's Covenant, Covenant Blood was shed. Jesus—the second Person of the Godhead—stepped in as the living sacrifice on our behalf and joined us to God.

Third, there is the *seal* of the covenant. In weddings, the marriage covenant is sealed first with the exchanging of rings and then a kiss at the altar near the end of the ceremony. Our Covenant with God is sealed by the Holy Spirit—the third Person of the Godhead. His presence in us is the seal or guarantee of our Covenant with Him.

Now that you know the three steps of the covenant process and three elements involved in it, there's one more thing you'll need to remember: *the covenant contradiction.* In marriage, the covenant contradiction is the thing that threatens to take the happy out of the couple's "happily ever after." In our Covenant with God, a Covenant contradiction is any natural obstacle that makes it appear impossible for God's promise to come to pass in our lives.

It's circumstances that rise up in front of us that tell us there's no way that what God said about us in His BLESSING could ever happen. It's the thoughts we have to contend with when after we read in the Bible that by Jesus' stripes we're healed, the doctor diagnoses us with some "incurable" condition. Or when, despite God's prosperity promises, we're facing a towering stack of unpaid bills.

You know the arguments you can have in your head in such situations. *Yeah, I know what the Bible says but it'll never work! I'm too far gone. My situation is too bad. I'm too old…too young…too short…too tall.* On and on the fight can go.

How do we win that fight? How do we overcome such Covenant contradictions?

By doing what Abraham did.

God told him and his wife they would have a child. He was 100 years old and his wife was 90. *How can we ever have a child?* they wondered. They couldn't. Yet they did.

How? Romans 4:16-21 provides the answer.

Therefore it is of faith, that it might be by grace; to the end the promise might be sure to all the seed; not to that only which is of the law, but to that also which is of the faith of Abraham; who is the father of us all, (As it is written, I have made thee a father of many nations,) before him whom he believed, even God, who quickeneth the dead, and calleth those things which be not as though they were. Who against hope believed in hope, that he might become the father of many nations, according to that which was spoken, So shall thy seed be. And being not weak in faith, he considered not his own body now dead, when he was about an hundred years old, neither yet the deadness of Sarah's womb: He staggered not at the promise of God through unbelief; but was strong in faith, giving glory to God. And being fully persuaded that, what he had promised, he was able also to perform.

Abraham never tried to reconcile the covenant contradiction. He just took Almighty God at His WORD and considered the blood covenant agreement he had with Him. That blood covenant made the contradiction make sense. It instilled such confidence in Abraham that years later, after his son Isaac was born, when God asked Abraham to sacrifice him, he raised the knife.

Why? Because he was fully persuaded that if that boy died, God would raise him from the dead. As The BOOK says, "by faith" Abraham "received him alive in a figure" (Hebrews 11:19).

As we study covenant in Scripture, we will see covenant contradictions arise time and again. We'll see that as soon as God reaches out to extend an opportunity for a covenant relationship with someone, along will come a natural obstacle. A contradiction will arise to try to keep God's promise from coming to pass.

But thank God, covenant men and women throughout time have refused the contradiction and pressed through in Faith to the end-result, to THE BLESSING promised by God. And we can too! We can renew our minds to the way God thinks, to what He says, and to what He wants us to do and get rid of every contradictory thought that comes into our minds. By coming to an understanding of covenant we too can become fully persuaded that God has provided a full and complete redemption for us. He has restored us back to relationship with Him, reinstated our BLESSING—and what He promised He is able also to perform!

GO DEEPER
WITH KENNETH & GREG

THE GREATEST
WEDDING CELEBRATION

And it shall come to pass, when The LORD thy God hath brought thee in unto the land whither thou goest to possess it, that thou shalt put *THE BLESSING* upon mount Gerizim, and the *curse* upon mount Ebal" (Deuteronomy 11:29).

Throughout history there have been many royal, well-attended weddings. None however compare to the wedding celebrated on two mountains in Israel's Promised Land more than 3,000 years ago. At that wedding, with as many as two million people not just in attendance but *participating,* the entire nation of Israel made a fresh commitment to their holy union with Almighty God.

The *solemn covenant renewal ceremony* unfolded in accordance with the instructions God had given them through Moses. Moses had told them that after they crossed the Jordan River into Canaan they were to gather between Mount Ebal and Mount Gerazim. There, in the hearing of all the people, the priests were to read the entire Law out loud, declaring the curse from one and the BLESS-ING from the other.

The Israelites, once they arrived at the appointed place, did exactly as God had commanded. In preparation for the ceremony they built an altar of unhewn stones on Mount Ebal, covered them with plaster and wrote on them all the words of God—the Law (Deuteronomy 23:5-6, 1 Peter 2:5, Joshua 8:32). Then, everyone assembled at the base of the two mountains. Representatives from six of Israel's twelve tribes gathered on Mount Gerizim, while representatives from the other six tribes gathered on Mount Ebal (Deuteronomy 27:12-13).

Once all the people were in place—men, women, children, priests and leaders—the ceremony began. From Mount Ebal, the Levites declared with a loud voice to all the people of Israel, "*Cursed* is the man who makes a graven or molten image, an abomination to The LORD...."

In response, all the people said, *Amen.*

"Cursed is he who dishonors his father or his mother," the priests continued.

Again, in response, all the people said, Amen (Deuteronomy 27:15, *Amplified Bible, Classic Edition*).

After the priests finished reading the "curses" recorded in the Law, from Mount Gerizim the Levites loudly declared the BLESSINGS. Continuing down the list of BLESSINGS until all of them had been read, they began:

> If you will listen diligently to the voice of The LORD your God, being watchful to do all His commandments which I command you this day, The LORD your God will set you high above all the nations of the earth. And all these BLESSINGS shall come upon you and overtake you if you heed the voice of The LORD your God (Deuteronomy 28:1-2, *Amplified Bible, Classic Edition*).

As in any wedding-vow renewal ceremony, those powerful words—etched in stone and given by Almighty God—were covenant declarations. They separated Israel from all other nations, established them as God's people, and set them on the strong foundation of their Blood-covenant relationship with Him.

Having recently crossed into the Promised Land, the Israelites needed that strong foundation. Many battles lay ahead. So did many opportunities to be deceived into participating in the evil practices of the Canaanites. For them to fully possess the Land the Israelites would have to drive out all its ungodly inhabitants. If they didn't, God had warned them long ago, "Those which ye let remain of them shall be *pricks in your eyes,* and *thorns in your sides,* and shall *vex you* in the land wherein ye dwell" (Numbers 33:55).

In His wisdom God knew the Israelites could never conquer Canaan without the power of His Blood-covenant WORD. For them to be victorious they would have to keep the words of that covenant in their ears, their mouths and their hearts. They would have to put their hope and trust in God's powerful presence (Joshua 1:8). Their success going forward depended on it.

So, at the outset, through this covenant-vow renewal ceremony, God assured them of His Love and commitment to them. He also reminded them of His Blood-covenant Friendship with them. With this reminder resounding in their ears, the people sealed this holy event with Blood-covenant sacrifices. On the altar they had built, they offered clean animals and burnt peace offerings to God.

Then, they all celebrated by enjoying a great covenant feast together, rejoicing before The LORD.

A CLEAR CHOICE

After hearing all the curses read, as well as the BLESSINGS, why would the Israelites rejoice? Because God was not cursing them. He wasn't threatening them or holding anything over their heads. His Blood covenant with Israel was for the purpose of sheltering and protecting them *from* the curse, so they could walk in THE BLESSING.

By presenting both THE BLESSING and the curse to them, He was giving them a clear choice. Although His desire was for them to choose to walk in THE BLESSING, He left the decision up to them. As He put it in Deuteronomy 30:19-20:

I call heaven and earth to record this day against you, that I have set before you *life and death, BLESSING and cursing:* therefore *choose life,* that both thou and thy seed may live: That thou mayest love The LORD thy God, and that thou mayest obey his voice, and that thou mayest cleave unto him: for *he is thy life,* and the length of thy days: that thou mayest dwell in the land which The LORD sware unto thy fathers, to Abraham, to Isaac, and to Jacob, to give them (Deuteronomy 30:19-20).

God was all for His people living the BLESSED life to its fullest. He did everything He could to make it possible for them to do so. But the choice was still theirs, just as the choice was Adam and Eve's, and as the choice is ours, today.

It's true: even as New Covenant believers, the degree of God's BLESSING we experience in our lives depends on the choices we make. To walk in the fullness of THE BLESSING that belongs to us through Christ Jesus we too must remember we've been separated unto Him. We too must constantly keep His Blood-Covenant WORD in our ears, our eyes, and our mouths and remember that He has said to us much as He did to the Israelites:

Be ye not unequally yoked together with unbelievers: for what fellowship hath righteousness with unrighteousness? and what communion hath light with darkness? And what concord hath Christ with Belial? or what part hath he that believeth with an infidel? And what agreement hath the temple of God with idols? for ye are the temple of the living God; as God hath said, I will dwell in them, and walk in them; and I will be their God, and they shall be my people. Wherefore come out from among them, and be ye separate, saith The LORD, and touch not the unclean thing; and I will receive you. And will be a Father unto you, and ye shall be my sons and daughters, saith The LORD Almighty (2 Corinthians 6:14-18).

God's WORD has been, and always will be, the transforming, consecrating, Blood-Covenant connection that separates His people from all others. That's why, today, we still have to hear it and hear it and hear it, and constantly renew our minds to it (Romans 10:17). To enjoy all the BLESSINGS that are ours, we have to choose life by choosing The WORD.

THE

EDEN

COVENANT

THE EDEN COVENANT

Significant, life-changing events leave lasting impressions. Looking back at them, we can usually remember exactly where we were and what was going on around us: like when you asked your sweetheart to marry you or found out you were having a baby, or when you got born again or were filled with the Holy Spirit.

For me, one such life-changing event was when *covenant* first started making sense to me. As a young preacher I was flying on one of the airlines to some meetings in Houston. After boarding, I settled into my seat and pulled out a small book by E.W. Kenyon called *The Blood Covenant.*

The book caught my eye because I had long been interested in Blood covenants. Having grown up very aware of my Native American heritage, I was familiar with the practices, traditions and symbolism that had historically accompanied them, particularly in the United States. I had also been aware for weeks there was something about covenant I still didn't know. God was dealing with me about it, and I sensed there was something in this book I needed to get.

As the flight got underway, I began to read. I read about how God had ordained covenant. I read about His covenant with Abraham. When I read how, through that covenant, everything God had belonged to Abraham and everything Abraham had belonged to Him, I began to see it! In God's agreement with Abraham, God promised to do *anything* for him. He promised to make Abraham great, make him rich, be his God, take care of him, protect him and give him land.

Then in Dr. Kenyon's book I came across Galatians 3:29, "And if ye be Christ's, then are ye Abraham's seed, and heirs according to the promise."

I'll never forget that moment. I was about cruising altitude, somewhere between Dallas and Houston. I remember because it was like a fog lifted or the clouds parted, and I saw clearly what my commitment to Jesus and my walk of Faith was all about.

Talk about a life-changing realization! Even during my first five to six years of being a Christian, I had known next to nothing about the Bible. Now though, looking through the lens of Blood covenant, the Bible was starting to become less of a mystery.

For the first time in my life, I saw myself *in* The BOOK. I saw myself in the Bible! Suddenly, this marvelous, old BOOK came to life—it was *my* story. It was *my* life, *my* connection, *my* agreement, *my* arrangement with God. I had just read that what was God's was Abraham's, and what was Abraham's was now *mine*. And as best as I could tell, God had pretty much promised Abraham everything!

Sitting in a bulkhead seat near the front of the plane, the revelation and reality of covenant exploded inside me.

You see, until my father in the Faith, Oral Roberts, eventually taught me better, for years I had heard the same lie most preachers had—that we had to be poor, especially as preachers. So, I told The LORD I needed more scriptures on this. And sure enough, here they came:

Christ hath redeemed us from the curse of the law, being made a curse for us: for it is written, Cursed is every one that hangeth on a tree (Galatians 3:13).

There went poverty out the door!

That THE BLESSING of Abraham might come on the Gentiles through Jesus Christ; that we might receive the promise of the Spirit through faith (verse 14).

Here came prosperity in to take its place!

With the help of Dr. Kenyon's little book, I began to discover that day that the entire New Testament (Covenant) was nothing *but* covenant. I couldn't help thinking of ALL the lies we as believers had been told—and perhaps believed and lived under for too long—all because we weren't taught, or didn't know, about covenant. I would never believe those lies again! Like Sir Henry Stanley, I had gotten a revelation of covenant, along with a sense of a new identity and level of power and authority equal to that of a king.

By the time we landed in Houston that day, I was a new man—I was a *covenant* man!

GOD'S LOVE AFFAIR WITH HUMANITY

All study and understanding of God's Blood covenants must start, and finish, with a revelation of these two things: God's glorious Love for mankind and the power of His WORD. As we've seen, *Love* is the driving force behind everything God says and does. It is the core of who He is. He is "the faithful God, which keepeth covenant and mercy with them that love him and keep his commandments to a thousand generations" (Deuteronomy 7:9).

To the human mind, God's Love for us is itself a contradiction. Because we've all sinned and fallen short of His glory, His Love for us is almost beyond belief. Yet we will see throughout this covenant study, His fierce, unconditional and eternal compassion and mercy are the essence of His very being.

The Apostle John, who called himself *the disciple Jesus loved* and the one to whom Jesus entrusted His own mother, summed up this revelation with these three short words: "God is Love" (1 John 4:8).

God's Love has been the motive and force behind all His covenants.

In the beginning, God—the BLESSED One—created the heavens and the earth and initiated the Eden Covenant by releasing BLESSING in and on His man and woman, crowning them with His glory and honor. And in the process of speaking that BLESSING into their destiny and their very being, He laid out this Eden Covenant, as well as His purpose for mankind and all creation. The Eden Covenant I am referring to is Isaiah 51:1-4, turning our lives back to the Garden. It says:

> Hearken to me, ye that follow after righteousness, ye that seek The LORD: Look unto the rock whence ye are hewn, and to the hole of the pit whence ye are digged. Look unto Abraham your father, and unto Sarah that bare you: for I called him alone, and BLESSED him, and increased him. For The LORD shall comfort Zion: He will comfort all her waste places; and he will make her wilderness like Eden, and her desert like the garden of The LORD; joy and gladness shall be found therein, thanksgiving, and the voice of melody. Hearken unto me, my people; and give ear unto me, O my nation: for a law shall proceed from me, and I will make my judgment to rest for a light of the people.

Those verses are directed to the seed of Abraham—and as we just saw, we as believers are Abraham's seed. The word *Zion* also applies to us because in Hebrews it's used to refer to the Body of Christ. We have inherited the Eden Covenant. By Faith in God, everything in the Garden of Eden is available to us.

That means when we read about how God created the universe in preparation for the Garden, we're reading about how He prepared for *us*. We're seeing the power and Love that backs our covenant with God.

Think of it: *Love* created the entire universe! *Love*—our heavenly Father—built it all to be a wonderful place where His beloved family could live and fellowship with Him. He didn't build it out of just some random material, either; He used a part of Himself.

The same apostle who said *God is Love* also said, "God is light" (1 John 1:5), and God used light as the foundation for our homeplace. His Love for us is so great that He worked His own essence into the very core of this physical, natural world in which we live. He made Himself the cornerstone of all creation.

He said, "Light be!" and light was (and still is). It exploded into space at the speed of 186,000 miles per second and never stopped. Within 24 hours it illuminated 90 billion, 700 million miles of a universe that science confirms is still expanding today.

That's how powerful God's WORD is! One eternal command from Him brought all creation into existence. Just two of His *Love*-filled, *light*-infused words released the light envelope into which our massive universe was to be placed.

To this day, God's words continue to carry this powerful, energizing, life-giving force we call *light*.

That's why the Eden Covenant, despite everything that tried to put an end to it, still exists. God's Faith-filled words, once spoken, stand forever because God and His WORD are One. As John 1 says:

> In the beginning was The WORD, and The WORD was with God, and The WORD was God. The same was in the beginning with God. All things were made by him; and without him was not any thing made that was made. In him was life; and the life was the light of men. And the light shineth in darkness; and the darkness comprehended it not (verses 1-5).

Notice, those verses refer to The WORD not as some*thing* but as Some*one*. Who is it? *Jesus!* Jesus is the *Light* of the world (John 8:12). He is the exact *image* of the Father (Colossians 1:15). He is The *WORD* made flesh (John 1:14) and by Him and for Him were all things created (Colossians 1:16-17).

This is how our homeplace came to exist: God, the Father (the eternal Creator), gave words of His power to His Son, Jesus. Then, Jesus, God the Son (the eternal WORD) gave utterance to those words. Then, God, the Holy Spirit (the eternal Power), executed those spoken words and brought them to pass.

When He did, instantly God's light energy became physical matter. Spiritual substance and material substance flowed together. The *light* of God's goodness and mercy expressed through His words released a form of His glory that framed the worlds. And the eternal power of His WORD is still holding it all together today (verses 2-3).

GOD'S CROWNING WORK

The crowning glory of God's creation, of course, was to be His precious family. So, once He completed the home He'd prepared for us—

God said, Let us make man in our image, after our likeness: and let them have dominion over the fish of the sea, and over the fowl of the air, and over the cattle, and over all the earth, and over every creeping thing that creepeth upon the earth. So God created man in his own image, in the image of God created he him; male and female created he them. And God BLESSED them, and God said unto them, Be fruitful, and multiply, and replenish the earth, and subdue it: and have dominion over the fish of the sea, and over the fowl of the air, and over every living thing that moveth upon the earth (Genesis 1:26–28).

When we talk about God making man in His own likeness, we're not talking about the kind of *likeness* we see between people in the natural. We're not talking about when all the family gets together and Aunt So-and-So looks at one of the kids and says, "Doesn't he look just like his daddy.... Isn't she just the spittin' image of her mama?"

No, we're talking here about the Most High God. We're talking about the ever-present, past and future "I AM," the Three-in-One (Father, Son and Holy Spirit), in whom, by whom, through whom all things were made. The Eternal One, Elohim[3] created man *exactly* like Himself.

In essence, He said, "Let man rule as We rule, BLESS as We BLESS, multiply as We multiply, be fruitful as We are fruitful, fill as We fill, subdue as We subdue, give as We give, possess as We possess!" And with that, He breathed man into being.

Just as God made all the hosts of heaven "by the breath of his mouth" (Psalm 33:6), with His mighty words of Faith and dominion

---

3 For a fuller understanding of the term *Elohim*, see Appendix A: The Covenant Names of God, p. 249.

God breathed into man the very Spirit and power of His own eternal life and being. He conferred on him the same power and authority in the earth realm that God Himself has in the spirit realm.

One day while I was studying these things, The LORD gave me a vision of the Father creating Adam. I saw a lifeless, grayish body God had formed from the dust of the earth. The LORD was holding up the body by its shoulders. It was just hanging there, but it was the exact same size and the exact image of the Father, Son and Holy Spirit. The lifeless body was as much a copy of the Father as Jesus was. Adam was an exact copy of Jesus!

As I watched, God spoke the eternal words of everlasting life into that lifeless body (Daniel 12:2), nose-to-nose and mouth-to-mouth. As the breath and Spirit of God flowed into its nostrils, that perfectly formed body was flooded with the glory, power and life force of God Himself, and that lifeless body came alive. What I saw in that vision lines up with Genesis 2:7: "And The LORD God formed man of the dust of the ground, and breathed into his nostrils the breath of life; and man became a living soul."

The Jewish sages commenting on the creation of man note that though the animals were also created living souls[4], only man was given the gift of articulate speech. Only man was made a "speaking spirit"[5] like God. The royal gift of speech was the ultimate tool of dominion God gave to His sons and daughters.

Having used His words—the power containers of His Faith—to release His life and power into the earth, He equipped His family with the ability to do the same. He authorized us to set in motion the destiny of our own environment (this planet) with Faith-filled words. So, like our heavenly Father, "we having the same spirit of faith, according as it is written, I believed, and therefore have I spoken; we also believe, and therefore speak" (2 Corinthians 4:13).

---

4 Genesis 1:30, *Complete Jewish Bible,* David H. Stern (Jerusalem: Jewish New Testament Publications Inc., 1998).

5 *The Chumash, Artscroll Series,* Mesorah Heritage Foundation, *Bereishis/Genesis,* Rabbi Nosson Sherman (Brooklyn: Mesorah Publications, Ltd.) p. 11.

THE EDEN COVENANT PROMISE

Although the word *covenant* doesn't appear in the Bible until Genesis 6, THE BLESSING of the Eden Covenant was actually the very first thing ever heard by the human ear. As we've just seen in Genesis 1:28, right after God breathed His life into Adam, He "BLESSED them, and…said unto them, Be fruitful, and multiply, and replenish the earth, and subdue it: and have dominion over the fish of the sea, and over the fowl of the air, and over every living thing that moveth upon the earth."

THE BLESSING crowned God's family with His glory and honor. It gave them power over the planet and everything in, on and around it. It empowered them to operate as His under-rulers on the earth.

In initiating the Eden Covenant, God also laid out His purpose for mankind: They were to keep expanding the Garden of Eden until it filled the whole earth with THE BLESSING and glory of God.

Adam was divinely designed to fulfill this glorious mission. He was a spirit being, an eternal man. His physical body, clothed with God's radiant glory, was infused with God's DNA. That DNA made him uniquely different from any of the animals.[6]

Adam also walked in a realm of authority no angel nor any other created being had ever been given. He was not created to be a manager over God's creation, but to rule over it. Like God, Adam's *nature* was to rule. He was made to have dominion as a king and priest unto God (Revelation 1:6).

A triune being with a spirit, a soul (comprised of mind, will and emotions) and a body, Adam had complete dominion on earth over all three worlds: the spiritual, intellectual and physical. His spirit was indwelt by God's Spirit. He was equipped with God's mind (1 Corinthians 2:16), so he had mental superiority over everything that walks, flies, crawls and swims.

Filled with God Himself, Adam had everything he needed to carry God's glory and expand His physical family throughout this

---

6 "Deoxyribonucleic Acid (DNA) Factsheet," National Human Genome Research Institute, https://www.genome.gov/about-genomics/fact-sheets/Deoxyribonucleic-Acid-Fact-Sheet (accessed 7/2023).

massive universe. Everything, that is, except a mate. At that point, Adam had no companion, apart from God, because in the beginning the first man and woman were not yet two separate people. They were literally, physically one. That's why Genesis 5:2 says that in the day God created them, He made them "male and female... and called *their* name Adam."

CUTTING THE EDEN COVENANT

Adam is translated from the word *Ish,* which is the Hebrew word for *human.* So, Adam was originally as much female as he was male. Like God, he had within him the traits of both. After he was created, however, God said, "It is not good that the man should be alone," and made a helpmate for him.

Causing a deep sleep to fall upon Adam, God "took one of his ribs, and closed up the flesh instead thereof; And the rib, which The LORD God had taken from man, made he a woman, and brought her unto the man" (Genesis 2:21-22).

We could say this was the first surgical procedure ever performed—and why not? It was at the capable, steady hands of the Great Physician, and it was in a perfectly safe, healthy, disease-free environment. We can also say that with the opening of Adam's side there was likely the shedding of some blood, which foreshadowed two future events:

- The piercing of Jesus' side by the spear of a Roman soldier, as He hung on the cross
- The shedding of Jesus' sinless blood for the new life of His soon-to-be Bride, the Church (2 Corinthians 5:21; 1 Peter 1:17-19).

The cut God made in Adam's side also resulted in the first human covenant because He did far more through that operation than remove a rib from Adam's body. He took the female characteristics out of the first *Adam* (human) and put them into another, separate *Adam* (human). So, when the first *Adam* awoke and saw the second one, he said, "This is now bone of my bones, and flesh of my flesh: she shall be called Woman, because she was taken out of Man" (Genesis 2:23).

Later, Adam named his new "Number Two *Adam*" companion, *Eve*. But God always saw the two Adams as one. So, after dividing them into *Ish* and *Isha*, man and woman, He reconnected them. How? Through the marriage covenant!

This is why "a man shall leave his father and mother and be joined to his wife, and they shall become one flesh" (verse 24, *New King James Version*). Marriage is literally an example of human covenant in the flesh.

THE EDEN COVENANT CONDITIONS

Once rejoined, *Ish* (male) and *Isha* (female)—together—were like God again. His intention for them, as it is for all married couples, was for them to work together as one. With God in their midst, they were to operate in agreement as a loving trinity of power.

The Garden of Eden was supplied by God with everything they needed. "Out of the ground made The LORD God to grow every tree that is pleasant to the sight, and good for food; the tree of life also in the midst of the garden, and the tree of knowledge of good and evil" (verse 9). God also provided for them an abundance of natural resources—including precious stones and gold. The Garden was a testing ground for His family. A proving place from which they could expand, discover and develop.

It also carried with it great responsibilities. Adam had been put there by God "to dress it and to keep it"(verse 15). The *Chumash*[7] or *Torah*, translation of that verse says: "God took the man and placed him in the Garden of Eden, to work it and to guard it."[8] Adam's job, in other words, was to use his authority *to keep and to guard* the Garden that God had planted and laid out for him. From there, the

---

7 *Chumash* is a Hebrew word which means "five," indicating the five books of Moses (the *Torah*, or Greek *Pentateuch*), published in book, or codex, form which often includes commentary. This differs from a *Sefer Torah* which is the same five books in scroll form.
8 *The Chumash*, Genesis 2:15, p. 13.

plan was for this first couple to spread *Love's* influence and glory. To take THE BLESSING beyond the Garden of Eden throughout the rest of the planet, finishing what God had begun.

First and foremost, of course, Adam and Eve were there to fellowship with God. To walk and talk with Love and enjoy their Father's presence every day (Genesis 3:8). Filled with His glory, as His children they had confidence in both the spiritual and the natural realms. They also had direct access to heaven's throne of grace (Luke 3:38; Hebrews 9:23, 4:16).

They, as well as their Father, were living the dream.

All Adam and Eve had to do to keep living that dream was abide by the Eden Covenant conditions to which they'd agreed. Those conditions included only one restriction: "The LORD God commanded the man, saying, Of every tree of the garden thou mayest freely eat: But of the tree of the knowledge of good and evil, thou shalt not eat of it: for in the day that thou eatest thereof thou shalt surely die" (Genesis 2:16-17).

It sounds like a simple request—and it would have been if not for this: In the Garden there lurked a spiritual outlaw (satan). Previously called *Lucifer,* a name that in Hebrew means *Morning Star* or *Light Bearer,* he was once known as "the anointed cherub" (Ezekiel 28:14). When iniquity was found in him, he was cast out of heaven (Ezekiel 28:15, Luke 10:18) and by the time he showed up in the Garden of Eden, he had become God's number-one enemy.

His new name, *satan,* which means "opponent or adversary" aptly described his evil nature. As a fallen angel, he had witnessed the creation of God's first family members and he coveted their dominion over the earth. So, he set about to steal it by speaking to Eve through the mouth of a serpent. Asking her a subtle question designed to plant a seed of doubt in her mind about God's WORD, he said, "Hath God said, Ye shall not eat of every tree of the garden?"

"We may eat of the fruit of the trees of the garden," Eve replied: "But of the fruit of the tree which is in the midst of the garden, God hath said, Ye shall not eat of it, neither shall ye touch it, lest ye die" (Genesis 3:1-3).

That was not what God said. Eve misquoted Him by adding to His words. We must never do that. He didn't say anything about not touching the fruit. Eve came up with that because she was deceived. She didn't have a revelation of their covenant agreement with God.

Because the truth of what God *did* say was weakened due to a lack of knowledge and mishandling of His WORD, Eve believed what satan said next: "Ye shall not surely die: For God doth know that in the day ye eat thereof, then your eyes shall be opened, and ye shall be as gods, knowing good and evil" (verses 4-5).

It was a lie, but Eve fell for it. Without realizing it, she let satan tempt her with a desire for something God had already given to her. She was deceived into thinking that God was withholding something from them when, in fact, He had given them everything! In doing so, she let satan steal The WORD of God from her. She let satan do to her what he always comes to do—which is steal, kill and destroy (John 10:10).

God has never changed (Malachi 3:6), and neither has the devil. He fell from heaven's authority, and he cannot change. He's doomed forever. At that moment though, he thought he'd found a way out because not only did Eve succumb to his temptation and eat the fruit, but she also turned and gave it to Adam, as well.

Adam had been right there the whole time. He could have used his authority to shut the serpent's mouth and drive the devil out of the Garden. Unlike Eve, "Adam was not deceived" (1 Timothy 2:14). That's why it was such a horrible sin on Adam's part when— knowing full well what he was doing—he too ate of the tree and broke God's covenant command.

Adam had the authority, but not the moral right to commit such an act of high treason against his Creator. So, as God said through His prophet, Hosea, God charged Adam and not Eve, for violating the covenant (Hosea 4:7).

THE EDEN COVENANT CONTRADICTION

The moment Adam bowed his knee to the devil, the Father and His family were separated. The glistening light of God's glory flowing from Adam and Eve's spirits, that covered and crowned their bodies, went out. In its place an unfamiliar and oppressive force overtook them.

Without their magnificent coverings of light, Adam and Eve's now-naked forms were exposed in all their never-seen-before earthiness. Flooded with guilt and shame, they ran and hid themselves among the trees. Having turned their backs on God and His Love, the dark force of fear—the evil nature of the devil to which they had joined themselves—gripped them. For the first time, death began overshadowing every aspect of their lives.

Desperate and exposed, they came up with the idea of sewing together fig leaves to cover their newly discovered nakedness (Genesis 3:7). It was man's first attempt to provide for himself. He had fallen to the level of relying on works of his flesh rather than on the power of God to meet his needs.

With Adam's act of treason also came the contradiction to the Eden Covenant, a contradiction that can be summed up in one small, simple word: *sin*. Sin became the major obstacle that threatened to dash all hopes of God's dream for a family ever becoming a reality.

With one bite, everything was seemingly lost.

Sin entered the world, and with it came death, and life was lost (Romans 5:12).

Shame came in, and innocence was lost (Genesis 3:7).

Fear came in, and Love was lost (verse 10).

Satan came in, and authority was lost (Luke 4:5-7).

Satan had already lost all his authority in heaven, and up to that point he'd had none on planet Earth. All authority here had been handed over by God the Father to Adam and Eve. But when they put their authority into satan's hands, they opened the door for him to rule over the earth—without having any covenant agreement with God.

That was a serious obstacle to the fulfillment of God's plan both for mankind and for the earth itself. As Adam and Eve were about to learn, the earth would now start to work against them. Adam would have to toil and sweat—which he had never done before—to get it to produce.

"The earth is The LORD's, and the fulness thereof" (Psalm 24:1). Designed to respond to its true owner, only when man is operating in his proper, God-given authority (and within his covenant rights) does creation function appropriately. So, when Adam and Eve fell, creation did too. Because of their rebellion against God, the earth rebelled against mankind.

Standing in stark contrast to the Eden Covenant contradiction, however, was the Eden Covenant seal—the tree of life. Planted by God in the center of the Garden, that tree was the guarantee of the covenant God made with man in Eden. While in the Garden, Adam and Eve had access to it. But as we will see in the next chapter, when they sinned, God sealed the Eden Covenant by blocking not only Adam and Eve's access to the tree of life, but all mankind's.

Why did their sin affect all of us? Because when creating the earth, God mandated every living thing to reproduce "according to its kind" (Genesis 1:11, *New King James Version*). We call this the *Law of Genesis*—corn reproduces corn, cows reproduce cows, and so on.

When Adam sinned, he became the first man to be born again—not from death to life, as we're familiar with today—but from life to death. So, after the Fall, he and Eve could only reproduce in mankind the seed of sin and death that was now planted in their spirits. They could only reproduce after their spiritual overlord, satan.

It might seem unfair that one man could blow it for the rest of us for all eternity, all because of just one tree. You might wonder why God set up a system that would leave us thousands of years later still suffering the very real consequences of Adam's decision—a decision that *we* didn't make.

Once you see what He had planned, however, you'll realize God's strategy in allowing it to play out that way was brilliant. He knew exactly what He was doing by giving the Eden mandate to Adam and Eve before they rebelled in the Garden of Eden. He had a reason for making covenant with them when they were innocent, holy and without sin; and putting in their hands the destiny of all mankind.

Yes, it meant that one man's *sin* could condemn us all. But it also meant that it would take only one man's *righteousness* to redeem us. It established the legal right and authority for a future "sinless man" (Jesus) to restore everything that Adam and Eve would lose—including the tree of life.

You see, in blocking mankind's access to that tree, God preserved it for our future (Revelation 2:7; 22:14). He sealed for us the Eden Covenant and pointed to the time when, on another tree, God would save His people. The time when Jesus, the promised Seed, the Second and last Adam, would be crucified on a tree, taking upon Himself the curse for our sins (Galatians 3:13).

God established at the very outset of Creation that our Redemption would come through a tree![9] From the beginning, He has given us great hope for our future (Jeremiah 29:11).

He even embedded that hope in the name *Adam*. Given by God to the first members of His earthly family, Adam is a neutral word which applied to both the first man and woman. As we've already seen, it means "human" or, literally, "red earth."

In ancient Hebrew, however, which consists of symbols that look more like pictures than letters, the name conveys a deeper meaning. Its spelling includes a series of symbols representing an *ox* (meaning strong leader), a *door* (meaning a pathway), and *water* (meaning life or death). Put all those together and *Adam* translates as "the strong leader that opens the doorway that leads to life or death."

Add in the fact that the symbol for *water* also represents Adam's *blood* and the translation of Adam's name becomes even more astounding. It becomes: *The strong leader who opens the doorway that leads to life or death by his blood!*

Amazingly, those symbols that make up Adam's name paint a picture of the plan of Redemption. They reveal God's intended purpose from the very start. They point us toward Jesus, our

---

9 The prophetic sign of mankind's Redemption coming through a tree can also be found in other places in the Bible, including: Numbers 21:4-9, where God delivered His people from deadly snake bites through a bronze serpent on a pole; Joshua 8:29, where Joshua ordered an enemy king to be "hanged on a tree;" Genesis 22:1-4, where Isaac carried wood for the burnt offering up the mountain where he was to be sacrificed.

Redeemer, who is referred to throughout Scripture as the *Second Adam* (1 Corinthians 15:45-50).

From the beginning of time, the First Adam was pointing to the Second Adam—Jesus, our "Strong Leader who opens the doorway that leads to life or death by His blood!"

TURNING OUR LIVES BACK TO THE GARDEN

The words of the Eden Covenant have stood throughout human history. Despite the seemingly insurmountable contradiction to it, its words, like all God's words will stand forever, until the Garden of Eden fills the earth.

Approximately 3,000 years after the Fall of mankind, King David wrote a beautiful song of hope about creation. Looking backward at the glory and authority Adam and Eve had in the beginning, and looking forward at the day when it would all be restored, he wrote:

> When I consider thy heavens, the work of thy fingers, the moon and the stars, which thou hast ordained; what is man, that thou art mindful of him? and the son of man, that thou visitest him? For thou hast made him a little lower than the angels, and hast crowned him with glory and honour. Thou madest him to have dominion over the works of thy hands; thou hast put all things under his feet: all sheep and oxen, yea, and the beasts of the field; the fowl of the air, and the fish of the sea, and whatsoever passeth through the paths of the seas (Psalm 8:3-8).

Like many of David's songs, that one was prophetic. Its lyrics offered a great sense of hope—that God has not given up on us.

Yes, man had failed, but all was not lost. Fellowship and relationship had been broken, yet Love would press through generations to secure the future of His beloved family. With His creation in place and every key player in position, He began preparing a series of covenants. Each of them interrelated, and progressive in revelation, they would increasingly unveil God's master plan for the Redemption of man.

GO DEEPER
WITH GREG

WHY THE BIBLE
IS ONE SEAMLESS STORY

In my grandmother's kitchen, all the years I was growing up, there sat a small box filled with cards right next to the coffee pot. On the cards were printed promises from the Bible. Every day that I was at her house, she would take a promise card from the front of the box and read it to me, then place it at the back of the group of cards. The next time, she would pull from the front so that she was always rotating through the promises of God, reminding herself— and me—of God's faithfulness.

To this day, I can remember her usually saying to me after reading from each card, something like: "Honey, every promise in God's WORD belongs to you."

My grandmother's promise card box probably only held about 100 cards, but there are tens of thousands of promises in the Bible, and 7,487 of them are from God directly to mankind. If my grandmother had known that, I feel sure she would have made it her life's mission to read them all to me.

I recently had a student tell me that there is a difference between Old Testament promises and New Testament promises. But there's actually not. Although those promises were written in different generations, different locations and even different centuries, they are all inspired by God, and they all belong to us through Jesus: "For all the promises of God in Him are Yes, and in Him Amen" (2 Corinthians 1:20, *New King James Version*).

Moreover, it's important to understand that prior to the death, burial and resurrection of Jesus, there was but one collection of sacred Scripture; there was no Old Testament. In fact, the word *testament*—translated from the Latin *Testamentum*—is an Old English word for *covenant*. It wasn't until after the New Covenant was written that the idea of an Old Testament and a New Testament was developed.

As you'll learn throughout this book, the Old Testament included covenants God made with individuals, with all of mankind, with a tribe and with the nation of Israel, but in all these covenants Jesus was the promised Seed. When He offered Himself as the required sacrifice, the New Covenant that was made available to all mankind was built and established on the previous one. So while we recognize two testaments in the structure of the Bible, the story of the covenants crosses the page, dividing the Old and the New. The Bible links the two together time and again. Take for example these verses from Jeremiah 31:

> "The day is coming," says The LORD, when I will make a new covenant with the people of Israel and Judah. This covenant will not be like the one I made with their ancestors when I took them by the hand and brought them out of the land of Egypt. They broke that covenant, though I loved them as a husband loves his wife, says The LORD. But this is the new covenant I will make with the people of Israel after those days, says The LORD. I will put my instructions deep within them, and I will write them on their hearts. I will be their God, and they will be my people (verses 31-33, *New Living Translation).*

Not only do those verses from Jeremiah reveal the connection between the two Covenants, they appear again in the New Testament in Hebrews 8:7-13. We also see the connection between the two Covenants in 2 Corinthians 3. There, the Apostle Paul, showing the seamless story of Covenant and comparing the New to the Old, wrote:

The old way, with laws etched in stone, led to death, though it began with such glory that the people of Israel could not bear to look at Moses' face. For his face shone with the glory of God, even though the brightness was already fading away. Shouldn't we expect far greater glory under the new way, now that the Holy Spirit is giving life? If the old way, which brings condemnation, was glorious, how much more glorious is the new way, which makes us right with God! In fact, that first glory was not glorious at all compared with the overwhelming glory of the new way. So if the old way, which has been replaced, was glorious, how much more glorious is the new, which remains forever! (verses 7-11, *New Living Translation*).

The thread of covenant that connects us today to the promises God made to His people under the First Covenant can also be seen in Hebrews 11. It encourages us to follow the example of great men and women of God who lived under the First Covenant. Rehearsing their exploits, it reminds us over and over that they did them by Faith. Going down the list, it says:

- It was by Faith that Abel brought a more acceptable offering to God than Cain did.
- It was by Faith that Enoch was taken up to heaven without dying.
- It was by Faith that Noah built a large boat to save his family from the flood.
- It was by Faith that Abraham obeyed when God called him to leave home and go to another land that God would give him as his inheritance.
- And even when he reached the land God promised him, he lived there by Faith.
- It was by Faith that even Sarah was able to have a child, though she was barren and was too old.
- It was by Faith that Abraham offered Isaac as a sacrifice when God was testing him.
- It was by Faith that Isaac promised BLESSINGS for the future to his sons, Jacob and Esau.

- It was by Faith that Jacob, when he was old and dying, BLESSED each of Joseph's sons and bowed in worship as he leaned on his staff.
- It was by Faith that Joseph, when he was about to die, said confidently that the people of Israel would leave Egypt.
- It was by Faith that Moses' parents hid him for three months when he was born.
- It was by Faith that Moses, when he grew up, refused to be called the son of Pharaoh's daughter.
- It was by Faith that Moses left the land of Egypt, not fearing the king's anger.
- It was by Faith that Moses commanded the people of Israel to keep the Passover and to sprinkle blood on the doorposts so that the angel of death would not kill their firstborn sons.
- It was by Faith that the people of Israel went right through the Red Sea as though they were on dry ground.
- It was by Faith that the people of Israel marched around Jericho for seven days, and the walls came crashing down.
- It was by Faith that Rahab the prostitute was not destroyed with the people in her city who refused to obey God.

How much more do I need to say? It would take too long to recount the stories of the faith of Gideon, Barak, Samson, Jephthah, David, Samuel, and all the prophets. By faith these people overthrew kingdoms, ruled with justice, and received what God had promised them. They shut the mouths of lions, quenched the flames of fire, and escaped death by the edge of the sword. Their weakness was turned to strength. They became strong in battle and put whole armies to flight.... All these people earned a good reputation because of their faith, yet none of them received all that God had promised. For God had something better in mind for us, so that they would not reach perfection without us (see verses 4-40, *New Living Translation*).

Do you see it? The Bible is all one seamless redemptive plan. It's the plan God had from the beginning. The first and last parts are so interwoven, it's impossible to understand the ministry of Jesus without knowing what preceded Him. God gave us both the First Covenant and the Second, the Old and the New, so let's study the whole BOOK and walk in the fullness of the Covenant He made with us.

CHAPTER 2 ENDNOTE

God charged and entrusted to Adam and Eve—and with them all mankind—what you could call planetary stewardship.

Stewardship of the earth and everything in it (and beyond it) has remained our God-given responsibility down to today. Nothing changed after the Fall. This part of our human existence is still expected of us by God. Sadly, however, like most things, after sin entered this atmosphere, our care for this world we live in has been misguided and perverted—things such as worshipping nature over God. Unbelievers in their secular mindsets have no knowledge of the truth of this assignment, and therefore try to manage the planet and the life on it in their own limited understanding, with its Creator nowhere in the equation.

But before you're tempted to cast stones of judgment against anyone, realize that Jesus' own disciples would someday be challenged by wind and waves, fish and bread, water and wine—along with many other physical *phenomena* surrounding His life and ministry—that couldn't possibly make sense to their natural thinking and experiences.

The truth is, today's Church should be leading in the care for nature and not allowing it to default to governments or well-meaning organizations. We are the ones equipped and empowered by God Himself with all authority, power and dominion in heaven and on earth to rule, to BLESS, to multiply, to be fruitful, to fill, to subdue, to give, to possess…to reign on behalf of our heavenly Father—with His breath in our lungs, His blood in our veins, and His creative power in and on our own words.

> The day is coming, says The LORD, when I will make a new covenant with the people of Israel and Judah. This covenant will not be like the one I made with their ancestors when I took them by the hand and led them out of the land of Egypt. They did not remain faithful to my covenant, so I turned my back on them, says The LORD. But this is the new covenant I will make with the people of Israel on that day, says The LORD: I will put my laws in their minds, and I will write

them on their hearts. I will be their God, and they will be my people. And they will not need to teach their neighbors, nor will they need to teach their relatives, saying, 'You should know The LORD.' For everyone, from the least to the greatest, will know me already. And I will forgive their wickedness, and I will never again remember their sins (Hebrews 8:7-13, *New Living Translation*).

When God speaks of a "*new* covenant," it means he has made the *first one* obsolete. It is now out of date and will soon disappear.

GOD'S

COVENANT

WITH

ADAM

CHAPTER THREE

GOD'S COVENANT
WITH ADAM

One time back in the early days of Kenneth Copeland Ministries, Gloria and I arrived home after having been on the road traveling and holding meetings night and day—and we were exhausted. My dad, A.W. Copeland, was in the office, and when we walked in, he smiled and handed me a piece of paper from one of those old calculators.

On that little piece of paper were figures he had tallied that showed all our expenses.

"Kenneth," he said, "I don't know if you realize what the expenses of this ministry have grown into."

"No sir, I don't," I told him. "I don't have any idea what they are. I thought you were handling that."

"Well, I am," he said, "and I believe you had better do something about this."

My dad was ever so kindly saying, "Boy, we are out of money!"

I looked at that piece of paper and saw we owed $5,000. *Dear LORD*, I thought, *there isn't that much money in the whole world!*

Honestly, I had never seen that much money at one time, in one place, in my life. There was no way we could pay off those bills—at least not based on our natural circumstances.

But thank God, I had been listening to Kenneth Hagin's teachings on prosperity. I had heard him preach Mark 11:23-24:

Truly I say to you, whoever says to this mountain, "Be taken up and cast into the sea," and does not doubt in his heart, but believes that what he says is going to happen, it will be *granted* him. Therefore I say to you, all things for which you pray and ask, believe that you have received them, and they will be *granted* you" *(New American Standard Bible*-95).

I had heard him preach John 16:23-24:

And when that time comes, you will ask nothing of Me [you will need to ask Me no questions]. I assure you, most solemnly I tell you, that My Father will *grant* you whatever you ask in My Name [as presenting all that I AM]. Up to this time you have not asked a [single] thing in My Name [as presenting all that I AM]; but now ask and keep on asking and you will receive, so that your joy (gladness, delight) may be full and complete *(Amplified Bible, Classic Edition).*

I had heard him preach 1 John 5:14-15:

And this is the confidence (the assurance, the privilege of boldness) which we have in Him: [we are sure] that if we ask anything (make any request) according to His will (in agreement with His own plan), He listens to and hears us. And if (since) we [positively] know that He listens to us in whatever we ask, we also know [with settled and absolute knowledge] that we have *[granted* us as our present possessions] the requests made of Him *(Amplified Bible, Classic Edition).*

Grant, grant, grant, grant. That was covenant talk!

As I said earlier, I didn't have much revelation of covenant back then, but at least Jesus—and Brother Hagin—did. And based on those scriptures, I knew enough to know what Gloria and I needed to do next.

After my dad showed me that piece of paper and caught me up to speed (and jerked some slack out of me, in the process), Gloria and I walked into his little office. I turned the chair around from the desk, got on my knees to pray, and opened my Bible.

Turning to Mark 11:24-25, I went over it again: "...Whatever you ask for in prayer, believe (trust and be confident) that it is granted to you, and you will [get it]. And whenever you stand praying, if you have anything against anyone, forgive him and let it drop (leave it, let it go), in order that your Father Who is in heaven may also forgive you your [own] failings and shortcomings and let them drop" *(Amplified Bible, Classic Edition)*.

Then I went over again what Jesus said in John 16:23: "My Father will grant you whatever you ask in My Name [as presenting all that I AM]" *(Amplified Bible, Classic Edition)*.

GRANT ESTABLISHED

When I finished reading those scriptures, Gloria and I said, "We can agree for this $5,000 because we have a *heavenly grant!*"

So, we wrote out exactly what we needed, and prayed and believed we received it. Then we took the calculator tape that read $5,000, along with our agreement grant and, according to 1 Peter 5:7, we rolled the care over on God, our Covenant Partner, and forgot about it.

About two weeks later, a delightful woman walked into my dad's office. "Who do I give this money to?" she asked. "The LORD laid it on my heart some time ago to give Brother Copeland's ministry $10,000."

When we put together the timeline, we realized if she had given the money when The LORD first laid it on her heart, the $5,000 debt wouldn't have been there. The ministry would have been $5,000 in the black instead of in the red.

The lesson to learn here is this: My Covenant Partner, the Almighty God, and His angels were doing their part in that situation. God always does His part. He's never late. And by walking in Faith for finances, Gloria and I were doing our part.

Faith is our part! For "the just shall live by faith," and we "walk by faith, not by sight" (Hebrews 10:38; 2 Corinthians 5:7).

Even though $5,000 was more money than I ever could have imagined coming up with myself, I realized back then that *Faith* didn't know the difference. Whether it's five cents, $5,000, or $5 million, Faith works just the same. So, Gloria and I put The WORD of God first place and made it our final authority. With the help of the Holy Spirit, we reprogrammed our minds with the truth of The WORD and brought our thoughts into line with it.

We refused to budge an inch off our Covenant promises, pled the blood, and commanded the devil to take his hands off our money. Never letting go of what Jesus said was rightfully ours, we refused to let the devil talk us into doubting God and His WORD.

Because of that, then and now, the devil cannot steal the authority invested in us, as believers.

Faith is a lifestyle, based on blood-backed, precious promises.

THE ADAM COVENANT PROMISE

Although Adam and Eve didn't yet realize it, a blood-backed promise was what they needed in the Garden of Eden after their sin separated them from the Father. God had said they would surely die if they ate of the tree of the knowledge of good and evil; and it had happened. Their bodies didn't instantly fall to the ground lifeless, but Adam and Eve died spiritually the moment they broke their precious Covenant relationship with God.

The fig leaves they'd sewn together to cover their physical nakedness had done nothing to cover their spiritual shame. So, when they heard the sound of God walking in the Garden in the cool of the day, they didn't joyfully join Him. Instead, they hid themselves from His presence among the trees of the Garden.

Genesis 3:9 tells us that God called out to Adam, "Where art thou?"

Professor Stephens has pointed out in his teachings that in the Hebrew text, God's question is phrased this way: *Why are you where you are?* That clarifies the situation. It wasn't that the Omniscient— All-Knowing—God didn't know where Adam was. Of course He knew. The more important question was: *Why are you there…and not here with Me?*

In asking that, God was giving Adam an opportunity to repent. But repenting was the last thing on Adam's mind. Notice his reply: "I heard Your voice in the garden, and I was afraid, because I was naked; and I hid myself" (verse 10, *New King James Version*).

Giving Adam a second opportunity to repent, God spoke to him again, and then to Eve:

And He said, "Who told you that you were naked? Have you eaten from the tree of which I commanded you that you should not eat?" Then the man said, "The woman whom You gave to be with me, she gave me of the tree, and I ate." And The LORD God said to the woman, "What is this you have done?" The woman said, "The serpent deceived me, and I ate." So The LORD God said to the serpent: "Because you have done this, you are cursed more than all cattle, and more than every beast of the field; on your belly you shall go, and you shall eat dust all the days of your life" (verses 11–14, *New King James Version*).

Neither Adam nor Eve took responsibility for their sin. Reacting and responding in fear, they blamed everybody else. First, Adam blamed his wife. Then he blamed God. Eve blamed the serpent.

Once everyone had their say and pleaded their case, with all guilty parties present, God delivered the promise of what would become the *Adam covenant.*

First to satan, the perpetrator: "And The LORD God said unto the serpent, Because thou hast done this, thou art cursed above all cattle, and above every beast of the field; upon thy belly shalt thou go, and dust shalt thou eat all the days of thy life: And I will put enmity between thee and the woman, and between thy seed and her seed; it shall bruise thy head, and thou shalt bruise his heel" (verses 14-15).

Eve was next: "Unto the woman he said, I will greatly multiply thy sorrow and thy conception; in sorrow thou shalt bring forth children; and thy desire shall be to thy husband, and he shall rule over thee" (verse 16).

And, finally, Adam: "And unto Adam he said, Because thou hast hearkened unto the voice of thy wife, and hast eaten of the tree, of which I commanded thee, saying, Thou shalt not eat of it: cursed is the ground for thy sake; in sorrow shalt thou eat of it all the days of thy life; thorns also and thistles shall it bring forth to thee; and thou shalt eat the herb of the field; in the sweat of thy face shalt thou eat bread, till thou return unto the ground; for out of it wast thou taken: for dust thou art, and unto dust shalt thou return" (verses 17-19).

It may have sounded more like a judge handing down a sentence than like a Father BLESSING His children. But really, it was the next installment of the covenants God would put in place to preserve His dream and His family. For tucked away in the depths of God's words was a hidden mystery that would take thousands of years to be revealed. We just read it in verse 15—let's look again at what God said to the serpent: "I will put enmity between thee and the woman, and between thy seed and her seed; it shall bruise thy head, and thou shalt bruise his heel."

These prophetic words were the promise of the Adam covenant. They contained the hidden secret of a virgin birth. They told of the coming *Seed*, the Redeemer (Jesus) and how He and the devil would bruise each other. Of how He would bring Redemption by paying the price for Adam's sin, restoring THE BLESSING, and reuniting the Father with His family.

The Adam covenant was the first of what we refer to as *seed* covenants (Galatians 3:29).

While it might appear that God was *forced* to initiate this new covenant to deliver Adam and Eve from the mess they'd made, God already had it prepared. He knew long before He ever created them that Adam and Eve (and all mankind with them) would end up naked, afraid and in trouble. That's why Revelation 13:8 speaks of "the Lamb [Jesus] slain from the foundation of the world." The

Adam covenant was part of God's plan to send the Lamb. It was His next step in leading mankind down the path of Redemption to Jesus and ultimately to eternal life with Him.

It was also the next step toward obliterating satan forever. Through the Seed promised in the Adam covenant, God would one day put a permanent end to satan's ability to deceive, hurt or subvert His people (Hebrews 2:14; Revelation 20:10). Even the animal kingdom would eventually be set free from the devil's influence. Instead of being subject to the curse that came on it when Adam sinned, creation itself would one day be "delivered from the bondage of corruption into the glorious liberty of the children of God" (Romans 8:21; Isaiah 11:6).

CUTTING THE ADAM COVENANT

Once God had issued the Adam covenant promise, He performed a covenant act. "For Adam also and for his wife The LORD God made long coats (tunics) of skins and clothed them" (Genesis 3:21, *Amplified Bible, Classic Edition)*. The first cutting of a Blood covenant between God and man, this is the first record of blood being shed in the earth.

Why did blood have to be shed? Because, as God had previously warned Adam, the price of disobeying God's command was death. It had to be. Not because Elohim was out to kill the people He created and loved, but because sin produces separation from Him—and apart from Him there is no life.

Blood is the only substance in existence precious enough to cover the cost of a life! One of the most mysterious of all physical substances, it's something that neither God nor the angels nor satan had. Yet Elohim breathed His own life into it and made sure that Adam had it, Eve had it, and even the animals had it.

God later explained through Moses the reason for this: "The life of the flesh is in the blood: and I have given it to you upon the altar to make an atonement for your souls: for it is the blood that maketh an atonement for the soul" (Leviticus 17:11).

Beginning with the Adam covenant, God used animals as a substitute to literally bear man's punishment, which was death. Their blood provided an *atonement* for man's sins. *Atone* means "to cover." Atonement was God's way of temporarily covering the darkness of sin while mankind waited for Jesus, the Redeemer.

Under Old Covenant Law, an animal sacrifice would cover sin for one year. But the sacrifice made by Jesus would last forever. His blood would not atone for sin. It would remit it. To *remit* means "to release, pardon, let go like it never happened."

The magnificent book of Hebrews lays this out very clearly: "Without the shedding of blood there is neither release from sin and its guilt nor the remission of the due and merited punishment for sins." But "where remission of these is, there is no more offering for sin" (Hebrews 9:22, *Amplified Bible, Classic Edition,* 10:18).

This is why under the New Covenant there's no need for us, as believers, to offer animal sacrifices. By the blood of Jesus, our sins have been remitted.

For Adam and Eve, however, such remission still lay in the future. So, God acted as the Mediator of the Adam covenant. He sacrificed animals for them, thereby setting the example for what His priests would do for His people, the Israelites, generations later.

In doing so, He also revealed another aspect of His character and nature; one that had not yet been seen. In Genesis 1 He was known as *Creator, Father, Son* and *Holy Spirit,* the plural *Elohim,* in the Hebrew. Here in Genesis 2 and 3, God reveals Himself as *Redeemer Creator.* Adding *Yahweh* or *Jehovah*[10] to His Name, He gives us a glimpse into the redemptive part of His nature.

Here we discover the tender, compassionate side of our Redeemer Creator. We find Him, after Adam and Eve's Fall, guiding and caring for the frightened couple out of His grace and mercy. We see even after they sinned, the God who is Love is still on the scene. He still has a covenant plan for them.

Executed out of Love, this first Blood covenant became a new and binding form of contract, sealed with the blood of innocent

---

10 For a fuller understanding of the names of God, see Appendix A: The Covenant Names of God, p. 249.

animals that for years to come would be killed in place of sinful man, rendering their life-filled blood as a covering for sin and death. It established the pattern for future covenants that allowed man *of his own free will* to commit to a relationship with Almighty God, or *El Shaddai* in the Hebrew, the God who is more than enough.

Unlike the Eden Covenant, which Adam and Eve broke with seemingly little thought, the value and seriousness of this new Adam covenant could not be missed. This was an agreement to be far more mindful of because now *blood* (life and death) was on the line.

The vast scope of the Redemption plan God had hidden in the Adam covenant, though, remained cloaked. A divine mystery, no fallen human or angel could have ever discerned it. For centuries the fullness of this plan stayed a secret (Colossians 1:26). None but God Himself could see how its fulfillment would allow Him, once again, to have relationship with His beloved family. Only He knew how it would make a way to unite to Him forever those who would willingly enter into a binding Blood Covenant agreement with Him.

From time to time, God did allow His prophets glimpses of the glorious salvation that lay ahead. But He only let them see just enough. Enough to keep everyone headed in the right direction— toward Israel, to be specific, the place where this great mystery would eventually unfold, the Covenant Capital of the world.

Meanwhile, step by step along this journey to man's Redemption, God was laying a trap for satan who, because of his near-sighted pride and arrogance, would fall headlong into it and bring about his own eternal destruction.

THE ADAM COVENANT SEAL

The seal of the Adam covenant was the skins of the innocent animals Adam and Eve wore as clothing. For them, those skins became the reminder or guarantee of God's Blood covenant. They're also a perfect example of God's eternal Love for us.

Reading about them reminds us that even when our love fails— as Adam and Eve's did—God's Love says, "I choose to continue loving and caring for you." That's huge. Think again about what Adam and Eve had done. They not only rejected God's Love by disobeying Him, afterward they rejected Him as their Provider by not seeking Him for help. Instead of trusting Him, they put their trust in their own works by sewing leaves together to wear.

Even so, however, God had not turned His back on them. He had stepped in as a loving and compassionate Father and provided better clothing for them.

Imagine how Adam and Eve must have felt wearing those skins afterward, day after day. Imagine the new physical sensations they felt. The deep sense of grief or loss they must have experienced as they realized the ramifications of what they had done. Think about Adam realizing he was responsible for the death of the animals he had once named and given an identity.

In addition to the animal skins, Adam and Eve also had another reminder to keep in the forefront of their minds. This second seal was their *Faith*—Faith in the day when sin would be dealt with once and for all.

Remember what God said to the serpent? "I will put enmity between thee and the woman, and between thy seed and her seed; it shall bruise thy head, and thou shalt bruise his heel" (Genesis 3:15). Adam and Eve were there and heard God speak those words.

That's where their *Faith* was—in God's WORD. Their Faith and His WORD became a vital reminder for them in this covenant process of redemption and restoration.

The same is true in our lives as believers today. It's how Gloria and I believed God for the $5,000 worth of bills to be paid that I told you about at the beginning of this chapter. Even though we didn't have much revelation of covenant at the time, we had learned enough to recognize covenant talk in the Bible when we read it. We understood passages like Mark 11 and John 16 to be *Faith* chapters!

Thankfully, we had also learned enough about Faith to know if we were ever going to see those bills paid, we would have to keep God's Covenant WORD in the forefront of our thinking. We would have to keep it in our mouths and in our hearts. The WORD produces life in the human spirit for the soul and physical body, so we knew we needed to do what Proverbs 4:20-22 says:

> My son, attend to my words; incline thine ear unto my sayings. Let them not depart from thine eyes; keep them in the midst of thine heart. For they are life unto those that find them, and health to all their flesh.

That's why, where that $5,000 was concerned, Gloria and I wrote out on paper in our heavenly grant exactly what we needed—so we could keep it before our eyes at all times. We took God's Covenant promises seriously—even *more* seriously than our financial need.

CONTRADICTION TO THE ADAM COVENANT

Adam and Eve would also need to take God's covenant promises seriously. They would have to hold onto them in the face of the Adam covenant contradiction. The contradiction lay in the fact that due to their now darkened sinful nature, God could no longer walk on the level of fellowship with them they'd once known. His relationship with mankind would now have to be at arm's length at best. Otherwise, the intense power of His glory would consume and destroy them.

What's more, because of their fallen condition, Adam and Eve could no longer remain in the Garden of Eden. As we've already discussed, the tree of life in the center of the Garden had sealed the Eden covenant. So, to preserve it for their future, God had to put it out of their reach.

> And The LORD God said, Behold, the man is become as one of us, to know good and evil: and now, lest he put forth his hand, and take also of the tree of life, and eat, and live for ever: Therefore The LORD God sent him forth from the garden of Eden, to till the ground from whence he was taken. So he drove out the man; and he placed at the east of the garden of Eden Cherubims, and a flaming sword which turned every

way, to keep the way of the tree of life (Genesis 3:22–24).

With God and man, Father and family, seemingly parted forever, satan figured he had finally arrived. He now had control of what had briefly been Adam and Eve's domain. With man bound by sin and death and Almighty God bound to a safe distance from mankind, he finally had free reign on earth.

The way satan saw it, he had succeeded at trapping both God and man. There was no way God would *ever* be able to change man and get him back to a place of holiness and righteousness. In fact, by banishing Adam and Eve from the Garden of Eden, God seemed to have conceded defeat.

He appeared to have shut down His plans for man to live forever like Himself, their physical bodies filled with His glory. Instead, they were doomed to death. God had even gone so far as to limit their lifespan: "And The LORD said, My spirit shall not always strive with man, for that he also is flesh: yet his days shall be an hundred and twenty years" (Genesis 6:3).

Because Adam had committed high treason and given the devil his authority, satan had become the god of this world (2 Corinthians 4:4). He had become the spiritual father of fallen mankind. Jesus confirmed this many years later when He told the religious men of His day: "Ye are of your father the devil, and the lusts of your father ye will do. He was a murderer from the beginning, and abode not in the truth, because there is no truth in him. When he speaketh a lie, he speaketh of his own: for he is a liar, and the father of it" (John 8:44).

Where did this leave Adam and Eve? Sadly, it left them stuck outside the Garden of Eden and separated from God.

What did their future on this earth look like? Although Adam's assignment to be fruitful and multiply was still intact, the ground was now cursed for his sake. It would bring forth thorns and thistles, and he would have to sweat to get it to produce. Eve would bring forth children but she would do it in sorrow.

It didn't sound like much of a life to look forward to. But the truth is, the devil didn't have much to look forward to either because, thank God, the promised Seed *was* coming!

Yes, there would be plenty of obstacles to overcome. This *Seed of woman* would have to stand the test that the first Adam failed, so He would have to be born into the world without a sin nature. He could *not* be born part man and part God. Mankind's Redeemer would have to be *all* man, since it was a man who broke the Covenant. Yet, somehow, God would have to accomplish this Redemption Himself.

Somehow, He had to find a way back into the earth. But how?

There would have to be more Blood covenants. Those Blood covenants would have to have more conditions and more promises. They would have to be able to overcome the seemingly insurmountable, natural obstacles that had arisen against these first two covenants.

This is where it begins to get complicated. It's also where we will see God's mastery and genius at causing all things to "work together for good to them that love God, to them who are the called according to his purpose" (Romans 8:28).

GO DEEPER
WITH GREG

TWO ADAMS—ONE FAILING, THE OTHER FULFILLING

As we've seen, the first man was created in God's image. An "image" is an exact likeness, a visible representation or reproduction of a thing or person. So, the first Adam was an exact likeness, a visible reproduction of Almighty God.

After Adam and Eve fell because of their disobedience to God, however, they began to reproduce after their own likeness. We see this confirmed in Genesis 5:3 that says, "Adam lived an hundred and thirty years, and begat a son *in his own likeness*, and *after his [own] image;* and called his name Seth."

Seth was actually Adam and Eve's third son. Their first two were Cain and Abel. But all of them were born into the likeness and image of sin—so was all mankind after them. We all inherited the first Adam's sinful nature. We were all born in his fallen image rather than in the likeness of the Father in whose image we all had originally been created.

Adam and Eve's attempt to cover up and hide their fallen condition with sewn-together fig leaves was fallen man's first attempt to use self-effort to cover his sin. It did not work, of course. So, God Himself covered their sin by shedding the blood of animals and clothing Adam and Eve with the skins.

By doing this, God was prophetically pointing to the Second Adam—Jesus, the Lamb of God, who would forever bring an *end to the curse.* The Second Adam would fulfill where the first Adam failed.

We see in the Gospels another prophetic picture of Jesus stepping in and fulfilling what the first Adam could not accomplish. There, we find Him, in the last week of His life, traveling with His disciples and coming across a *fig tree*. Jesus, being hungry, went over to the tree and began looking for figs. Finding there were none, Jesus, the Second Adam, cursed the tree, saying: "No man eat fruit of thee *hereafter for ever*" (Mark 11:14). The next day when He and His disciples passed by the tree again, they saw that it had dried up from the roots.

For years I puzzled over this incident. I couldn't figure it out: What did the tree do wrong? Mark 11:13 says that it wasn't the season for fig trees to produce their fruit, so why would Jesus expect to find any? Why curse the tree when it wasn't the tree's fault that it hadn't yet produced figs?

Then one day I saw it: Jesus was making a prophetic declaration! He was pointing back to the first Adam's attempt to *cover* his sin with fig leaves and letting us know that era was over. He was making a statement: *NO MORE COVERING! NO MORE HIDING! NO MORE CONDEMNATION! NO MORE SHAME!*

He was declaring that He, the Second Adam, had come and was about to pay the ultimate price for removing all that guilt, condemnation and shame once and for all—and for *all* mankind!

HOW TO NIP BAD FRUIT IN THE BUD

In studying the Adam covenant, another thing I puzzled over for years was why God didn't intervene *before* Adam and Eve ate of the forbidden tree. Why didn't He do something to save them and all the rest of us a lot of heartache and headaches? I simply could not make sense of it.

Then one day, the Holy Spirit took me back in Scripture to the very moment God created man (the first Adam) in His image.

And God BLESSED them, and God said unto them, Be fruitful, and multiply, and replenish the earth, and *subdue it*: and *have dominion* over the fish of the sea, and over the fowl of the air, and *over every living thing* that moveth upon the earth (Genesis 1:28).

There was my answer—"...*subdue* the earth...*have dominion* over every living thing!"

The moment God spoke those words to the first Adam, releasing them into the atmosphere for the rest of eternity—it was done! God *had* intervened. God *had* equipped Adam and Eve to *subdue* the serpent and *dominate* satan! In that instant, "dominion" had been imparted into the "image" (the first Adam) of God. All earthly authority had been deposited into a physical being.

For God to have stepped into the situation to intercept the devil's scheme to deceive Eve and manipulate Adam—He would have had to break His own WORD. He would have had to break His very first Blood covenant with the first Adam. That was something God *could not* do. He is *incapable* of breaking His WORD. He cannot lie (Numbers 23:19). So, it is impossible for Him to break covenant.

I cannot tell you how many times over the years I have heard people ask in some moment of crisis or grief, "Where was God when this happened? Why didn't He do something?"

Again, the answer is: "*Subdue* the earth...*have dominion* over every living thing!"

Some time ago, I heard a statement that has really helped me, personally, in some tough times when hard questions surfaced in my mind. The statement was simply: "Never trade what you know for what you don't know." In other words, stick with what you know. Don't ever let go of what you *know* to be the truth.

In the face of every challenge, keep reminding yourself God *cannot* lie. Keep rehearsing in your mind the fact that the same authority and dominion God gave to the *first* Adam, He intended for you. Keep declaring out loud that the same authority and dominion God gave to the *Second* Adam has been transferred to you (Matthew 28:18-20).

In short, put yourself in remembrance.

And while you're at it, use these scriptures to help establish yourself in your place of authority and dominion in the Second Adam:

- Seven "I AM" declarations Jesus made: *The Bread* (John 6:35); *The Light* (John 8:12); *The Door* (John 10:9); *The Good Shepherd* (John 10:11); *The Resurrection and Life* (John 11:25); *The Way, Truth and Life* (John 14:6); *The Vine* (John 15:5)
- Where the first Adam failed, the Second Adam finished (John 19:30)
- God's *grace* is greater than the first Adam's *sin* (Romans 5:15-19)
- *Death* came through the first Adam, but *life* through the Second (1 Corinthians 15:21-23)
- The first Adam became a *living soul,* but the Second Adam a *life-giving spirit;* the first Adam is of the *earth,* and the Second from *heaven;* we have borne the image of the *earthly,* and shall bear the image of the *heavenly* (1 Corinthians 15:45-49)
- The Second Adam tasted death for *every* man (Hebrews 2:9)
- The blood of the Second Adam *speaks better things* than the blood of Abel (Hebrews 12:24)
- The Second Adam will change our *earthly bodies* into *glorious bodies* like His (Philippians 3:20-21)
- The *same glory* the Father gave the Second Adam *has been given to us* (John 17).

GOD'S

COVENANT

WITH

NOAH

CHAPTER FOUR

GOD'S COVENANT WITH NOAH

One of my heroes of the Faith is Bishop David Oyedepo, pastor of Faith Tabernacle in Ota, Nigeria. A remarkable person, he's what I would call a modern-day *Covenant man*. I'm certain a major part of that has to do with his living on the continent of Africa. The land of Stanley and Livingstone, people there in general have been very aware of *Blood covenants* for generations.

Faith Tabernacle began in 1983, and for years the people gathered as a church and spent much of their time just praising and worshipping God. The bishop had learned early on about the power of praising God for what He had already promised in His WORD, and standing fast until results came. So, whenever the church encountered any kind of need or challenge, they just focused on what their Covenant with God afforded them as believers.

As they continued to do this year after year, the church kept growing. Eventually they ran out of room. That's when they decided to buy land outside the major city of Lagos—land that at the time was nothing but 500 acres of jungle; full of lions, monkeys and other wildlife.

Fast forward about twenty-five years. That's when Bishop Oyedepo and I met. It was 2008, and America and much of the world was in a global financial crisis with real estate bottoming out. Faith Tabernacle, however, was experiencing a boom. They had 2,000 acres cleared and newly developed, with buildings and infrastructure—including a facility seating 50,000 people. The project had cost US$250 million and it was just Phase 1. The miracle was they did it debt free, with no American money, and ALL in one year!

How could such a feat be accomplished, in bad financial times? And out in the middle of a jungle?

Simple: *Covenant*—but not just any covenant; one bought and paid for by the precious blood of Jesus.

God, by His Spirit, instructed Bishop Oyedepo to build, and the bishop and his people knew they had a Blood Covenant with Jehovah Jireh—The LORD their Provider. So what if all kinds of officials and professionals said it could not be done? The people at Faith Tabernacle were confident that through the direction and power of the Holy Spirit, the project would be completed. They trusted that the One who had given the directive would "supply all [their] need according to his riches in glory by Christ Jesus" (Philippians 4:19).

Meanwhile, they continued to praise and worship their Covenant-honoring God, which kept Him on the jobsite (Hebrews 13:15; Psalm 22:3). Their acts of praise were a declaration that He is faithful to keep His promises. Their worship was their Faith in action, effectively calling into being things that don't yet exist (Romans 4:17).

The power of God's WORD, combined with their praise, produced a great harvest, and the project was completed. What's more, in 2008 when Bishop and I met, he told me that the $250 million for Phase 2 was already in the bank.

Leroy Thompson, others and I call this a "sweatless" anointing. Remember how God told Adam that, due to the curse, he would have to toil and sweat to get the ground to produce a harvest for himself (Genesis 3:18)? We, as believers, have been redeemed from the curse. We can release our Faith in God's WORD and watch His power produce over and above what we could ever imagine possible—and with a whole lot less *toil* (Ephesians 3:20). That's why it's called a "sweatless" anointing. It's also called working by Faith!

Bishop Oyedepo and his congregation are, by most modern-day standards, extremely aware of covenant. They understand it because of the traditions and culture in which they were raised. Their fore-fathers are the ones who taught the likes of Stanley and Livingstone about covenant. I believe that it is—in part—because of their innate understanding of covenant that they were able to act so confidently on God's WORD. Due to their grasp of covenant's purpose, power and potential, they took His WORD seriously and received their guaranteed result, against all odds.

Now, in contrast, consider Adam and Eve. They lived in the best of times and conditions, and were intimately acquainted with God Himself. Yet they were readily talked out of their Covenant rights and benefits by the serpent. The Adam covenant God cut with them afterward was a wake-up call, not only for Adam and Eve, but for all mankind. From then on, people knew to take the covenant of Blood very seriously, seeing it as a matter of life and death.

GOD'S IDEA OF A NEW BEGINNING

Whether in Adam and Eve's day or Stanley and Livingstone's, on the continent of Africa or in America, a Blood covenant has al-ways been the most powerful and binding agreement between two parties in existence. And it always will be. That's because covenant originated from the heart of God. It was the outflow of His divine wisdom, Love, mercy and compassion for us.

After mankind fell into the oppressive grip of satan, however, that outflow was put to the test. Despite God's Blood covenant with Adam, people sinned to the point where it seemed God's Love and mercy would be stretched to its limits. Really, however, it was just beginning to unfold. The divine rescue of humanity was still on the horizon (Genesis 3:15). God's Faith-filled prophetic words were still in motion, creating, establishing and working.

Even so, the curse of sin and death spawned by Adam and Eve's rebellion began taking its toll. Jealousy, rage and every other evil trait of man's new overlord, satan, began to surface in God's once-holy family. Adam and Eve's firstborn, Cain, became the first man to rise up in anger and take the life of another human being—that of his own brother, Abel. Genesis 4:10 tells us that when God confronted Cain, He said, "What hast thou done? the voice of thy brother's *blood* crieth unto me from the ground."

I learned from Professor Stephens that the Hebrew word used for *blood* in this verse is the plural form. That indicates the generations of Abel's seed, who would never be born and walk the earth, were witness to his murder and were crying out. Blood cried out, and God heard it. That is the base of the Blood covenant.

As sin's seed sown in man kept producing, mankind soon brought forth even more wicked fruit. The evil spawned by the sin lodged within people's spirits kept increasing.

> And God saw that the wickedness of man was great in the earth, and that every imagination of the thoughts of his heart was only evil continually. And it repented The LORD that he had made man on the earth, and it grieved him at his heart. And The LORD said, I will destroy man whom I have created from the face of the earth; both man, and beast, and the creeping thing, and the fowls of the air; for it repenteth me that I have made them (Genesis 6:5-7).

Even in the middle of all the corruption, violence, wickedness and despair, however, God was able to find Himself a man...Noah.

Unlike the other people of his day, Noah was "a just man and perfect in his generations, and Noah walked with God.... And God said unto Noah, The end of all flesh is come before me; for the earth is filled with violence through them; and, behold, I will destroy them with the earth" (verses 9-13).

Imagine waking up one morning like Noah and hearing God tell you in your "quiet time" with Him that He was going to destroy the earth! What would you do? Try and talk Him out of it or just go with it? Either way, such news would definitely grab your attention. So, no doubt, Noah was listening intently as God went on to say:

> Behold, I, even I, do bring a flood of waters upon the earth, to destroy all flesh, wherein is the breath of life, from under heaven; and every thing that is in the earth shall die. But with

thee will I establish my covenant; and thou shalt come into the ark, thou, and thy sons, and thy wife, and thy sons' wives with thee. And of every living thing of all flesh, two of every sort shalt thou bring into the ark, to keep them alive with thee; they shall be male and female (verses 17-19).

God then laid out for Noah the blueprints of the *ark*. He told him exactly how and with what to build it (verses 14-16). Noah may not have known it, but God was preparing him to become the patriarch of a new family line. He was about to enter a new Blood covenant through which God would one day produce the promised *Seed*, the Redeemer.

Born *eight* generations after Adam, it would eventually be recorded in the *eighth* chapter of Genesis that Noah and his family of *eight* people would exit their floating life-haven to begin their new life in God on the earth.

Is it coincidence that number eight keeps popping up in connection with Noah?

Not according to E.W. Bullinger, nineteenth century Anglican theologian and biblical scholar. He writes: "[Eight] is seven plus one. Hence it is the number specially associated with *Resurrection* and *Regeneration*, and the beginning of a *new era* or order. When the whole earth was covered with the flood, it was Noah 'the eighth person' (2 Peter 2:5) who stepped out on to a new earth to commence a new order of things. 'Eight souls' (1 Peter 3:20) passed through it with him to the new or regenerated world."[11]

In this again, we see God's great Love and mercy. Although He executed judgment on the earth by means of the Flood, before He did, He assured Noah that he and his family would get through it—along with the animal kingdom as they had known it. He set the stage for the hope of a new covenant on the other side; a new beginning for mankind and all the earth, as well as a new day and new place in life for Blood covenants.

---

11 *Number in Scripture*, E.W. Bullinger, Fourth edition revised (London: Eyre and Spottiswoode, (Bible Warehouse) Ltd., 1921.

THE NOAH COVENANT PROMISE

Noah found favor and grace in the sight of God (Genesis 6:8). He was also a man of Faith. For "without faith it is impossible to please him [God]: for he that cometh to God must believe that he is, and that he is a rewarder of them that diligently seek him" (Hebrews 11:6).

With the future of the world in his hands, Noah believed what God told him and did everything exactly as God had commanded (Genesis 6:22).

[Prompted] by faith Noah, being forewarned by God concerning events of which as yet there was no visible sign, took heed and diligently and reverently constructed and prepared an ark for the deliverance of his own family. By this [his faith which relied on God] he passed judgment and sentence on the world's unbelief and became an heir and possessor of righteousness (that relation of being right into which God puts the person who has faith) (Hebrews 11:7, *Amplified Bible, Classic Edition*).

Noah had never seen rain and floods. He had never seen a boat at all, much less one on which every species of animal could be transported under one roof (Genesis 2:6). But that didn't matter. Noah had a working relationship with God and trusted Him.

Though he endured heavy ridicule for his actions by the people of his day, Noah's Faith was in God and His promise of deliverance. He walked in close fellowship with God. So, if God told him to do something—like build a massive boat that had never existed before, and build it on *dry* ground—then that's exactly what Noah was going to do. He knew God well enough by Faith to know He could not lie (Numbers 23:19). His WORD was then, and is now, His bond. Once He said it, it was absolute truth forevermore.

Sure enough, when the ark was completed, just as God said, the Flood came.

On the very same day Noah and Shem, Ham, and Japheth,

the sons of Noah, and Noah's wife and the three wives of his sons with them, went into the ark, they and every [wild] beast according to its kind, all the livestock according to their kinds, every moving thing that creeps on the land according to its kind, and every fowl according to its kind, every winged thing of every sort.... And they that entered, male and female of all flesh, went in as God had commanded [Noah]; and The LORD shut him in and closed [the door] round about him (Genesis 7:13–14, 16, *Amplified Bible, Classic Edition*).

Look again at that last verse. Who does it say shut the door to the ark? God! Noah received it by Faith, but once he and his family were on the ark, God closed them in. Talk about a safe place! The Creator of heaven and earth, the King of the universe, shut the door on the ark. There was no way that ark could sink!

As the rain came down and the ark began rising, Noah and his family discovered yet again that the Covenant WORD of God is exact and never changes. Faith in His covenant promise provided for them everything they needed. It preserved their lives through a world upheaval.

Gloria and I have experienced God's Covenant provision and protection for decades now. So have Bishop Oyedepo and the people of Faith Tabernacle. God's WORD is the same yesterday, today and forever. It will provide everything any of us need and get us through any situation—and it will do the same for you (Malachi 3:6; Hebrews 13:6).

Noah and his family spent more than a year together on the ark. Then God gave them the *all's-clear* sign. The water had receded. The land had dried out. So, they could start life fresh and anew.

As soon as their feet touched dry ground, Noah performed an action that demonstrated true covenant Faith. He initiated it out of his own will, indicating he had an understanding and awareness of Blood covenant perhaps never seen up to this point. "Noah builded an altar unto The LORD; and took of every clean beast, and of every clean fowl, and offered burnt offerings on the altar" (Genesis 8:20).

This apparently touched the heart of God. Noah, out of his

gratitude, respect and close fellowship with God, had gone all-out and expressed his love in a bold and trusting way. How could the heavenly Father not be pleased with His Blood covenant partner?

> And The LORD smelled a sweet savour; and The LORD said in his heart, I will not again curse the ground any more for man's sake; for the imagination of man's heart is evil from his youth; neither will I again smite any more every thing living, as I have done. While the earth remaineth, seedtime and harvest, and cold and heat, and summer and winter, and day and night shall not cease (Genesis 8:21-22).

Notice that in addition to making a covenant with Noah and his family, God also established an agreement with the animals. (See Genesis 9:10-11.) Then, He literally set up a new world order. He established times and seasons that mankind and even nature could count on, because they would operate like clockwork. At Creation, God had created the sun, moon and stars for signs, days and years. Now, everything would align according to the four seasons, bringing another level of order to a world that had been in chaos.

God's expression of Covenant lovingkindness didn't end there, however. He had never given up on the original BLESSING He'd given to Adam and Eve. So, as Genesis 9 records:

> God BLESSED Noah and his sons, and said unto them, Be fruitful, and multiply, and replenish the earth. And the fear of you and the dread of you shall be upon every beast of the earth, and upon every fowl of the air, upon all that moveth upon the earth, and upon all the fishes of the sea; into your hand are they delivered. Every moving thing that liveth shall be meat for you; even as the green herb have I given you all things. But flesh with the life thereof, which is the blood thereof, shall ye not eat (verses 1-4).

With these words of promise, *Elohim* [God the Father, the Son and the Holy Spirit] opened the door for man to add to his regular diet the meat of animals, but with one stipulation: *Don't eat their blood.*

Again, God was reemphasizing the value—even sacredness—of blood. Because the life of any being is in the blood, it would continue to be the key to all creation's justification and redemption. Therefore, blood was to be honored and reverenced by man (and animal). In fact, God went on to promise in this Noah covenant:

And surely your blood of your lives will I require; at the hand of every beast will I require it, and at the hand of man; at the hand of every man's brother will I require the life of man. Whoso sheddeth man's blood, by man shall his blood be shed: for in the image of God made he man (verses 5-6).

Those were serious words; a command with consequences if disobeyed. God was requiring a new level of Faith and obedience from man. He was specifically forbidding murder and charging man to judge anyone who committed it. Remember, when Cain murdered Abel, it was not against the law. The book of the Law had yet to come to pass. It was developed through covenant promises from God to Moses, the lawgiver. Therefore, this promise to Noah put into mankind's hands a greater degree of responsibility.

God had found in Noah, the one man—in a godless world of evil—who still loved and revered Him. The one man with whom He could entrust THE BLESSING He intended for us all. Finding that "one man" would become God's pattern in cutting covenant.

His covenant with Noah changed this planet and the world's system forever. It kept His plan for mankind on course, opening the door to even greater covenants with future generations who would eventually restore God's family to their original close fellowship with Him.

CUTTING THE NOAH COVENANT

The altar upon which Noah presented his offerings to The LORD is the first such altar mentioned in the Bible. And with the shedding of blood on that altar, the covenant between God and Noah was cut. How did Noah know about Blood covenant sacrifice? How did he know to build an altar?

Most likely he learned about those things from his grandfather, Methuselah. One of Adam's great-great-grandsons, Methuselah lived 969 years. Adam lived 930 years. So, the two had many years together on this earth. And since Methuselah didn't die until the year of the Flood, he had plenty of time to pass along to Noah all he had learned about animal sacrifices and cutting covenant.

As I've said before, such knowledge is rare today in our "civilized" societies. In recent centuries, we have become removed from the understanding of Blood covenants and their vital importance in our lives. That's sad, particularly for believers. Without a knowledge of God's system of Blood covenant, we tend to have more difficulty receiving His BLESSING.

That's why I so appreciate the depth of revelation spiritual leaders like Bishop Oyedepo have. Because of his understanding of Blood covenants, he can explain them very plainly. As he put it:

> We understand from scriptures that the Bible is a book of covenants and that is why we have the Old and New Testaments, which also mean Old and New Covenants…. A covenant is a *deal* enacted by God based on well-defined terms and sealed with an oath. The *deal* is contained in the book of *deals* called the Bible. However, to draw on it, there are demands that should be kept.[12]

Bishop Oyedepo's practical, down-to-earth words echo the insights of another favorite of mine, 19th-century theologian Andrew Murray, who wrote:

---

12 "Examining the Covenants of Scriptures for Our Dominion in Christ!" *Flatimes,* Bishop David Oyedepo, Winners' Chapel, https://flatimes.com/examining-covenant-scriptures-dominion-christ-david-oyedepo/ (accessed 6/2023).

Blessed is the man who truly knows God as his Covenant God; who knows what the Covenant promises him; what unwavering confidence of expectation it secures, that all its terms will be fulfilled to him; what a claim and hold it gives him on the Covenant-keeping God Himself. To many a man, who has never thought much of the Covenant, a true and living faith in it would mean the transformation of his whole life.[13]

Those statements also remind me of Psalm 89. There, God declares His absolute resolve to fulfill His covenant promises to King David, saying:

My mercy will I keep for him for evermore, and my covenant shall stand fast with him. His seed also will I make to endure for ever, and his throne as the days of heaven. If his children forsake my law, and walk not in my judgments.... Nevertheless my lovingkindness will I not utterly take from him, nor suffer my faithfulness to fail. My covenant will I not break, nor alter the thing that is gone out of my lips. Once have I sworn by my holiness that I will not lie unto David (verses 28–30, 33-35).

When it comes to entering a Blood covenant, this is God's heart, not just toward David, but toward all of us.

THE NOAH COVENANT SEAL—THE RAINBOW

The seal of God's Blood covenant with Noah and his family is both famous and widely recognizable. To this day, it is a hard-to-miss reminder of God's promise to Noah and all mankind. It is also one that quite literally remains in God's face. Positioned between heaven and earth, that seal is the *rainbow*. As God said to Noah and his sons:

---

13 Andrew Murray, *The Two Covenants* (Fort Washington: Christian Literature Crusade, 1974), Chapter 1.

This is the token of the covenant which I make between me and you and every living creature that is with you, for perpetual generations: I do set my bow in the cloud, and it shall be for a token of a covenant between me and the earth. And it shall come to pass, when I bring a cloud over the earth, that the bow shall be seen in the cloud: And I will remember my covenant, which is between me and you and every living creature of all flesh; and the waters shall no more become a flood to destroy all flesh. And the bow shall be in the cloud; and I will look upon it, that I may remember the everlasting covenant between God and every living creature of all flesh that is upon the earth. And God said unto Noah, This is the token of the covenant, which I have established between me and all flesh that is upon the earth (Genesis 9:12-17).

The rainbow is not just a natural, earthly phenomenon. In heaven, there's a rainbow that surrounds God's throne. The Prophet Ezekiel saw it in the vision he had of the four living creatures in heaven. He said:

Above the dome that was over their heads was something like a throne that looked like a sapphire. On it, above it, was what appeared to be a person. I saw what looked like gleaming, amber-colored fire radiating from what appeared to be his waist upward. Downward from what appeared to be his waist, I saw what looked like fire, giving a brilliant light all around him. This brilliance around him looked like a rainbow in a cloud on a rainy day (Ezekiel 1:26-28, *Complete Jewish Bible*).[14]

The Apostle John provided us with an amazingly similar description. In Revelation 4, he said a door was opened to him in heaven: "And...behold, a throne was set in heaven, and one sat on the throne. And he that sat was to look upon like a jasper and a sardine stone: and there was a rainbow round about the throne, in sight like unto an emerald" (verses 2-3).

---

14 *Complete Jewish Bible*, David H. Stern (Jerusalem: Jewish New Testament Publications Inc., 1998).

God put a rainbow around His throne so that in any direction He looked, His eyes would forever see the sign of the covenant through which He had obligated Himself to Noah and his descendants. To this day, no matter how hard satan and his band of demons try to wreak havoc on earth, God is continually reminded of His promise to BLESS His people and to never flood the whole earth again.

CONTRADICTION TO THE NOAH COVENANT

God did us all a great favor by putting that constant reminder in front of Himself. We needed it to be there because, before long, people were doing things that might tempt Him to send another flood. The trouble started with Noah and his sons: Shem, Ham and Japheth. After they got the ark unpacked, they settled in on dry ground, and Noah planted a vineyard.

> And he drank of the wine, and was drunken; and he was uncovered within his tent. And Ham, the father of Canaan, saw the nakedness of his father, and told his two brethren without. And Shem and Japheth took a garment, and laid it upon both their shoulders, and went backward, and covered the nakedness of their father; and their faces were backward, and they saw not their father's nakedness. And Noah awoke from his wine, and knew what his younger son had done unto him. And he said, Cursed be Canaan; a servant of servants shall he be unto his brethren. And he said, BLESSED be The LORD God of Shem; and Canaan shall be his servant. God shall enlarge Japheth, and he shall dwell in the tents of Shem; and Canaan shall be his servant (Genesis 9:21-27).

Shocking, isn't it? Noah, deemed righteous in his generation and held in high regard by God, got drunk after sampling the fruit of his labor. While he was passed out, one of his sons shamed and humiliated him. So, he proceeded to BLESS and curse his sons and grandsons according to God's judgment on this act. As a result, Noah's sons and subsequent descendants were split permanently.

We see in this the contradiction to the Noah covenant—evil still threatened to prevail. Yes, God had hit the *reset* button for mankind with the Flood. But the Flood did not wipe out the devil. He was still the god of this world with Adam's authority. And since man's sin nature hadn't changed, sin continued to pose a natural obstacle to this new agreement.

In Genesis 11 (just two chapters after God established His covenant with Noah) we see the threat of evil once again becoming serious. We find mankind disobeying God's command to fill the earth (Genesis 9:1) and instead congregating in Babylonia. Although the people came into unity there, which is characteristic of God, sadly,. this post-Flood generation unified *against* their Creator.

> And the whole earth was of one language, and of one speech. And it came to pass, as they journeyed from the east, that they found a plain in the land of Shinar; and they dwelt there. And they said one to another, Go to, let us make brick, and burn them thoroughly. And they had brick for stone, and slime had they for morter. And they said, Go to, let us build us a city and a tower, whose top may reach unto heaven; and let us make us a name, lest we be scattered abroad upon the face of the whole earth (Genesis 11:1-4).

One theory explaining the desire those people had to build a tower is they wanted to be able to escape another flood. They did not understand God's promise. Nor did they trust Him, it seems, because they set about to exalt themselves and become equal to or greater than Him.

God, who sees through man's reasonings and judges the intentions of his heart (Jeremiah 17:9-10), intervened, of course. But thankfully, total annihilation of mankind to bring an end to evil was no longer an option for Him. So, this time He intervened without any destruction:

> And The LORD came down to see the city and the tower, which the children of men builded. And The LORD said, Behold, the people is one, and they have all one language; and

this they begin to do: and now *nothing will be restrained from them,* which they have imagined to do. Go to, let us go down, and there confound their language, that they may not understand one another's speech. So The LORD scattered them abroad from thence upon the face of all the earth: and they left off to build the city (verses 5-8).

Why did The LORD scatter the people? He answered that question Himself: They were united and nothing they set out to do would be impossible for them (verse 6). Which, given their evil inclinations, could ruin everything.

There was one encouraging sign seen among men, though. After the cutting of the Noah covenant, people in general retained a respect for covenant relationships. Where Blood covenants had once only existed between God and man, people began implementing them among themselves. By imitating God's practices and patterns, they began emphasizing the true value of covenant.

As man began populating the earth, individuals, families, clans, tribes, communities—even whole nations—began implementing the principles and practices of covenant in everyday relationship. People cut covenant in situations, for example, where trust and commitment were absolutely necessary. They established covenants regarding family or business matters. They used them to ensure government stability and military strength.

According to E. W. Kenyon, there are three primary scriptural reasons people entered covenants with one another:

1. "If a strong tribe lives by the side of a weaker tribe, and there is danger of the weaker tribe being destroyed, the weaker tribe will seek to 'cut the Covenant' with the stronger tribe that they may be preserved."
2. "Two businessmen entering into a partnership might 'cut the Covenant' to ensure that neither would take advantage of the other."
3. "If two men loved each other as devotedly as David and Jonathan…they would 'cut the Covenant' for that love's sake."[15]

---

15 E.W. Kenyon, *The Blood Covenant* (New Kensington, Penn: Whitaker House, 2019) p.8.

Numerous examples of covenant relationships established for these very reasons found in the Bible include:

- King Abimelech of the Philistines cutting covenant with Abraham to maintain peace and good business dealings between them (Genesis 21).

- Dishonest Laban cutting a covenant with his son-in-law, Jacob, that would set up physical boundaries to keep peace between them and their families. This covenant followed an intense confrontation in which Laban's sons claimed Jacob's riches and said he "got all this glory" from their father. The first instance where the word *glory* appears in the Bible, *glory* is used there to refer to wealth (Genesis 31).

- Ruth and her mother-in-law, Naomi, entering a covenant relationship after the death of their husbands, and Ruth declaring to Naomi, "Intreat me not to leave thee, or to return from following after thee: for whither thou goest, I will go; and where thou lodgest, I will lodge: thy people shall be my people, and thy God my God" (Ruth 1:16).

- Jonathan, the son of King Saul of Israel, cutting covenant with David "because he loved him as his own life" (1 Samuel 18:3, *Amplified Bible, Classic Edition*).

With the cutting of covenant becoming more common among people in their earthly relationships came hope. Hope that, perhaps in the future, mankind would give greater attention to subsequent covenants with the Almighty God. People everywhere were, after all, descendants from the eight souls who had survived the catastrophic Flood.

The Flood was now part of mankind's history. People who had heard of it had good reason to believe God when He handed out warnings such as, "The earth also is defiled under the inhabitants thereof; because they have *transgressed* the laws, *changed* the ordinance, *broken* the everlasting covenant. Therefore hath the curse devoured the earth, and they that dwell therein are desolate:

therefore the inhabitants of the earth are burned, and few men left" (Isaiah 24:5-6).

Surely, people's knowledge of covenant principles combined with their knowledge of the past would cause them to take The LORD and His covenants with them more seriously. Surely, despite mankind's failures, there was still hope.

WHEN GOD'S PEOPLE AGREE

I began this chapter by sharing with you the amazing story of my Faith-filled, Covenant-conscious friend, Bishop Oyedepo of Nigeria. The Covenant awareness and mindset that the bishop and people of Faith Tabernacle demonstrated in the early years of their church produced astounding, supernatural results. Honestly though, I haven't told you the half of the story!

What makes Faith Tabernacle's journey such a testimony of God's faithfulness to our Blood Covenant is the contradictions they have faced and overcome. Among those contradictions is the fact that Nigeria is one of the poorest countries in the world. To some people, that may not be a surprise, given the headlines we see in the news about the challenges facing this West African nation. But what's surprising is Nigeria has one of the highest Gross National Product (GNP) ratings per capita in the world.

GNP is a global formula, or standard, used to measure a country's economic activity. It provides an overall indication of a nation's financial health. Yet 40 percent of Nigerians live below the poverty line, which means there's been a huge divide there between the rich and the poor.[16]

Faith Tabernacle's ministry and national influence, however, has helped establish what is now the new Nigerian middle class. In effect, Bishop Oyedepo, by training his congregation to be Faith people, has not only benefitted the church but also improved the nation's economy and demographics. It's all because of Faith in the

---

16   "Forty percent of Nigerians live in poverty: stats office," Alexis Akwagyiram, *Reuters, Business News,* May 4, 2020, https://www.reuters.com/article/us-nigeria-economy-poverty/forty-percent-of-nigerians-live-in-poverty-stats-office-idUSKBN22G19A (accessed 6-2023).

Blood Covenant of Almighty God, a revelation the bishop recalls having to first receive in his own life.

Bishop once told me: "I had no trouble with healing and praise. I had no trouble with anything else in The WORD, but the money part was a real puzzle to me. I read your book *The Laws of Prosperity,* and Mama Gloria's book *God's Will Is Prosperity.* I fasted and prayed and was seeking God. But it was while reading Mama Gloria's book that it hit me: *It's a covenant!*"

Then, the Bishop looked me in the face and said this: "Brother Copeland, when I read, 'Seek ye first the kingdom of God and His righteousness, and *all these things* will be added unto you,' I realized that is a *blood-backed statement.* The only thing left is just the *doing* of it. I don't even have to think about it anymore. I just praise and praise and praise until something happens. The way we do everything is with praise! Once we have a mandate from God, we don't question anymore. We just praise and worship, and everything happens. I ask no further questions because that is a Blood Covenant promise. I say to The LORD, 'You do it. I take it. Thank You very much!'"

Today, I'm pleased to report to you that, as of this writing, Faith Tabernacle owns about 17,000 acres. Called *Canaanland,* Ota, the area owned by the church has become its own city. It has roads, banks, a university, a primary and secondary school, a publishing company, a power plant, homes, a post office, and stores. On Sundays, Faith Tabernacle's *Winner's Chapel*—which seats 54,000 people—has five services. That was all part of Phase 1. Phase 2 is set to go with *another* $250 million that's already in the bank, and without ever having to raise the money!

Right now they are building a worship center properly named "The Ark."[17] Scheduled to be dedicated in 2024, it will seat 100,000 people. A hotel and a shopping center are to be built along with it. Of course, the building is already too small, but knowing Bishop Oyedepo, he already has something else planned.

How do they do it all?

The bishop told me, "We just let God do it!"

---

17 To see architectural renderings of "The Ark," please turn to the back of this book.

Here's a people with great understanding of the power of a Blood Covenant relationship with Almighty God. They make their *petition* and believe they receive their *grant*. When any contradiction or lie against God's WORD dares to raise its ugly head, they don't get upset. They simply ignore the contradiction and PRAISE and WORSHIP their way through it until they see a manifestation of the mighty things of God. Hallelujah!

GO DEEPER
WITH GREG

THE HIGH VALUE OF COVENANT

From the beginning, God placed a high value on blood, both that of humans and animals. As He said in Leviticus 17:14, *"The life of all flesh is the blood thereof."* So, it's no surprise that blood plays such a vital role in the covenant process. It's also no surprise that the Hebrew word used to refer to a binding or bond between two parties is *berit*.

In Hebrew, *berit* means "to cut." It is the biblical word used to describe a compact made by "passing between pieces of flesh." In the Old Testament it is most often translated *covenant*.

Berit first appears in Genesis 6 when God approached Noah about cutting a covenant. It's used another 270 to 280 times—depending on which translation of the Bible you read—in reference to covenants initiated by God, as well as to those among men.

In the covenants God cut with Adam—the Eden Covenant and the Adam covenant—Adam stood as the covenant representative of the human race (Genesis 3:17-24; Romans 5:12-19). So did Noah in the covenant God cut with him. The Abraham covenant, as we will see in the next chapter, was the first time God partnered with a man (Abraham) who would represent all people who chose to live by *Faith* (Habakkuk 2:4; Romans 1:17; Galatians 3:11; Hebrews 10:38). The next Man to stand in that role was Jesus, who represented the entire human race (past, present, future) in the New Covenant (1 Corinthians 15:45; Romans 5:15).

The "representative" roles men like Adam, Noah and Abraham

stood in when God cut covenant with them differ from those we see in human covenants. Like the marriage covenant between a husband and wife, human covenants are cut between two equal parties in what is commonly described as a bilateral covenant. In bilateral covenants the bond was sealed by both parties. Each vowed, often by oath, that having equal privileges and responsibilities, they would carry out their assigned roles.

Because this was the case between two human parties, some Bible scholars have concluded that God's covenants with man are also bilateral. But they are not. That would be impossible.

Remember, all Blood covenants man has ever cut with God were initiated by God. And He, being God, is always the greater party. He is always the stronger, wealthier, wiser party. He is, after all, the ALL-SUFFICIENT ONE (Genesis 17:1). So, any covenant with Him would be *unilateral*. That means we can either accept or reject it, but never alter it. It is what it is: It's God bringing everything He is and has to the table, thereby putting us in a favorable position because we have *everything* to gain!

As we begin to study the various signs and acts of covenant, this is important to remember: While God's covenants often demonstrate a level of *equality* between God and man, that's only because God in His Covenant lovingkindness chose to raise us up to His level. He chose to restore us to our original place of relationship and authority with Him. Again, He has everything to give. We have everything to receive.

So, with this understanding of covenant as our foundation, let's look at the typical steps both parties would take to enter a Blood covenant:

1.   First, a covenant site was chosen where everyone involved could see the ceremony. Then an animal was selected and killed in a unique way. The animal was cut down the backbone and the two halves of its body made to fall opposite each other, creating a *walk of blood* between the walls of the animal's flesh (Genesis 15:9-10).

2.   As the covenant ceremony began, a representative of

each party took off his coat and gave it to the other. Using the coats to symbolize their *authority,* each covenant partner declared, "This is who I am and all that I am." They gave themselves to one another in commitment (1 Samuel 18:4; Luke 15:22-24).

3. Next, the representatives removed and exchanged weapon belts. This indicated the giving of their strength and a determination that the enemies of either party would now be their mutual enemies. They declared, "Even if it results in death, I stand with you" (1 Samuel 18:4).

4. Following the exchange of belts, the representatives began walking the path of blood between the animal halves. The path formed a figure eight. The symbol of eternity, the eight represented a never-ending commitment to this solemn and binding oath. Each walked the path twice, stopping in the middle and declaring to the other: "Even as this animal has died, I will stand with you even in the middle of death. Standing in the blood, I make promises I can never break." These promises were THE BLESSINGS of the covenant. Also, in the middle of the *walk of blood,* the representatives swore by God to keep the promises, thus making God third party to the covenant (Genesis 15:17).

5. Following the walk of blood was a name change that declared to all, "We are one family, our names are one" (Genesis 17:5, 15).

    In the New Covenant, we see this name change reflected in the words written by the Apostle Paul: "For this cause I bow my knees unto the Father of our LORD Jesus Christ, *of whom the whole family in heaven and earth is named*" (Ephesians 3:14-15).

    Today we, as believers, have as much right to use the Name of Jesus as He does. We are Jesus' family. We are His born-again, Blood-Covenant brothers and sisters, born of the same Father. We are joint heirs with Him and have been given the power of attorney to use His Name (John 14:14; Romans 8:16-17; Hebrews 2:11).

6. Once the Blood covenant ceremony was complete, the two parties became covenant *Friends*. Proverbs 18:24 tells us, "A man that hath friends must show himself friendly: and there is a friend that sticketh closer than a brother." In the Hebrew covenant way of thinking, that level of *Friend* could only exist if a Blood covenant had been cut. Jesus became our Blood Covenant sacrifice so we could attain to this level of *Friendship* with God:

Greater love hath no man than this, that a man lay down his life for his *friends*. Ye are my *friends*, if ye do whatsoever I command you. Henceforth I call you not servants; for the servant knoweth not what his lord doeth: but I have called you *friends*; for all things that I have heard of my Father I have made known unto you (John 15:13-15).

The unbreakable bond of relationship created through Blood covenant can be summed up in one Hebrew word: *hesed*. We will study this at length in the chapters that follow. For now, you simply need to know that *hesed* is God's *Covenant lovingkindness*—His mercy, grace, kindness, goodness, favor, loyalty. *Hesed* is actually a legal term pertaining to covenant. Yet, it tenderly expresses God's heart of Covenant Love for us.

Hesed is what moved Jesus to tell His disciples during their last covenant meal together, "I have *earnestly and intensely desired* to eat this Passover with you *before I suffer*" (Luke 22:15, *Amplified Bible, Classic Edition*). *Hesed* was the reason He ended their meal together with the words: "Do this in *remembrance* of me" (verse 19). With those Blood Covenant words, Jesus was saying:

- I hold you in my heart (Jeremiah 31:3)
- I crown you "with lovingkindness and tender mercies" (Psalm 103:4)
- You are ever before Me (Psalm 16:8)
- I have Covenant plans to BLESS and surprise you (Jeremiah 29:11)

- Ask, and I will give to you. Seek, and I will reveal to you. Knock, and I will open to you (Matthew 7:7).

Almighty God's loyalty is forever. Zechariah prophesied to Israel, "He that toucheth you toucheth the apple of his eye" (Zechariah 2:8). That means God's enemies should think twice before messing with you—His blood-bought Covenant people—because touching you is like poking Him in the eye, and that's dangerous!

God promises His Covenant people today: "I will never leave thee, nor forsake thee" (Hebrews 13:5).

Jesus said it like this: "I am with you always, even unto the end of the world" (Matthew 28:20).

GOD'S
COVENANT
WITH
ABRAHAM

CHAPTER FIVE

GOD'S COVENANT WITH ABRAHAM

There's a song I often sing at our meetings that's become one of my favorites. The music and lyrics are so anointed because they speak of the Father's consuming Love for us, His people, and the compassion that compelled Jesus to sacrifice His life for us. It's a tender song of His Faith for our future and His constant remembrance of our Covenant with Him. The song is titled, "When He Was on the Cross (I Was on His Mind)."[18] It's based on Romans 5:8, Hebrews 12:2 and Isaiah 53:10-11.

Notice the words of the song's second verse:

The look of love was on His face, thorns were on His head/
The blood was on His scarlet robe, stained a crimson red/
Though His eyes were on the crowd that day, He looked ahead in time/
For when He was on the cross, I was on His mind.

We've consistently seen throughout our study that from day one, God has always "looked ahead in time." He has always been working to get us back to Eden, to a place where we can dwell in BLESSING. From before the foundation of the world, He's been planning, preparing, and providing a way—the Way—for us to enter into that

---

18 "When He Was on the Cross," written by Ronald Payne and Ronny Hinson, 1984

final Blood Covenant with Him that guarantees our destiny and our eternal relationship with Him.

We just closed the chapter on how God mercifully stopped the people from building the tower of Babel. He divided them and disrupted their disastrous plot by giving them new and different languages that caused them to scatter. Even then, however, God was looking ahead in time and had a plan to redeem that situation. Even then, He was foreseeing the day when He would give His people new tongues and languages that, instead of scattering them, would draw to Him people from all nations.

Acts 2 records what happened when that day eventually came. It tells us that as Jesus' disciples waited in an upper room in Jerusalem after His ascension:

> When the day of Pentecost was fully come, they were all with one accord in one place. And suddenly there came a sound from heaven as of a rushing mighty wind, and it filled all the house where they were sitting. And there appeared unto them cloven tongues like as of fire, and it sat upon each of them. And they were all filled with the Holy Ghost, and began to speak with other tongues, as the Spirit gave them utterance. And there were dwelling at Jerusalem Jews, devout men, out of every nation under heaven. Now when this was noised abroad, the multitude came together, and were confounded, because that every man heard them speak in his own language…the wonderful works of God (Acts 2:1-6, 11).

Although that was a New Covenant event, a man named Abram born thousands of years earlier opened the door for it by accepting God's invitation to enter covenant with Him. As John Walvoord, a twentieth century theologian, tells us, "[God's] covenant with Abraham is one of the important and determinative revelations of Scripture. It furnishes the key to the entire Old Testament and reaches for its fulfillment into the New…[setting] the mold for the entire body of Scriptural truth."[19] It also demanded of Abram and his wife, Sarai, a long and demanding walk of Faith.

---

19 *The Millennial Kingdom*, John F. Walvoord (Grand Rapids: Dunham, 1959) p. 139.

THE ABRAHAM COVENANT PROMISE

Abram's covenant story starts in Genesis 12. There, we find that God instigated His relationship with Abram just as He did with His previous covenant partners—with a BLESSING. Only this time God's promise of BLESSING went over the top. He said to Abram:

Get thee out of thy country, and from thy kindred, and from thy father's house, unto a land that I will show thee: and I will make of thee a great nation, and I will *BLESS* thee, and make thy name *great;* and thou shalt be a *BLESSING:* And I will *BLESS* them that *BLESS* thee, and curse him that curseth thee: and in thee shall all families of the earth be *BLESSED* (Genesis 12:1-3).

There was a lot of BLESSING in those words! Even the *curse* attached to them was a *BLESSING.* When God said, "[I will] curse him that curseth thee," He was promising to deal with the one person ultimately responsible for the curse—satan himself.

What's more, God's promise to Abram of abundant BLESSING carried with it only one condition. Where Noah had to build an ark and gather all species of the animal world—by *Faith*—Abram had to leave his world of seventy-five years and by Faith go to a new land and build a new life, with a new God that until now he had never known.

So Abram departed, as The LORD had spoken unto him.... And Abram took Sarai his wife, and Lot his brother's son, and all their substance that they had gathered, and the souls that they had gotten in Haran; and they went forth to go into the land of Canaan [present-day Israel]; and into the land of Canaan they came.... And The LORD appeared unto Abram, and said, Unto thy seed will I give this land: and there builded he an altar unto The LORD, who appeared unto him (Genesis 12:4-5, 7).

Shortly after Abram arrived in Canaan, Scripture records that the people there began calling him "Abram the Hebrew" (Genesis 14:13).

Hebrew means "the one who crossed over." The term fit Abram in more than one sense. He had indeed "crossed over" the Jordan and Euphrates rivers when he left Ur (his father's homeland and present-day Iraq) to go to Canaan (Genesis 11:28-32; Joshua 24:3). But this *crossing over* also involved more than just geography.

Abram's world at the time was full of idol worshippers. Most people had rebelled against God's ways and sided with evil, so they noticed when Abram broke ranks and crossed over to God's side. They also noticed as God continued to BLESS His newfound covenant Friend and partner. For Abram became a very rich man (Genesis 13:2).

Despite his wealth, however, even after Abram crossed over, he lacked one thing. He and Sarai had no children. That weighed heavily on him, so when God spoke to him again, He addressed the situation.

The WORD of The LORD came unto Abram in a vision, saying, Fear not, Abram: I am thy shield, and thy exceeding great reward. And Abram said, LORD God, what wilt thou give me, seeing I go childless, and the steward of my house is this Eliezer of Damascus? And Abram said, Behold, to me thou hast given no seed: and, lo, one born in my house is mine heir. And, behold, the word of The LORD came unto him, saying, This shall not be thine heir; but he that shall come forth out of thine own bowels shall be thine heir. And he brought him forth abroad, and said, Look now toward heaven, and tell the stars, if thou be able to number them: and he said unto him, So shall thy seed be. And he believed in The LORD; and he counted it to him for righteousness (Genesis 15:1-6).

CUTTING THE ABRAHAM COVENANT

Once Abram believed God, he was ready to step out by Faith into the next phase of their covenant relationship. So, The LORD stepped out of heaven and met with him to initiate the actual *cutting* process:

> And he said unto him, Take me an heifer of three years old, and a she goat of three years old, and a ram of three years old, and a turtledove, and a young pigeon. And he took unto him all these, and divided them in the midst, and laid each piece one against another: but the birds divided he not.... And it came to pass, that, when the sun went down, and it was dark, behold a smoking furnace, and a burning lamp that passed between those pieces. In the same day The LORD made a covenant with Abram, saying, Unto thy seed have I given this land, from the river of Egypt unto the great river, the river Euphrates (Genesis 15:9-10, 17-18).

What Abram witnessed moving along the covenant walk of blood that night was the fire and glory of God. The "smoking furnace and burning lamp" was God manifesting Himself between those pieces of flesh, consecrating His covenant with His partner, Abram. I am totally convinced that as God's glory illuminated the darkness, Abram could see the actual footprints of his Creator in the covenant blood of animals as He walked in a figure eight—the sign of *eternity,* indicating God's never-ending, absolute commitment to this solemn and binding oath.

Abram himself did not take the *covenant walk of blood* alongside God. Although it was the custom, in this case Abram's participation was unnecessary. For this covenant was different than all the others.

The Abraham covenant was *not* an arrangement between God and Abraham (mankind). Abraham, Sarah and their descendants were only the beneficiaries. They were simply the designated recipients of the covenant's benefits. The covenant itself was between God the Father and God the Son, Jesus.

This is why there was no *curse* attached. There was no reason for there to be. Because this covenant was between two sinless beings who could not fail, there was only BLESSING associated with it.

Can you see the similarities between the Abrahamic covenant and the New Covenant? Both are eternal agreements between Father and Son, with the Abraham covenant being foundational to the new one soon to come.

THE CONTRADICTION AND
THE COVENANT NAME CHANGE

The covenant promise God had made to Abram was clear: Abram would have a son of his own to be his heir. But there was an obvious natural obstacle to that covenant promise. Abram and Sarai had never conceived because Sarai was—and had always been—barren. In addition, they were both now beyond childbearing age.

Sarai initially came up with her own plan to deal with that obstacle. She decided to help both God and Abram by allowing her Egyptian servant Hagar to be the surrogate mother of Abram's heir. In Sarai's mind there seemed to be no doubt Abram would have *his* heir. God said he would. But the way Sarai figured it, there would have to be another woman involved for this to happen.

Sarai certainly didn't see herself as being the mother to the heir of God's promise to Abram. How could she be? At her age? Particularly since, being barren, she had never been able to get pregnant, she certainly couldn't figure out how it could happen now.

So, Sarai took herself out of the equation. Like Eve before her, she came up with a natural solution to the problem. She gave Hagar to Abraham. Hagar conceived and gave birth to Ishmael when Abram was eighty-six years old.

This, however, was not God's solution to the covenant contradiction. So when Abram was ninety-nine years old, The LORD appeared to him again and said to him:

I am the Almighty God; walk before me, and be thou perfect.

And I will make my covenant between me and thee, and will multiply thee exceedingly. And Abram fell on his face: and God talked with him, saying, As for me, behold, my covenant is with thee, and thou shalt be a father of many nations (Genesis 17:1-4).

With those words, God not only reaffirmed his covenant with Abram, He introduced Himself in a way He never had before to Abram or anyone else, by the Name *I AM El Shaddai—"I AM the Almighty God," (the God who is more than enough).* In other words, God said, *"I am the Supreme, the Almighty God! I am All-Mighty in ability! I have all! I can do all! I am the great Provider! Whatever you need, I have it! Whatever you could possibly desire, I am able to supply it!"*

Imagine the grandeur and magnitude that flew all over Abram the moment he heard those words. They hit him with such force, he fell face down on the ground. Yet God was just getting started. He went on to institute a covenant name change and introduced Abram and Sarai to their new identities.

First, He told Abram: "As for me, behold, my covenant is with thee, and thou shalt be a father of many nations. Neither shall thy name any more be called Abram, but *thy name shall be Abraham;* for a father of many nations have I made thee. And I will make thee exceeding fruitful, and I will make nations of thee, and kings shall come out of thee" (Genesis 17:4-6).

Then, "God said unto Abraham, As for Sarai thy wife, thou shalt not call her name Sarai, but Sarah shall her name be. And I will BLESS her, and give thee a son also of her: yea, I will BLESS her, and she shall be a mother of nations; kings of people shall be of her" (Genesis 17:15-16).

Notice, God inserted a "ha" in Abram's name and an "ah" into Sarai's, by adding to each the letter "H." That letter is drawn from God's Hebrew Name, *YHWH,* which in our English Bible is translated *LORD.*[20] "H" in Hebrew (pronounced *hey*) can mean "look, behold, breath or light." It's associated with the breathy sound made

---

20 For a fuller understanding of the term *YHWH,* see Appendix A: The Covenant Names of God, p. 249.

when God spoke all creation into existence. "By The WORD of The LORD were the heavens made; and all the host of them by the breath of his mouth" (Psalm 33:6).

It's no surprise that God chose to include this particular part of His Name to give to Abraham and Sarah. They needed a creative miracle, and "H" speaks of His creative ability. They needed a supernatural impartation of life that would produce for generations to come, so God gave each of them part of His life-giving identity, which made a world of difference not only for them, but for all mankind forever.

THE ABRAHAM COVENANT SEAL

After giving Abram and Sarai their new names, The LORD revealed how the covenant was to be sealed. That seal would require the blood of Abraham and take the form of a reminder that no *man* could forget.

And God said unto Abraham, Thou shalt keep my covenant therefore, thou, and thy seed after thee in their generations. This is my covenant, which ye shall keep, between me and you and thy seed after thee; Every man child among you shall be circumcised. And ye shall circumcise the flesh of your foreskin; and it shall be a token of the covenant betwixt me and you. And he that is eight days old shall be circumcised among you, every man child in your generations, he that is born in the house, or bought with money of any stranger, which is not of thy seed. He that is born in thy house, and he that is bought with thy money, must needs be circumcised: and my covenant shall be in your flesh for an everlasting covenant. And the uncircumcised man child whose flesh of his foreskin is not circumcised, that soul shall be cut off from his people; he hath broken my covenant (Genesis 17:9-14).

Here, for the first time ever, God was requiring man's blood essentially be mingled with the sacrificial blood of animals. This foreshadowed what Jesus would one day be required to do as our Covenant sacrifice on Calvary's cross. Dr. Kenyon wrote that God's new requirement of circumcision "meant that all Abraham had or ever would have was laid on the altar. It meant that God must sustain and protect Abraham to the very limit."[21]

Abraham had everything to gain in this arrangement! As we've already seen, God is always the *stronger* covenant Partner, and He was committing Himself and all His resources to defend and protect the *weaker* covenant partner, Abraham (and his descendants). In turn, Abraham's cutting of his own flesh and the shedding of his blood (and that of all his male descendants) served as the outward evidence of an inward commitment to God.

Life would flow through that bloodline mark of the circular scar (a "circle" symbolizing a forever Covenant) and would keep flowing until the *Seed*, Jesus, entered the earth realm through the door of Abraham's covenant bloodline. That bloodline would not be reckoned through Ishmael, however. Despite being Abraham's firstborn, he was not the heir God had promised. That heir, God said, would come through Sarah.

> Then Abraham fell upon his face, and laughed, and said in his heart, Shall a child be born unto him that is an hundred years old? and shall Sarah, that is ninety years old, bear? And Abraham said unto God, O that Ishmael might live before thee! And God said, Sarah thy wife shall bear thee a son indeed; and thou shalt call his name Isaac: and I will establish my covenant with him for an everlasting covenant, and with his seed after him (Genesis 17:17–19).

Abraham wasn't the only one who laughed to himself when God told him Sarah would be the mother of his heir. When Sarah heard about it she laughed as well (Genesis 18:10-15). But as Abraham and Sarah continued to speak their new covenant names— names now imbedded with the "H" from YHWH—within months, Isaac was conceived.

It's no wonder God instructed Abraham to name his and Sarah's

---

21 E.W. Kenyon, *The Blood Covenant* (New Kensington, Penn: Whitaker House, 2019) p. 16.

son Isaac, which means "he laughs." A year later, when this wonderful baby boy was born to a 100-year-old father and 90-year-old mother, Sarah said, "God hath made me to laugh, so that all that hear will laugh with me. And she said, Who would have said unto Abraham, that Sarah should have given children suck? for I have born him a son in his old age" (Genesis 21:6-7).

Sarah's laugh had changed. She was no longer laughing because she thought God's promise too good to be true. She was laughing for joy. For she herself had "received strength to conceive seed, and was delivered of a child when she was past age, because she judged him faithful who had promised" (Hebrews 11:11).

Imagine the joy Isaac's birth also gave Sarah's heavenly Father. He knew her miraculous conception would make a way for another even more *miraculous conception*...thirty-nine generations later. Through her, His Blood Covenant promises would extend from Abraham to Isaac, then Isaac to Jacob. Three family patriarchs, one eternal Covenant, all making way for the promised *Seed* of woman, mankind's hope for Redemption and THE BLESSING abiding on *all* peoples of the world.

THE UNEXPECTED CONTRADICTION

Watching Isaac grow up, Abraham and Sarah seemed to have finally arrived at their golden years. It seemed they could now sit back, relax and let Isaac take things from here. As Gloria and I learned years ago, however, there are no "retirement years" when it comes to the Faith journey. Followers of God must *always keep the switch of Faith turned on.*

Abraham was no exception, for as Genesis 22 says:

It came to pass after these things that God tested Abraham, and said to him, "Abraham!" And he said, "Here I am." Then He said, "Take now your son, your only son Isaac, whom you love, and go to the land of Moriah, and offer him there as a burnt offering on one of the mountains of which I shall tell you." So Abraham rose early in the morning and saddled his donkey, and took two of his young men with him, and Isaac his son; and he split the wood for the burnt offering, and arose and went to the place of which God had told him (Genesis 22:1-3, *New King James Version*).

Remember what I said earlier about how in God's covenant with Abraham, for the first time ever, God was requiring that a man's blood essentially be mingled with the sacrificial blood of animals? Now we are seeing that *three* different sources of blood would be tied into this agreement: the customary blood of animals, the blood of Abraham's circumcision, and the blood of Abraham and Sarah's son, Isaac, the one covenant promise for which they spent decades believing God.

If you know how this account plays out, you're probably saying to yourself, B*ut I thought....* And you're right. As it turned out, Isaac was never actually sacrificed. God provided a substitute for him. But Abraham didn't know God was going to do that. So, again, he had to keep his Faith engaged.

To be clear, God does not ask people to kill their children. In this instance, though, He *was* requiring the blood of Isaac. Why? To put a demand on Abraham's Faith. God needed His covenant Friend to be willing to sacrifice his only son by Faith so that, in turn, He could do the same for all humanity when the time came.

Sure enough, Abraham proved he was willing. He was up bright and early the next morning, packing and getting ready to head out. When they arrived at the place Isaac was to be sacrificed, Abraham made this very revealing statement to the servants who were traveling with them: "I and the lad will go yonder and worship, and come again to you" (Genesis 22:5).

How could he have been so sure that both he and Isaac would come back?

Because God had told Abraham before Isaac was born that He would confirm His and Abraham's covenant with Isaac—AND—with his *descendants* (Genesis 17:19, 21:12). That meant Isaac still had decades to live and children to father. How God worked all that out was up to Him (Hebrews 11:17-19). He had already done the impossible for them, and He would undoubtedly do it again!

And Abraham took the wood of the burnt offering, and laid it upon Isaac his son; and he took the fire in his hand, and a knife; and they went both of them together. And Isaac spake unto Abraham his father, and said, My father: and he said, Here am I, my son. And he said, Behold the fire and the wood: but where is the lamb for a burnt offering? And Abraham said, My son, God will provide himself a lamb for a burnt offering: so they went both of them together (Genesis 22:6-8).

Talk about putting feet to your Faith! Abraham absolutely did. From that moment on, he and Isaac walked in unity through each step of preparing Isaac to be sacrificed—from building an altar and arranging the wood, to tying up Isaac and laying him on the altar. All the while with Abraham believing—fully convinced, even—that he would bring Isaac back home alive.

And Abraham stretched forth his hand, and took the knife to slay his son. And the angel of The LORD called unto him out of heaven, and said, Abraham, Abraham: and he said, Here am I. And he said, Lay not thine hand upon the lad, neither do thou any thing unto him: for now I know that thou fearest God, seeing thou hast not withheld thy son, thine only son from me. And Abraham lifted up his eyes, and looked, and behold behind him a ram caught in a thicket by his horns: and Abraham went and took the ram, and offered him up for a burnt offering in the stead of his son (Genesis 22:10-13).

The magnitude of God's Blood covenant with Abraham cannot be overstated. It was key to restoring our BLESSING—our place of dominion, authority, power, health, wealth and total fellowship with God. It was Abraham's willingness to sacrifice his only son for God that granted Almighty God legal permission to do the same in return. As Abraham's covenant Partner, God could now bypass satan, who had usurped Adam's authority, and send His only Son, Jesus—whom He loved so much—to sacrifice Himself for our sins and, in the process, crush the devil's head.

But that's not all! Hebrews 11 tells us the rest of the story: "By faith Abraham, when he was tried, offered up Isaac: and he that had received the [Blood covenant] promises offered up his only begotten son, of whom it was said, That in Isaac shall thy seed be called: accounting that God was able to raise him up, even from the dead; from whence also he received him in a figure" (Hebrews 11:17-19).

Do you see it? Abraham's Faith set the stage for Jesus' resurrection. When he put Isaac on that altar, Abraham fully expected to sacrifice him and see God raise that boy from the dead!

Abraham eventually even foresaw the coming of the Messiah. Jesus confirmed it during His earthly ministry. Speaking to the Jews, He said: "Your father Abraham rejoiced to see my day: and he saw it, and was glad" (John 8:56).

TWO FATHERS—AND THEIR SONS

As one of the original patriarchs in the Old Covenant (Testament), and one about whom much is written in the New, Abraham was given many titles throughout Scripture, but there are two that particularly stand out.

First, Abraham was known as a father—as the *father of nations* and as the *father of the Faith:*

And Abram fell on his face: and God talked with him, saying, As for me, behold, my covenant is with thee, and thou shalt be a *father of many nations.* Neither shall thy name any more be called Abram, but thy name shall be Abraham; for a *father of many nations* have I made thee (Genesis 17:3-5).

Therefore it is of faith, that it might be by grace; to the end the promise might be sure to all the seed; not to that only which is of the law, but to that also which is of the *faith of Abraham;* who is *the father of us all,* (as it is written, I have made thee a father of many nations,) before him whom he believed, even God, who quickeneth the dead, and calleth those things which be not as though they were (Romans 4:16-17).

The second name given by God to Abraham is the one that is perhaps most endearing—that of Friend. Specifically, he is called the Friend of God. As God said to Abraham's descendants generations later, "thou, Israel, art my servant, Jacob whom I have chosen, the seed of *Abraham my friend*" (Isaiah 41:8).

Notice, in that verse not only does God call Abraham His Friend, He refers to His Old Covenant people as "Israel" and "Jacob." Because God calls them by two names, it sounds like He's talking about two people, but He's not. He's using the names that were given to Abraham's grandson.

He too, like his grandfather Abraham, had a covenant name change. At birth he was given the name Jacob, which means "supplanter, schemer, trickster, swindler" (Genesis 32:27, *Amplified Bible, Classic Edition*)—and he initially lived up to that name. Later, though, Jacob made a covenant commitment to God, promising to give Him a tenth of all his increase.

Once he made that commitment, it became obvious that THE BLESSING of Abraham was working in his life and the angels of God had been assigned to him to protect him. For he became very wealthy. Even his father-in-law, Laban, (who had cheated Jacob and tried to keep him poor) saw God's BLESSING on him and eventually asked to make a covenant with him.

In addition to his wealth, Jacob also displayed two other characteristics.

First, he humbled himself before God and said, "I am not worthy of the least of all the mercy and loving-kindness and all the faithfulness which You have shown to Your servant, for with [only] my staff I passed over this Jordan [long ago], and now I have become two companies" (Genesis 32:10, *Amplified Bible, Classic Edition*).

Second, he absolutely would not quit. He was determined to fulfill what his grandfather Abraham and his father, Isaac, were called of God to do. On one occasion, the Bible says that Jacob wrestled with God all night and said, "I will not let You go unless You declare a BLESSING upon me" (Genesis 32:26, *Amplified Bible, Classic Edition*).

Because of these two characteristics, there came a covenant name change. Later, just as God appeared to Abram again in Genesis 17 and changed his name to Abraham, "God appeared unto Jacob again...and BLESSED him. And God said unto him, Thy name is Jacob: thy name shall not be called any more Jacob, but Israel shall be thy name: and he called his name Israel" (Genesis 35:9-10).

Israel means "a prince with God."

So, we now can see the meaning of the term "children of Israel." We still use that term today. It is not the nation of *Jacob,* it is the nation of *Israel.* With Jacob's covenant name change, a nation was born. In 1948, we saw it happen again. Israel was the only nation to be born out of World War II.

Although Israel bears the name of Abraham's grandson, as we've seen, Abraham himself was the one God named "father of many nations." Because Abraham is clearly identified by God as a father, I believe he is a picture for us of God "the Father," just as his son Isaac is a clear picture of God "the Son" (Jesus).

Let's look at some examples of events in Abraham's life that point to this fact.

NO. 1—THE TWO SONS OF ABRAHAM

In his later years, Abraham went on to father many sons (Genesis 25:1-4). Scripture, however, primarily focuses on his first two: Ishmael and Isaac. For us, as believers, recognizing the difference between them is important because in New Covenant writings, Abraham's firstborn, Ishmael, represents the flesh, while Isaac represents the spirit. As Galatians 4:28-29 says, "Now we, brethren, as *Isaac* was, are *children of promise.* But as then he that was born *after the flesh* [Ishmael] persecuted him that was born *after the Spirit* [Isaac], even so it is now."

Like Abraham, God "the Father" also has many sons, and Scripture focuses on the important difference between two in particular—the first Adam, and the Second Adam, Jesus. They too represent the difference between flesh and spirit, the Holy Spirit and our reborn spirits.

- "Which was the son of Enos, which was the son of Seth, which was the son of Adam, which was *the son of God*" (Luke 3:38).
- "For as *in Adam all die,* even so *in Christ shall all be made alive*" (1 Corinthians 15:22).
- "*The first man Adam* was made *a living soul; the last [second] Adam* was made a *quickening spirit.* Howbeit that was not first which is spiritual, but that which is *natural;* and afterward that which is *spiritual*" (1 Corinthians 15:45-46).

NO. 2—THE SON AFTER THE FLESH IS SENT AWAY

After Isaac was born, Abraham faced a difficult decision due to a conflict that erupted in the family. The trouble started during a feast Abraham held the day Isaac was weaned.

And Sarah saw the son of Hagar the Egyptian, which she had born unto Abraham, mocking. Wherefore she said unto Abraham, Cast out this bondwoman and her son: for the son of this bondwoman shall not be heir with my son, even with Isaac. And the thing was very grievous in Abraham's sight because of his son. And God said unto Abraham, Let it not be grievous in thy sight because of the lad, and because of thy bondwoman; in all that Sarah hath said unto thee, hearken unto her voice; for in Isaac shall thy seed be called. And also of the son of the bondwoman will I make a nation, because he is thy seed (Genesis 21:9-13).

That last statement is very important. It points to the Second Covenant ratified by the blood of Jesus which says: "And if you belong to Christ [are in Him Who is Abraham's Seed], then you are Abraham's offspring and [spiritual] heirs according to promise" (Galatians 3:29, *Amplified Bible, Classic Edition).*

Although sending away Ishmael grieved Abraham, it had to be done. Isaac was the one through whom God's plans would be accomplished; and Ishmael *(the son after the flesh)* could not share in the inheritance with Isaac.

In this, Abraham became a type of God the Father in that after the Fall He, too, sent away His first son, Adam, from the Garden of Eden. After sending Adam away, God, too, shifted His attention to another *Seed* through His prophetic words to the serpent: "I will put enmity between thee and the woman, and between *thy seed* and *her seed;* it shall bruise thy head, and thou shalt bruise his heel" (Genesis 3:15).

Abraham sending Ishmael away and God sending Adam away is a clear picture: Spiritually, God places no hope or confidence in who we are in the first Adam—only in who we are in Christ, the Second. Therefore, we too are to cast away any hope we may have in our own Adam-like nature and rest in all that Jesus is for us. As the Apostle Paul wrote:

> For we are the circumcision, which worship God in the spirit, and rejoice in Christ Jesus, and have no confidence in the flesh. Though I might also have confidence in the flesh. If any other man thinketh that he hath whereof he might trust in the flesh, I more: circumcised the eighth day, of the stock of Israel, of the tribe of Benjamin, an Hebrew of the Hebrews; as touching the law, a Pharisee; concerning zeal, persecuting the church; touching the righteousness which is in the law, blameless. But what things were gain to me, those I counted loss for Christ. Yea doubtless, and I count all things but loss for the excellency of the knowledge of Christ Jesus my LORD: for whom I have suffered the loss of all things, and do count them but dung, that I may win Christ, and be found in him, not having mine own righteousness, which is of the law, but that which is through the faith of Christ, the righteousness which is of God by faith (Philippians 3:3-9).

NO. 3—THE FATHER SACRIFICES HIS SON

God also allowed His close Friend Abraham to share the experience of having to give up his own son for the purposes of God. Abraham's willingness to do this revealed that he truly was a *father of the Faith*. In following through on what seemed like a horrible request from God, Abraham never once doubted, wavered or hesitated. He never stopped trusting.

Abraham was confident that God's promise would be kept and that Isaac, once sacrificed, would be resurrected on the spot. As we've seen, because of his Faith in God, Abraham offered up Isaac, "accounting that God was able to raise him up, even from the dead; from whence also he received him in a figure" (Hebrews 11:19).

Let's take a moment and answer the question: What is Faith?

First of all, Faith is an invisible force. It is the creative force of the Almighty God, the force released in the first words spoken in Genesis 1, when God said, "Let there be light." The primary use of words is for the release of power and for communication to God's people.

A clear definition of Faith is found in Hebrews 11:1 *(Amplified Bible, Classic Edition)*:

Now faith is the assurance (the confirmation, the title deed) of the things [we] hope for, being the proof of things [we] do not see and the conviction of their reality [faith perceiving as real fact what is not revealed to the senses].

Romans 10:17 says, "Faith cometh by hearing, and hearing by The WORD of God."

Abraham's Faith mirrored God's Faith not only in his willingness to offer Isaac, but also in this: Just as Abraham and Isaac were together both physically and purposefully in what they were doing, so were God "the Father" and God "the Son" united in their willingness to make the sacrifice to redeem mankind.

Isaiah 53:10-11 goes so far as to say:

It pleased The LORD to bruise him [Jesus]; he hath put him to grief: when thou shalt make his soul an offering for sin, he shall see his seed, he shall prolong his days, and the pleasure of The LORD shall prosper in his hand. He [God the Father] shall see of the travail of his [Jesus'] soul, and shall be satisfied: by his knowledge shall my righteous servant justify many; for he [Jesus] shall bear their iniquities.

In all the thirty-three years of Jesus' life leading up to the crucifixion, He and the Father had been together. They had never been separated until that one final moment on the Cross. Only then was Jesus, like Isaac, suddenly unsure of His Father's purpose. But the victory was won. The presence of His Father was restored to Him, and Jesus cried with His last breath, "Father, into thy hands I commend my spirit" (Luke 23:46).

With those words Jesus let us know that His executioners didn't kill him. No, by Faith He released His spirit. The first man to receive what His death provided was a thief hanging next to Him on a cross.

NO. 4—THE FATHER'S HEART FOR HIS SON

As Abraham prepared to leave this earth, he did something else for his Blood-Covenant son, Isaac, that provides us with a picture of God the Father's heart for His Son: He made arrangements for Isaac to be provided with a wife. Calling his eldest servant to him, Abraham said, "Swear by The LORD, the God of heaven, and the God of the earth, that thou shalt not take a wife unto my son of the daughters of the Canaanites, among whom I dwell: but thou shalt go unto my country, and to my kindred, and take a wife unto my son Isaac" (Genesis 24:3-4).

Like Abraham, God's heart, too, is that a bride should be found and prepared for His Son. The unnamed servant who has been sent out to do this is the Holy Spirit. We as believers collectively are the Bride He is preparing, as a gift from the Father to His Son, Jesus.

We are those about whom Jesus said:

- "All that the Father *giveth me shall come to me;* and him that cometh to me *I will in no wise cast out*" (John 6:37).
- "Father, the hour is come; glorify thy Son, that thy Son also may glorify thee: As thou hast given him power over all flesh, that *he should give eternal life to as many as thou hast given him*" (John 17:1-2).

The Apostle Paul wrote:

For the husband is the head of the wife, even as Christ is the head of the church: and he is the saviour of the body.... Husbands, love your wives, even as Christ also loved the church, and gave himself for it; that he might sanctify and cleanse it with the washing of water by The WORD, that he might present it to himself a glorious church, not having spot, or wrinkle, or any such thing; but that it should be holy and without blemish.... For this cause shall a man leave his father and mother, and shall be joined unto his wife, and they two shall be one flesh. This is a great mystery: but I speak concerning Christ and the church (Ephesians 5:23, 25-27, 31-32).

We, the Church, are the Bride God will give as a gift to His beloved Son, Jesus. And we eagerly look and long for the marriage supper of the Lamb.

GO DEEPER
WITH KENNETH

THE LOVE OF GOD...
UNDERSTANDING *HESED*

As we've said from the beginning, all study and understanding of God's powerful Blood covenants must start and finish with an awareness and revelation of the breadth, length, depth and height of the glorious Love our heavenly Father has for us (Ephesians 3:17-20). *Love* is who God is (1 John 4:7-17). He is not power. He is Love. He uses His power on behalf of His Love.

As Professor Greg Stephens has already pointed out, in the Old Covenant (Testament), the primary Hebrew word used to communicate God's immeasurable Love is *hesed*. The root word of *hesed* means "to be good or kind." Most often translated in the Bible as *lovingkindness, hesed* speaks of the unfathomable, unconditional and eternal Love, compassion and mercy of God.[22] It can also be joined with the word *covenant*—covenant lovingkindness—to give a richer sense of when two parties enter a deeper level of relationship, as with the covenant between God and Noah.

God's *hesed* Love first appears in Scripture at a seemingly unlikely moment: just before the destruction of Sodom. Two angels had arrived in the city, spent the night there with Abraham's nephew, Lot, and his family, and escorted them to safety just in time to escape the city's fiery demise. Afterward, Lot said to the angels: "Behold now, thy servant hath found grace in thy sight, and

---

22 *The New Strong's Exhaustive Concordance of the Bible* (Nashville: Thomas Nelson Publishers, 1996) H2617, *checed*.

thou hast magnified thy mercy *[hesed]*, which thou hast showed unto me in saving my life" (Genesis 19:19).

This was God's *covenant lovingkindness* in action. It was God doing what only He can do; what He yearns to do in His extravagant and tender compassion, which is…to BLESS.

God's desire to show His *hesed* toward Abraham's family in that situation was so great, He even told Abraham in advance that the city where Lot lived was in danger. He went to visit Abraham and said, "Because the cry of Sodom and Gomorrah is great, and because their sin is very grievous; I will go down now, and see whether they have done altogether according to the cry of it, which is come unto me; and if not, I will know" (Genesis 18:20–21).

God in His great mercy *[hesed]* never desires for anyone to perish (2 Peter 3:9). In addition, He and Abraham were covenant partners. As close covenant Friends, they had a holy and deep Love for one another (Genesis 18:19; 2 Chronicles 20:7; Isaiah 41:8; James 2:23). So, because of their Friendship and partnership, God went first to consult with Abraham about the matter.

Abraham responded by interceding for the lives of righteous souls who might be living in Sodom. Pleading with God to save them and the city, Abraham said, "Peradventure there be fifty righteous within the city: wilt thou also destroy and not spare the place for the fifty righteous that are therein?… And The LORD said, If I find in Sodom fifty righteous within the city, then I will spare all the place for their sakes" (Genesis 18:24, 26).

Then, Abraham asked if God would spare the city for the sake of forty-five…and kept going until eventually, the number got down to ten. When The LORD said, "I will not destroy it for ten's sake," (verse 32) Abraham was satisfied. He may have assumed that surely The LORD could find in Sodom at least ten righteous people.

But there were not even ten. So, the city perished.

Because Abraham pled with Almighty God for their lives, however, Lot and his two daughters did not perish. They escaped destruction because of God's covenant lovingkindness and disposition *to be kind*. Their deliverance was birthed out of covenant Friendship, where each party was completely invested in the other. God had Abraham on His mind, Abraham had God on his mind…and Lot reaped the benefits of that relationship.

As we saw in Chapter 1, marriage is a perfect example of covenant relationship. It's about always having the other person in your heart and on your mind. Once you say, "I do!" you don't have any more independent thoughts or vision. Nothing happens in your life anymore without having that covenant relationship right there in your heart. At least, that's the way God intended for it to be.

To this day, Gloria and I don't have independent thoughts. She's on my mind, and I'm on hers. Whenever anyone asks me to do something, my first thought is, *How will this affect Gloria?* If I go to town to go shopping, I always end up looking for something to buy for her, and even get excited about it. Why? Because of the marriage covenant between us.

In the same way, God's covenant of strong Friendship with Abraham was an ever-present *remembrance*. Almighty God gave Himself to His Friend Abraham—a forever commitment.

*   *   *   *   *

We find God's consuming *hesed* Love for His covenant people spoken about throughout the Bible:

- "And The LORD passed by before [Moses], and proclaimed, 'The LORD! The LORD! a God merciful *[hesed]* and gracious, slow to anger, and abundant in loving-kindness and truth, keeping mercy and loving-kindness for thousands, forgiving iniquity and transgression and sin'" (Exodus 34:6-7, *Amplified Bible, Classic Edition*).

Hesed and *compassion* are Love's trademarks.

- "Wherefore it shall come to pass, if ye hearken to these judgments, and keep, and do them, that The LORD thy

God shall keep unto thee the covenant and the mercy *[hesed]* which he sware unto thy fathers" (Deuteronomy 7:12).

- "But my mercy *[hesed]* shall not depart away from him, as I took it from Saul, whom I put away before thee" (2 Samuel 7:15).
- "Surely goodness *[hesed]* and mercy shall follow me all the days of my life: and I will dwell in the house of The LORD for ever" (Psalm 23:6).

Mercy is *hesed,* which is the lesser being BLESSED by the greater on an equal level.

- "But the mercy *[hesed]* of The LORD is from everlasting to everlasting upon them that fear him, and his righteousness unto children's children" (Psalm 103:17).
- "O give thanks unto The LORD; for he is good: for his mercy *[hesed]* endureth for ever" (see Psalm 136:1-26).
- "Can a woman forget her sucking child, that she should not have compassion *[hesed]* on the son of her womb? yea, they may forget, yet will I not forget thee. Behold, I have graven thee upon the palms of my hands; thy walls are continually before me" (Isaiah 49:15-16).
- "For this is as the waters of Noah unto me: for as I have sworn that the waters of Noah should no more go over the earth; so have I sworn that I would not be wroth with thee, nor rebuke thee. For the mountains shall depart, and the hills be removed; but my kindness *[hesed]* shall not depart from thee, neither shall the covenant of my peace be removed, saith The LORD that hath mercy on thee" (Isaiah 54:9-10).
- "Incline your ear, and come unto me: hear, and your soul shall live; and I will make an everlasting covenant with you, even the sure mercies *[hesed]* of David" (Isaiah 55:3).
- "The LORD hath appeared of old unto me, saying, Yea, I have loved thee with an everlasting love:

therefore with lovingkindness *[hesed]* have I drawn thee" (Jeremiah 31:3).

- "For thus saith The LORD of hosts; After the glory hath he sent me unto the nations which spoiled you: for he that toucheth you toucheth the apple of his eye" (Zechariah 2:8).

- "For God so loved the world, that he gave his only begotten Son, that whosoever believeth in him should not perish, but have everlasting life" (John 3:16).

- "...So that the world may know that You have sent Me, and have loved them as You have loved Me" (John 17:23, *New King James Version).*

- "But God shows and clearly proves His [own] love for us by the fact that while we were still sinners, Christ...died for us" (Romans 5:8, *Amplified Bible, Classic Edition).*

- "But God, who is rich in mercy, for his great love wherewith he loved us, even when we were dead in sins, hath quickened us together with Christ, (by grace ye are saved)" (Ephesians 2:4-5).

- "Behold, what manner of love the Father hath bestowed upon us, that we should be called the sons of God: therefore the world knoweth us not, because it knew him not" (1 John 3:1).

- "He that loveth not knoweth not God; for God is love" (1 John 4:8).

GOD'S
COVENANT
WITH
MOSES

CHAPTER SIX

GOD'S COVENANT WITH MOSES

A braham went beyond valuing his own Blood covenant relationship with God; he also taught his descendants to value it. That's one of the things that stood out about him. As God said in Genesis 18:19, "I have loved [known] him because he commands his children and his household after him that they keep the way of [The LORD]."[23]

Because of Abraham's faithfulness to pass along the lessons he had learned from God, his covenant family developed into a covenant nation. What's more, the Abrahamic covenant became the foundation for the covenants God made in subsequent generations. His covenant with Abraham continued with Abraham's son, Isaac; then Isaac's son, Jacob (Israel); and so on, down to Moses and David and even the Promised Seed of the New Covenant.

With each generation, God revisited and reaffirmed His covenant and made the necessary personal connection with Abraham's heirs. One such heir who proved to be particularly vital in perpetuating the succession of the covenant line was Joseph. Born in the fourth generation of Abraham's descendants, Joseph was the eleventh of Jacob's (Israel's) twelve sons. He walked in THE BLESSING passed down from his father, and his Faith was tested in an unusual way.

The tests began at the hands of Joseph's brothers. Jealous because Joseph was their father's favorite son, they came to hate him so much they plotted to kill him (Genesis 37:3-4, 18). God's

---

23 *The Chumash, Artscroll Series,* Mesorah Heritage Foundation, *Bereishis/Genesis,* Rabbi Nosson Sherman (Brooklyn: Messorah Publications, Ltd.) p. 83.

covenant BLESSING however, working on Joseph's behalf, kept him alive. And instead of being killed, he was sold into slavery by his brothers and taken to Egypt.

There, Joseph was put to work in the home of Potiphar, a wealthy captain of Pharaoh's guard. Even while serving as a slave, the favor and BLESSING of God on Joseph soon became apparent, so Potiphar set his young Hebrew slave over his entire estate. As Joseph continued to succeed in his new position, he enriched Potiphar even more (Genesis 39:2-6).

Then, Potiphar's wife wrongly accused Joseph of sexually assaulting her, and he was thrown into prison. But even iron bars could not keep THE BLESSING of God from this seed of Abraham. So, as before, Joseph was eventually appointed overseer of the entire prison, greatly benefiting everyone there (Genesis 39:21-23).

While in prison, Joseph also gained a reputation for being gifted by God to interpret dreams. This eventually landed him an audience with Egypt's pharaoh, who needed a dream interpreted. Joseph told him the dream was about a coming famine. He also told Pharaoh how to prepare Egypt for the famine and became a national hero and a world leader.

As it turned out, Joseph also became a savior and benefactor to his own family, who, during the years of famine, relocated from Canaan to Egypt (Genesis 41-42). God prospered His original covenant family of Jacob's seventy descendants; and soon THE BLESSING that had so manifested in Joseph's life was fully restored and intact in the growing tribe of Israel (Jacob).

(Remember what we discussed in Chapter 5 about the names Jacob and Israel. Just as Abraham's name was changed in Genesis 17, later, Jacob's name was changed to *Israel*, which means, "Prince of God." This is why in the Middle East, his descendants are not referred to as the Nation of Jacob, but the Nation of Israel.)

After the death of Joseph and the pharaoh he served, a new pharaoh—and entire generation of Egyptians—arose who knew nothing of Joseph. They became fearful of the strength and overwhelming number of Israelites living among them (Exodus 1:7-9). So, the new pharaoh made the Hebrew people the Egyptians' servants.

Therefore they did set over them taskmasters to afflict them with their burdens. And they built for Pharaoh treasure cities, Pithom and Raamses. But the more they afflicted them, the more they multiplied and grew. And they were grieved because of the children of Israel. And the Egyptians made the children of Israel to *serve* with rigour: And they made their lives bitter with hard bondage, in morter, and in brick, and in all manner of *service* in the field: all their *service,* wherein they made them *serve,* was with rigour (verses 11-14).

The Israelites' enslavement lasted for 400 miserable years, just as God had prophesied to Abraham on the night they cut covenant (Genesis 15:13). At the end of those 400 years, God's people cried out under their heavy bondage of slavery (Psalm 105), and He heard them. His great heart of *hesed* (Covenant lovingkindness and mercy) was moved by their bitter groaning, and He remembered His covenant with Abraham.

This wasn't a case of a 400-year-old promise that God had forgotten. No, the Hebrew word for *remember,* particularly when referring to a Blood covenant, is *zakar.* It is more than head activity. Any time God remembers, He acts.

The *zakar* kind of remembering is what we're to do when we take Communion. Jesus said, "This do in remembrance of me" (1 Corinthians 11:24). Such remembrance invokes action (Luke 1:54-55). It conveys the idea that each covenant person is aware of the other all the time, with both *continually* thinking of each other.

Covenant awareness was what prompted God to take action based on the promise He had made to His Friend, Abraham. It is still what motivates God to this day. It is what compels God to move on behalf of individuals and on behalf of nations.

His covenant awareness is the reason God has so BLESSED the United States. Our first President, George Washington, established a covenant with Him. History records that at his inauguration, President Washington opened his Bible to the seventeenth chapter of Genesis, laid his hand on the covenant God made with Abraham, and lifted his other arm toward heaven. He made a vow to lead our nation and honor the God of Israel. Then he walked arm-in-arm with the new nation's senators and elected officials down the streets of New York to St. Paul's Chapel. There, they prayed and dedicated this land to Almighty God.

A COVENANT FAMILY
BECOMES A COVENANT NATION

When God remembered His covenant with Abraham after the Israelites' 400 years in Egypt, He called Moses to deliver them from slavery. Much like Noah and Joseph, Moses would help preserve the bloodline through which would come God's *Promised Seed* of Redemption for all mankind.

Although he was a Hebrew by birth, Moses had an Egyptian upbringing. Through a series of divinely directed events, he had been miraculously spared from death as an infant and raised in the royal household of Egypt's pharaoh (Exodus 2:1-10). As a young man, Moses had killed an Egyptian citizen while trying to defend a Hebrew slave, and had to flee to the desert for his life. There, Moses became a shepherd, got married and started a family.

While tending sheep near Mount Sinai (later known as *the mountain of God)*, Moses encountered the God of the Hebrews for the first time. Speaking to him out of a burning bush, God said:

> I am the God *[Elohim, God the Father, the Son, and the Holy Spirit]* of thy father, the God of Abraham, the God of Isaac, and the God of Jacob.... And I am come down to deliver them out of the hand of the Egyptians, and to bring them up out of that land unto a good land and a large, unto a land flowing with milk and honey.... Come now therefore, and I will send thee unto Pharaoh, that thou mayest bring forth my people the children of Israel out of Egypt (Exodus 3:6, 8, 10).

Notice, God identified himself to Moses as "the God of Abraham, the God of Isaac, and the God of Jacob." But when He told Moses of his assignment, instead of using the name Jacob, He referred to His people as "the children of Israel."

By that time, Moses was perfectly prepared to deliver those people out of Egypt and lead them through the wilderness. After forty years there he knew that wilderness well. Everywhere in the wilderness the Israelites' journey would take them, Moses had already been there.

Having grown up in pharaoh's household, Moses was also well-equipped to speak to him. He didn't have a stuttering problem, as many have thought. He did tell God when He called him, "I *am* slow of speech, and of a slow tongue" (Exodus 4:10). But that was because he hadn't spoken Hebrew in forty years and was no longer fluent in the language.

With the promise that his brother Aaron would be by his side and speak for him, Moses agreed to go back to Egypt. There, he confronted Pharaoh for the release of the Israelites. Ten plagues later, with nearly all of Egypt and its people affected, Pharaoh gave in to Moses' demand to set the Israelite slaves free.

After a miraculous crossing of the Red Sea and a three-month journey through the wilderness, God had His covenant family, Israel, exactly where He wanted them. Anywhere from one million to three million descendants of Abraham gathered at the foot of Mount Sinai, where they could get reacquainted with the God of their fathers, Abraham, Isaac and Jacob (Israel)—and more importantly, reestablish their own covenant with Him.[24]

And Moses went up to God, and The LORD *[LORD here is Jehovah, the name of God's power]* called to him out of the mountain, Say this to the house of Jacob and tell the Israelites: You have seen what I did to the Egyptians, and how I bore you on eagles' wings and brought you to Myself. Now therefore, if you will obey My voice in truth and keep My covenant, then you shall be My own peculiar possession and treasure from among and above all peoples; for all the earth is Mine. And you shall be to Me a kingdom of priests, a holy

---

24 Six hundred thousand men on foot left Egypt in the Exodus (Exodus 12:37). This does not factor in a likely equal number, or more, of women and children (Exodus 12:37), bringing the total to at least 1.2-3 million.

nation [consecrated, set apart to the worship of God]. These
are the words you shall speak to the Israelites (Exodus 19:3-6,
Amplified Bible, Classic Edition).

Having heard from The LORD, Moses descended the holy
mountain and conveyed to the people God's intentions. Within
three days these chosen people had the Ten Commandments with
more to come—the beginnings of God's covenant with Moses.

Abraham's covenant had been simple: God had given him
requirements, commandments and instructions—all face to face—
along with a promise (Genesis 26:3-5). Abraham had listened to
God, obeyed, and been BLESSED.

Now that the Israelites numbered in the millions, however,
more was required. It became necessary for God to give them a
written covenant, one that would guide them on how to conduct
their lives, their families, their businesses, their nation, even their
worship of God. Why? So they could continue to walk in THE
BLESSING.

THE MOSES COVENANT PROMISE

God's covenant with Moses had far more words than any of the
others. It contained the entire moral, civil and ceremonial Law for
the nation of Israel.

Unlike God's covenant with Abraham, which was based on obedience that came from a heart of Faith and a promise of BLESSING
that came in the form of a simple oath, the Moses covenant included
many regulations. Its promise of BLESSING came with a long and
complicated list of conditions that included consequences and even
curses, which was something new.

There were also plenty of *"Thou shalt nots"* in the Moses covenant. Even God's command, "Thou shalt love The LORD thy God
with all thine heart, and with all thy soul, and with all thy might"
(Deuteronomy 6:5), carried with it a sense of strict obedience,
rather than the outflow of complete trust and love. At the same

time though, the Moses covenant also laid out the wonderful results of walking in covenant with the Creator:

> And it shall be, when The LORD thy God shall have brought thee into the land which he sware unto thy fathers, to Abraham, to Isaac, and to Jacob, to give thee great and goodly cities, which thou buildedst not, and houses full of all good things, which thou filledst not, and wells digged, which thou diggedst not, vineyards and olive trees, which thou plantedst not; when thou shalt have eaten and be full.... But thou shalt remember The LORD thy God: for it is he that giveth thee power to get wealth, that he may establish his covenant which he sware unto thy fathers, as it is this day (Deuteronomy 6:10-11, 8:18).

God said to the Israelites (and He says to us), be aware of your covenant. This is THE BLESSING covenant! THE BLESSING is threefold: spiritual life, healing and divine health, and prosperity. That's the plan of God. The curse is threefold: spiritual death, sickness and disease, and poverty. Therefore, you make the choice.

The Moses version of the Abrahamic covenant also differed from God's previous covenants in that mediators were included for the first time. Moses, Aaron and the Levites would now go to God on behalf of the people. The mediators and the added covenant conditions and consequences served to remind Israel that Abraham, in himself, was not qualified to cut covenant with God. He could only receive THE BLESSING of the covenant. And he could only do that by *Faith,* which is believing God to be gracious and kind and merciful.

After all, God was the Greater One initiating the agreement, and He knows full well the heart and fallen state of all mankind. So, to enter covenant with God, Abraham, like anyone else (including us), had to believe that God would keep His WORD.

The reason God added conditions and consequences to His covenant with Moses was to reveal to the Israelites their fallen nature. He wanted them to realize they could not keep His covenant requirements through their own self-effort—that it would never work (Galatians 3:19). God wanted them to see that instead, they needed a Savior, someone who could do the impossible, the unattainable for them.

The *Law*, as God's covenant with Moses came to be commonly known, was never intended to justify or *save* anyone. Its purpose was not to *save* the Hebrews. The purpose of the Law was to reveal sin and invite the Israelites into Blood-covenant *relationship* with their God, which has been His intent all along.

You can see this in the Ten Commandments.

God started them out by declaring: "I am The LORD thy God, which have brought thee out of the land of Egypt, out of the house of bondage. Thou shalt have no other gods before me" (Exodus 20:2-3). In my Bible, I marked it like this: *Thou shalt have no other gods before Me. I am your Source!*

Next, God said, "Thou shalt not make unto thee any graven image, or any likeness of any thing that is in heaven above, or that is in the earth beneath, or that is in the water under the earth: Thou shalt not bow down thyself to them, nor serve them." In other words, *Don't bow down to those things; you have dominion over them!* "For I The LORD thy God am a jealous God, visiting the iniquity of the fathers upon the children unto the third and fourth generation of them that hate me; and showing mercy unto thousands of them that love me, and keep my commandments" (verses 4-6).

Those are not just commandments. God didn't just stick them out there to make things difficult for people. There's an explanation that goes along with them. There's a reason for all ten, and the result of each one is good—it's THE BLESSING of Abraham, Isaac and Jacob (Israel).

The same is true of the civil law God gave Israel. All of it is squarely based on those first ten, and it was all given for people's good. Their civil law told them what to do in certain situations. It said if you bring harm to a person, you need to recompense him. For example, an eye for an eye, and a tooth for tooth (Exodus 21:24) isn't about extracting vengeance. It's about taking care of other people. Civil law said, if you kill another man's oxen, you must replace it. If what you did cost him money, you need to pay him.

All these articles of the law had to be written down. Not only the Israelites but all the rest of us needed to be able to "watch to see" what The LORD has said to us. So, God gave Moses much the same instructions He gave the prophet Habakkuk: "Write the vision, and make it plain upon tables, that he may run that readeth it." (See Habakkuk 2:1-3.)

We are a BLESSED people of God to have in our possession this most precious of all books, the Holy Bible, or our personal copy of the covenants.

NOT A WAY TO EARN SALVATION, A RESPONSE TO IT

How can we be certain that the Law of Moses wasn't given to the Israelites so they could earn their salvation?

Because the Law was given *after* God *saved* Israel from slavery in Egypt. By the time God wrote out His covenant Law for them, their salvation had already manifested! In fact, they had already come up with a song to celebrate it. After seeing their enemies drown after their miraculous crossing of the Red Sea, they had sung: "I will sing unto The LORD, for he hath triumphed gloriously: the horse and his rider hath he thrown into the sea. The LORD is my strength and song, and he is become my salvation" (Exodus 15:1-2).

God offered Israel the free grace of salvation long before they observed a single task of the Law. So, clearly, salvation was never about human performance. It was never about checking off a list of do's and don'ts.

Think back how God saved…

- Adam and Eve from themselves by removing them from the Garden
- Noah and the human race from corruption
- Abraham and Sarah's promised seed
- Isaac, Jacob and Joseph.

The Law came in response to God's salvation, not as the way to achieve that salvation: Moses made this clear when he said to the Israelites in Deuteronomy 24:18, "You shall [earnestly] remember that you were a slave in Egypt and The LORD your God redeemed you from there; therefore I command you to do this" *(Amplified Bible, Classic Edition).*

The same applies to us as New Covenant believers. Observance of the Law—of God's WORD—is for us a matter of thankfulness and gratitude for the opportunity to have a relationship with God. It's our response to God's saving grace. Our obedience to any commandments, our commitment to live righteously, becomes a thank-you to our merciful and gracious God who has saved us.

For the Israelites, the challenge came when they (and the rest of humanity) began to replace an opportunity for relationship with God with a list of rules. When rather than living by Faith in their covenant with God, and using the Law as a guide on how to conduct themselves as His covenant partners, they tried to use the Law to establish their own righteousness.

A few years ago, in my prayer time, a vision illustrating this very challenge played out right in front of my eyes. I laughed out loud as I saw this guy and what he was doing. It reminded me of an old Buster Keaton[25] slapstick silent comedy.

I saw a man trying to hang long, heavy curtains. He would try to hang them up, and they would immediately fall all over him. He got all tangled up in those curtains while struggling to hang them.

I said, "Look at that guy!"

And sure enough, the curtains ended up in a mess, piled all over the floor.

I noticed in the corner a huge, heavy, solid-gold curtain rod that looked more like a beam from a bridge. I realized the man had been attempting to hang the long and heavy curtains *without* a rod!

As I looked closer, I saw the word *Faith* written on one curtain, on another *righteousness,* on another *healing* and on another *prosperity.* By now, the man had become hopelessly tangled up in them.

---

25 Comedian and pioneer filmmaker of silent movie comedies in the 1920s

Next, I saw words written in red letters on one side of the gold curtain rod that was standing in the corner. They were the words of Mark 12:30-31: "Love The LORD thy God with all thy heart, and with all thy soul, and with all thy mind, and with all thy strength... and thy neighbour as thyself."

Then, I heard the desperate cry of the man's heart and, suddenly, the situation wasn't funny anymore. I heard him cry: "Oh God, what is the matter with my Faith? Why doesn't it work? I believe in healing, and I'm still sick. I believe in prosperity, and I can't pay my bills. What is the matter with me?"

I knew in my spirit by The LORD that the man had known the rod was standing in the corner, but he had ignored it.

Again, as I looked closer, I could see piled up in those curtains that had so weighed the man down, little snakes crawling around in there, nipping at his heels. I wondered what in the world snakes were doing crawling around in *righteousness, Faith, prosperity* and *healing*.

The answer was: It was fear!

Then I heard The LORD shout...*HANG THE ROD, NOT THE CURTAINS! THE CURTAINS ARE ALREADY ATTACHED TO THE ROD!*

I share that to say: Hang the rod. Hang the rod of *Love!*

Understand, every law of God, including spiritual law, is of Love because God is Love. There is no spiritual law without God and His Love. If you hang the curtain rod—the law of Love—first, rather than the curtains, there will be no fear because perfected Love casts out fear (1 John 4:18). All the "snakes" in our lives are gone when there is no fear.

A step out of *Love* is a step into *fear*, which is satan's territory. And fear has torment (1 John 4:18). The torment is in the fear. The man trying to hang those curtains was tormented. He could not get his Faith to work and receive the victory in his finances, his health or in his walk of righteousness.

Walking in Covenant Love toward God and others allows the Holy Spirit to flow because Faith—the currency of heaven—works by Love (Galatians 5:6).

The Apostle Paul summed it up best with this: "Love worketh no ill to his neighbour: therefore love is the fulfilling of the law" (Romans 13:10).

A person who hangs the rod first, who wholeheartedly loves God and others as much as himself, will never steal, take his neighbor's wife, commit murder or worship other gods. Therefore, no external laws or punishments are needed to keep that person in line (Galatians 5:22-23; Romans 2:14-15).

CUTTING THE MOSES COVENANT

God's covenant with Moses did not replace His previous covenant with Abraham (Galatians 3; Hebrews 6). In fact, for centuries the prophets spoke of *two* coexisting covenants, of God's covenants with Abraham and Moses running parallel to each other (Ezekiel 16; Galatians 3). Both of those Blood covenants would ultimately flow into the Cross—the New Covenant of Blood. The Abraham covenant being fulfilled there, and the Moses covenant being abolished.

Until that time came however, the cutting of the Moses covenant required a steady flow of blood sacrifices offered at the tabernacle, and later at the Temple, under Moses. There were voluntary offerings, mandatory offerings, festival sacrifices, Sabbath sacrifices, daily sacrifices and sacrifices for certain diseases. With every variety of sacrifice, God was very particular about the handling of the animals' blood. There were times when it was sprinkled, and times when it was taken in behind the veil in the holy of holies (as on the Day of Atonement).

Because of this complicated system of shedding and sacrificing animal blood, the Moses covenant is often referred to as the *Blood covenant.* Death and blood were everywhere. Yet it was never enough and never good enough. The many sacrifices offered were a physical illustration of the spiritual truth: Mankind's sin was too great; no amount of animal substitution could ever satisfy the justice required.

Until the blood of Jesus was shed however, substitutionary blood still had to be provided. As God said in Leviticus 17:11, "For the *life* of the flesh is in the *blood*: and I have given it to you upon the altar to make an atonement for your souls." Even the blood of animals has always been very precious to God. But because the blood of mankind is even more precious to Him, through the Moses covenant God allowed the blood of animals to serve as a covering for man's sin.

We see this in the Bible again and again in the following passages:

Exodus 24:4-8

And Moses wrote all the words of The LORD, and rose up early in the morning, and builded an altar under the hill, and twelve pillars, according to the twelve tribes of Israel. And he sent young men of the children of Israel, which offered burnt offerings, and sacrificed peace offerings of oxen unto The LORD. And Moses took half of the blood, and put it in basons; and half of the blood he sprinkled on the altar. And he took the book of the covenant, and read in the audience of the people: and they said, All that The LORD hath said will we do, and be obedient. And Moses took the blood, and sprinkled it on the people, and said, Behold the blood of the covenant, which The LORD hath made with you concerning all these words.

Hebrews 9

Verses 1-3: Then verily the first covenant had also ordinances of divine service, and a worldly sanctuary. For there was a tabernacle made; the first, wherein was the candlestick, and the table, and the showbread; which is called the sanctuary. And after the second veil, the tabernacle which is called the Holiest of all.

Verses 6-10, 16-23: Now when these things were thus ordained, the priests went always into the first tabernacle, accomplishing the service of God. But into the second went the high priest alone once every year, not without blood, which he offered for himself, and for the errors of the people: The Holy Ghost this signifying, that the way into the holiest of all was not yet made manifest, while as the first tabernacle was yet standing: which was a figure for the time then present, in which were offered both gifts and sacrifices, that could not make him that did the service perfect, as pertaining to the conscience; which stood only in meats and drinks, and divers washings, and carnal ordinances, imposed on them until the time of reformation.... For where a testament is, there must also of necessity be the death of the testator. For a testament is of force after men are dead: otherwise it is of no strength at all while the testator liveth. whereupon neither the first testament was dedicated without blood. For when Moses had spoken every precept to all the people according to the law, he took the blood of calves and of goats, with water, and scarlet wool, and hyssop, and sprinkled both the book, and all the people, saying, This is the blood of the testament which God hath enjoined unto you. Moreover he sprinkled with blood both the tabernacle, and all the vessels of the ministry. And almost all things are by the law purged with blood; and without shedding of blood is no remission. It was therefore necessary that the patterns of things in the heavens should be purified with these; but the heavenly things themselves with better sacrifices than these.

Hebrews 10:1-4 (Amplified Bible, Classic Edition)

For since the Law has merely a rude outline (foreshadowing) of the good things to come—instead of fully expressing those things—it can never by offering the same sacrifices continually year after year make perfect those who approach [its altars]. For if it were otherwise, would [these sacrifices] not have stopped being offered? Since the worshipers had once for all been cleansed, they would no longer have any guilt or consciousness of sin. But [as it is] these sacrifices annually bring a fresh remembrance of sins [to be atoned for], *because the blood of bulls and goats is powerless to take sins away.*

Zechariah 9:9-12

Rejoice greatly, O daughter of Zion; shout, O daughter of Jerusalem: behold, thy King cometh unto thee: he is just, and having salvation; lowly, and riding upon an ass, and upon a colt the foal of an ass. And I will cut off the chariot from Ephraim, and the horse from Jerusalem, and the battle bow shall be cut off: and he shall speak peace unto the heathen: and his dominion shall be from sea even to sea, and from the river even to the ends of the earth. As for thee also, by the blood of thy covenant I have sent forth thy prisoners out of the pit wherein is no water. Turn you to the strong hold, ye prisoners of hope: even to day do I declare that I will render double unto thee.

Thankfully, we as believers are no longer subject to a Law under which we can only hope to gain the good graces of Almighty God through continual blood sacrifices. No, our hope now—our Blood Covenant sacrifice—is Jesus Himself. And as we will see in our study of the New Covenant, we do not even need the innocent blood of Jesus shed on our behalf and applied again and again, as with Moses' covenant. Jesus' blood was offered on the mercy seat once and for all (Hebrews 9:12). We simply use the power and authority of *His Name*, the Name of Jesus, that's backed by His blood.

THE MOSES COVENANT SEAL

The seal, or reminder, of Moses' covenant was the *Sabbath*. God introduced it to the Israelites in principle a couple of months before the Law was given. When, a month into their wilderness journey, they ran out of food, God started raining down on them a heavenly food, called manna. He told them to gather it, however, only six days a week. On the sixth day, they were to gather enough for two days, and on the seventh day they were to rest.

When they reached Mount Sinai, The LORD made this Sabbath rest part of the Law. He commanded the Israelites:

Remember the *sabbath* day, to keep it holy. Six days shalt thou labour, and do all thy work: But the seventh day is the *sabbath* of The LORD thy God: in it thou shalt not do any work, thou, nor thy son, nor thy daughter, thy manservant, nor thy maidservant, nor thy cattle, nor thy stranger that is within thy gates: For in six days The LORD made heaven and earth, the sea, and all that in them is, and rested the seventh day: wherefore The LORD BLESSED the sabbath day, and hallowed it (Exodus 20:8-11).

This Sabbath rest requirement was new to the Israelites. From the days of Adam until the Moses covenant, there had never been any mention of it. Certainly, the oral tradition had been passed down from generation to generation about God having rested on the seventh day, when He finished Creation. But that was only given as an example. With the Moses covenant, keeping the Sabbath became mandatory and was quite a serious matter with God.

While God's instructions about gathering the manna in the wilderness were simple, practicing the Sabbath according to the Law of Moses presented some challenges. Under the Law, in addition to the weekly day of rest on Saturdays, other Sabbaths were required. Certain feasts included in the Law were considered Sabbaths. There were even high Sabbaths, some of which could be on a Wednesday or Thursday.

Although most Christians don't know it, this was the case the week Jesus was crucified. As John 19:31 says, the day Jesus died the Jews were concerned "because it was the preparation, that the bodies [of Jesus and the two other men who were crucified alongside Him that day] should not remain upon the cross on the sabbath day, (for that sabbath day was an high day)...."

Because the Sabbath was on a high day that week, it was on Wednesday, not Friday. That is important to know! Why? Because Jesus said in Matthew 12:40, "For as Jonas was three days and three nights in the whale's belly; so shall the Son of man be three days and three nights in the heart of the earth."

That statement would be untrue if Jesus died on Friday and

then rose on Sunday. But contrary to what has been religiously taught, that's not what happened. Jesus was crucified on Wednesday and did exactly what He said. He spent three days and three nights in the heart of the earth and on Sunday He rose from the dead!

When the Israelites began trying to keep the Sabbath, of course, Jesus' death and resurrection was still thousands of years in the future. So, they weren't thinking about Him. Instead, God's Sabbath laws revealed to them their own inability to measure up to His standards. Their sin nature always thwarted them. No amount of human effort could enable them to perfectly *obey* the Law, not 100 percent.

As you read the following scriptures, take note of the various aspects and details of God's Sabbath requirements that are revealed in them. Paying special attention to the portions emphasized by italics, consider the lifestyle, intent and purpose of the Sabbath that God so wisely worked into the daily and monthly schedules of His covenant people.

Exodus 16:23-30

And he [Moses] said unto them, This is that which The LORD hath said, To morrow is the rest of the holy *sabbath* unto The LORD: bake that which ye will bake to day, and seethe that ye will seethe; and that which remaineth over lay up for you *to be kept until the morning.* And they *laid it up till the morning,* as Moses bade: and it did not stink, neither was there any worm therein. And Moses said, Eat that to day; for to day is a sabbath unto The LORD: to day *ye shall not find it in the field.* Six days ye shall gather it; but on the seventh day, which is the sabbath, *in it there shall be none.* And it came to pass, that there went out some of the people on the seventh day for to gather, and they found none. And The LORD said unto Moses, How long refuse ye to keep my commandments and my laws? See, for that The LORD hath *given you the sabbath,* therefore he giveth you on the sixth day the *bread of two days;* abide ye every man in his place, let no man go out of his place on the seventh day. So the people rested on the seventh day.

Exodus 31:12-17

And The LORD spake unto Moses, saying, Speak thou also unto the children of Israel, saying, Verily my sabbaths ye shall keep: *for it is a sign between me and you* throughout your generations; that ye may know that I am The LORD *that doth sanctify you.* Ye shall keep the sabbath therefore; for it is holy unto you: every one that defileth it shall surely be *put to death:* for whosoever doeth any work therein, that soul shall be *cut off* from among his people. Six days may work be done; but in the seventh is the sabbath of rest, holy to The LORD: whosoever doeth any work in the sabbath day, he shall surely be *put to death.* Wherefore the children of Israel shall keep the sabbath, to observe the sabbath throughout their generations, for a *perpetual covenant.* It is a sign between me and the children of Israel for ever: for in six days The LORD made heaven and earth, and on the seventh day *he rested, and was refreshed.*

[God didn't rest because He was tired. He rested because He was finished.]

Leviticus 19:30

Ye shall keep my sabbaths, and *reverence my sanctuary:* I am The LORD.

Leviticus 23:3

Six days shall work be done: but the seventh day is the *sabbath of rest, an holy convocation;* ye shall do no work therein: it is the sabbath of The LORD in all your dwellings.

Ezekiel 20 *(Amplified Bible, Classic Edition)*

Verses 10-16: So I caused them to go out from the land of Egypt and brought them into the wilderness. And I gave them My statutes and showed and made known to them My judgments, which, if a man keeps, he must live in and by them. Moreover, also I gave them My Sabbaths to be a sign between Me and them, that they might understand and realize that I am The LORD Who sanctifies them [separates and sets them apart]. But the house of Israel rebelled against Me in the wilderness; they walked not in My statutes and they despised and cast away My judgments, which, if a man keeps, he must even live in and by them; and they grievously profaned My Sabbaths. Then I thought I would pour out My wrath on them in the wilderness and uproot and consume them. But I acted for My name's sake, that it should not be profaned before the [heathen] nations in whose sight I brought them out. Yet also I lifted up My hand to *swear* to them in the wilderness that I would not bring them into the land which I had given them, flowing with milk and honey, which is the ornament and glory of all lands—because they despised and rejected My ordinances and walked not in My statutes and profaned My Sabbaths, for their hearts went after their idols.

Verses 18-20: But I said to their sons in the wilderness, You shall not walk in the statutes of your fathers nor observe their ordinances nor defile yourselves with their idols. I The LORD am your God; walk in My statutes and keep My ordinances, and hallow (separate and keep holy) My Sabbaths, and they shall be a sign between Me and you, that you may know, understand, and realize that I am The LORD your God.

Verse 21, 24: Yet the sons rebelled against Me; they walked not in My statutes, neither kept My ordinances which, if a man does, he must live in and by them; they profaned My Sabbaths. Then I thought I would pour out My wrath on them and finish My anger against them in the wilderness.... Because they had not executed My ordinances but had despised and rejected My statutes and had profaned My Sabbaths, and their eyes were set on their fathers' idols.

Despite all the fiery warnings God gave the Israelites about the dire consequences of not taking the Sabbath off, once the Israelites finally entered their Promised Land, God made a surprising exception to His own Law. During the seven-day battle to take the city of Jericho, He had the Israelites break their Sabbath rest by marching (which was considered "work") seven times around the city on the seventh day of the week (Joshua 6).

Why? God did the work by miraculously bringing down the massive walls of Jericho that day!

This confirms the fact that *obedience* has always been a matter of the *heart*. It was never about keeping rules and regulations. And by the time God's people reached Jericho (forty years after their exodus), He finally had a people whose hearts were with Him…for the most part.

CONTRADICTIONS TO THE MOSES COVENANT

Of all the covenants God ever made with the people of Israel, the one He cut with Moses was the most detailed and demanding. Even the early Church continued to wrestle with the requirements it placed on the Hebrew people (Acts 15). Debates continue to surround those requirements to this day.

When the Moses covenant was given, God's covenant with Abraham, Isaac and Jacob (Israel) was, technically, still in place. But the Israelites had failed miserably at keeping its terms. Even so, upon receiving the Law of Moses, these descendants of Abraham boasted of their ability to maintain their part of the agreement.

In their ignorance, they were not aware that in the nearly three months they'd spent traveling from Egypt to Mount Sinai, they had already failed four major *Faith* tests. And they had failed them after witnessing firsthand the supernatural workings of God's mercy and grace on their behalf!

In just a short period of time, the Israelites had seen God…

- loosen Pharaoh's grip through plagues that only the Egyptians suffered.
- load them up with gold and supplies that the Egyptians freely gave. (That was compensation! The Egyptians paid them for the time they'd spent and work they'd done there.)
- heal them physically so they were able to make the journey in full strength.

- deliver them across a sea that had them backed up, stalled with no natural way of escape, and Pharaoh coming hard behind them.
- destroy the entire Egyptian army before their very eyes.
- provide them with food, water and rest stops along the way.
- keep them warm at night and cool during the day.

Whatever Faith the Israelites may have had in the beginning was negated when, just days after their epic deliverance from Egypt, they began complaining and striving with each other. So when put to the test, their Faith failed four times. Those four *Faith failures* became contradictions, obstacles, to the relationship God sought with Israel through the Moses covenant.

FAITH FAILURE NO. 1—EXODUS 14

Verses 5-6, 9: And it was told the king of Egypt that the people fled: and the heart of Pharaoh and of his servants was turned against the people, and they said, Why have we done this, that we have let Israel go from serving us? And he made ready his chariot, and took his people with him…. [and] the Egyptians pursued after them, all the horses and chariots of Pharaoh, and his horsemen, and his army, and overtook them….

Verses 10-12: And when Pharaoh drew nigh, the children of Israel lifted up their eyes, and, behold, the Egyptians marched after them; and they were sore afraid: and the children of Israel cried out unto The LORD. And they said unto Moses, Because there were no graves in Egypt, hast thou taken us away to die in the wilderness? wherefore hast thou dealt thus with us, to carry us forth out of Egypt? Is not this the word that we did tell thee in Egypt, saying, Let us alone, that we may serve the Egyptians? For it had been better for us to serve the Egyptians, than that we should die in the wilderness.

Verses 15-16: And The LORD said unto Moses, Wherefore criest thou unto me? speak unto the children of Israel, that they go forward: But lift thou up thy rod, and stretch out thine hand over the sea, and divide it: and the children of Israel shall go on dry ground through the midst of the sea.

Verses 21-22: And Moses stretched out his hand over the sea; and The LORD caused the sea to go back by a strong east wind all that night, and made the sea dry land, and the waters were divided. And the children of Israel went into the midst of the sea upon the dry ground: and the waters were a wall unto them on their right hand, and on their left.

Verses 27-28: And Moses stretched forth his hand over the sea, and the sea returned to his strength when the morning appeared; and the Egyptians fled against it; and The LORD overthrew the Egyptians in the midst of the sea. And the waters returned, and covered the chariots, and the horsemen, and all the host of Pharaoh that came into the sea after them; there remained not so much as one of them.

Verse 31: And Israel saw that great work which The LORD did upon the Egyptians: and the people feared The LORD, and believed The LORD, and his servant Moses.

FAITH FAILURE NO. 2—EXODUS 15:22-26

So Moses brought Israel from the Red sea, and they went out into the wilderness of Shur; and they went three days in the wilderness, and found no water. And when they came to Marah, they could not drink of the waters of Marah, for they were bitter: therefore the name of it was called Marah. And the people murmured against Moses, saying, What shall we drink? And he cried unto The LORD; and The LORD showed him a tree, which when he had cast into the waters, the waters were made sweet....

It was there at Marah that The LORD set before them the following decree as a standard to *test their faithfulness* to Him. He said, "If thou wilt diligently hearken to the voice of The LORD thy God, and wilt do that which is right in his sight, and wilt give ear to his commandments, and keep all his statutes, I will put none of these diseases upon thee, which I have brought upon the Egyptians: for I am The LORD that healeth thee." He is still the healing God, filled with mercy and compassion!

FAITH FAILURE NO. 3—EXODUS 16

Verses 1-3: And they took their journey from Elim, and all the congregation of the children of Israel came unto the wilderness of Sin, which is between Elim and Sinai, on the fifteenth day of the second month after their departing out of the land of Egypt. And the whole congregation of the children of Israel murmured against Moses and Aaron in the wilderness. And the children of Israel said unto them, Would to God we had died by the hand of The LORD in the land of Egypt, when we sat by the flesh pots, and when we did eat bread to the full; for ye have brought us forth into this wilderness, to kill this whole assembly with hunger.

Verses 11-12: And The LORD spake unto Moses, saying, I have heard the murmurings of the children of Israel: speak unto them, saying, At even ye shall eat flesh, and in the morning ye shall be filled with bread; and ye shall know that I am The LORD your God.

FAITH FAILURE NO. 4—EXODUS 17:1-7
(AMPLIFIED BIBLE, CLASSIC EDITION)

All the congregation of the Israelites moved on from the Wilderness of Sin by stages, according to the commandment of The LORD, and encamped at Rephidim; but there was no water for the people to drink. Therefore, the people contended with Moses, and said, Give us water that we may drink. And Moses said to them, Why do you find fault with me? Why do you tempt The LORD and try His patience? But the people thirsted there for water, and the people murmured against Moses, and said, Why did you bring us up out of Egypt to kill us and our children and livestock with thirst? So Moses cried to The LORD, What shall I do with this people? They are almost ready to stone me. And The LORD said to Moses, Pass on before the people, and take with you some of the elders of Israel; and take in your hand the rod with which you smote the river [Nile], and go. Behold, I will stand before you there on the rock at [Mount] Horeb; and you shall strike the rock, and water shall come out of it, that the people may drink. And Moses did so in the sight of the elders of Israel. He called the place Massah [proof] and Meribah [contention] because of the faultfinding of the Israelites and because they tempted and tried the patience of The LORD, saying, Is The LORD among us or not?

These weren't the only times the Israelites provoked God. This generation of Israelites wound up provoking Him ten times. They repeatedly proved that neither they nor any other fallen human being would ever be able to keep up with all the conditions and regulations of Moses' covenant. It was impossible, because if you failed to keep just one of those conditions, you failed them all.

This was the absolute *holy* standard of the Father. Had He not set it up that way, He would not have been a *just* God. He selected a nation out of the seed of Abraham to represent Him to all other nations of people, and to all generations. So, in giving Israel the Moses covenant, He was bringing the entire world to court.

He was revealing the fallen condition of man's heart, showing us that pursuing rules rather than relationship always produces rebellion. At the same time, He was preparing the way for the New Covenant that would usher in a level of freedom—and relationship with the Father—never seen nor experienced before, not even by Adam.

GO DEEPER
WITH KENNETH

ACTIVATE YOUR COVENANT

The Israelites were heirs of Abraham's covenant with God even while they were living as slaves in Egypt. So, when they cried out, God, in His Covenant lovingkindness and mercy, demonstrated to them His faithfulness and supernaturally delivered them. Afterward however, even though God's covenant with Abraham belonged to them and was still in place, they didn't have the *Faith* necessary to activate it.

They did not believe God loved them.

FAITH BEGINS RIGHT WHERE YOU ARE

When I first started attending Oral Roberts University and serving Brother Roberts as part of his flight crew, I was also his driver, which afforded me the opportunity to see firsthand the anointing on his life and ministry. I saw the power of God at work to heal and deliver. In meeting after meeting, I saw the miraculous take place. And the more I saw, the more I wanted that same anointing that was on Brother Roberts to be on this ministry. Like Brother Roberts, I wanted to see people set free—as God had set His people, Israel, free.

The first time I heard this powerful man of God minister to his partners, I also wanted to become a partner. It was just all over me. I remember watching as I saw people sow into his ministry and connect their Faith with his. I saw how they were tangibly joining with him in ministry. *That* was covenant!

When Brother Roberts encouraged people who weren't yet partners with him to sign up and pledge to give ten dollars a month, I
was ready to do it. However, I was so broke as they say, I couldn't pay
attention. I had no money at all. Still, I was determined to become a
partner of Oral Roberts Ministries.

In that first partner meeting, the ushers passed out envelopes
to the people along with short, wooden pencils for them to use to
fill out their offering envelopes. Looking at the pencil I held in my
hand and recognizing it was all I had to give at that moment, I put
it in the envelope. I also checked the box on the envelope indicating
that I was now a partner with Oral Roberts Ministries.

Isn't that how God made His Covenant with us?

"God so loved the world, that He gave His only..." (John 3:16).

So, I gave my "only"!

About that time in the meeting, I heard someone behind me
say, "Hey, you!" When I turned around, it was a woman trying to
get my attention. She had no idea who I was but said, "During this
entire meeting The LORD has been worry warting me to give you
ten dollars."

I said, "Give it here, lady. I'll take it. Thank you!" Then I caught
the usher, put my ten-dollar bill in the envelope, and put the pencil
in my pocket. I was a partner!

As soon as I returned home, I could hardly wait to tell Gloria
we were partners with Oral Roberts Ministries for ten dollars per
month. Gloria said, and I quote, "Kenneth, where will we ever get
ten dollars a month?"

I realized she had not heard the partner message. So, I preached
it to her the best I could remember. "Gloria," I said, "we can have
Oral Roberts' anointing for ten dollars a month." She became as excited as I was, and we are still partners today with Richard Roberts
and Oral Roberts University.

Here's my point: Every covenant must be activated by *Faith*. And
you and I are the ones who must put Faith into action. That's the reason The LORD instructed Gloria and me to always call our Partners
"Covenant Partners." We are in covenant with our Partners to pray

for them every day, ministrywide. Gloria and I pray for our Partners at every meal. They are ever on our minds.

It's one thing to know we have a covenant, as millions of Israelites knew. It's another thing to live in that covenant and experience the full extent of its benefits.

How do you possibly do that?

To begin with, once you hear The WORD of God, once you hear God's promises to you—as Israel had, over and over—then you apply corresponding action. You act. You do something, and you do whatever you do in Faith. Faith is an act.

For me, I activated my covenant relationship with Brother Roberts and his ministry by giving what I was able to give—a pencil—while believing for more. And when the "more" came, I gave it too! On top of that, Gloria joined her Faith with mine when I told her what I had done.

Of course, we've had differences of opinion about things, but we discuss them and base our conversations on what The BOOK says. For instance, in 1968 I was preparing to preach at Grace Temple Church in Fort Worth, Texas. The Spirit of God directed me in the evening service to preach from the thirteenth chapter of Romans. My chosen text was the first verse: "Let every soul be subject unto the higher powers. For there is no power but of God: the powers that be are ordained of God." I was going to center up on verse 4, which says, "For he is the minister of God to thee for good. But if thou do that which is evil, be afraid; for he beareth not the sword in vain: for he is the minister of God, a revenger to execute wrath upon him that doeth evil"; and then continue through the rest of the chapter.

However, I landed *hard* on the eighth verse:

"Owe no man any thing, but to love one another: for he that loveth another hath fulfilled the law."

In my mind, there went the airplane.

Gloria was in another room, so I called for her. I still had my Bible in my hand with my finger on those words, "Owe no man any thing, but to love one another."

I could tell by the look on her face that her dream home had just vanished.

This incident shows the heart of Gloria Jean Copeland.

She put her finger on my Bible—at that verse—and boldly stated, "If that's what The BOOK says, that's what we're going to do."

We entered a binding covenant based on Deuteronomy 28:12: "The LORD shall open unto thee his good treasure, the heaven to give the rain unto thy land in his season, and to BLESS all the work of thine hand: and thou shalt lend unto many nations, and thou shalt not borrow."

That's THE BLESSING.

Now in the curse of the Law, the Bible says in verses 43 and 44: "The stranger that is within thee shall get up above thee very high; and thou shalt come down very low. He shall lend to thee, and thou shall not lend to him: he shall be the head and thou shalt be the tail."

Once that was established with us, Galatians 3:13-14 came alive in our hearts and this ministry: "Christ hath redeemed us from the curse of the law, being made a curse for us: for it is written, Cursed is every one that hangeth on a tree: that THE BLESSING of Abraham might come on the Gentiles through Jesus Christ; that we might receive the promise of the Spirit through faith."

Our ministry's statistics show that, by entering into a divine Covenant with the God who is more than enough, as of January 2023, our savings by not borrowing was $52,889,703. Had we borrowed to build a church, had we borrowed to buy trucks, cars, airplanes, we could not have said to our Partners, "Every dollar you sow into this ministry goes to win souls." It would not have been true because a lot of interest would have gone to banks and people we don't even know.

In Hebrews 5:10, Jesus is called the High Priest of these days after the order of Melchizedek. Hebrews 7:1-2 says, "For this Melchisedec, king of Salem, priest of the most high God, who met Abraham returning from the slaughter of the kings, and BLESSED him; to whom also Abraham gave a tenth part of all; first being by interpretation King of righteousness, and after that also King of

Salem, which is, King of peace." Read the entire book of Hebrews. It's all there.

That means He, Jesus, is my Financier.

I said many years ago, "I will preach that Jesus saves, Jesus heals, Jesus baptizes in the Holy Spirit, and He is the soon-coming King. I will preach that He is the One who makes us whole spirit, soul, body, financially and socially."

I heard Him say in my spirit, *I am coming so soon that I want this non-compromised Word-of-Faith message preached from the top of the world to the bottom and all the way around the middle.* I give praise, honor and thanksgiving that He entrusted me with that assignment. Because of His grace, and the insights and concepts of Faith, we have been able to do it.

I personally preached a three-week tour of northern Canada, where I was invited to a village that had no name—just map co-ordinates. We have fulltime staff in Australia. Jerry Savelle, Jesse Duplantis and I preached on Guadalcanal in the Solomon Islands. That is squarely on the equator. Not to mention Nigeria, Micronesia and other islands of the South Pacific.

PUTTING YOUR ANGELS TO WORK

You and I have a Covenant with God that, as we activate it by Faith, enables us to experience His BLESSINGS in every area of our lives. For example, I'm eighty-six years old as I'm writing this, and I'm in better physical condition now than I have ever been. And I'm thrilled to report that I no longer fight the *battle of the bulge*— carrying around more weight in my body than I should—as I once did for too long.

Medically, my ideal body fat is 15 percent. For years, I went from having 40 percent, to 30 percent body fat, then up to 35 percent. I constantly felt like I had to starve myself to fight it. Today? I just hit 14.7 percent!

The day I enrolled at Oral Roberts University, I weighed 240 pounds. As of this writing, I weigh 158 pounds. I'm well. I'm strong, and the dreams of my life have come to pass. I'm where I wanted to be when I was thirty years old, which is about eighty-plus pounds lighter, and it's all because of my Covenant with my God to live to be 120 years old (Genesis 6:3). I promised Him when I agreed to do that, I would get in the best spiritual condition possible. That my soul: my mind, will, and emotions, would be in the best condition possible. And my physical body would be in the best physical condition possible.

For that to happen, my diet had to change. Exercise had to be part of my lifestyle along with a steady diet of His WORD, which included listening to Brother Hagin on my phone. (You could say Brother Hagin speaks to me on the phone, and Faith comes!)

I stood on what my Covenant with God says in Exodus 23:25: "Ye shall serve The LORD your God, and *he* shall bless thy bread, and thy water; and I will take sickness away from the midst of thee."

That's a Covenant promise we can all activate in our lives by Faith, and I have since the day I first read it. What really helped me, though, was when I realized who was doing the talking and who was available 24/7 to help me and *BLESS my bread and my water.*

Look back a few verses and you'll see to whom I am referring. In verses 20-21, God says, "Behold, I [God] send an *Angel* before thee, to keep thee in the way, and to bring thee into the place which I have prepared. Beware of *him,* and obey *his* voice, provoke *him* not; for *he* will not pardon your transgressions: for my name is in *him.*"

God is talking to us there about our angels. He assigns angels to us, just as He did for all of Israel. Now, keeping that in mind, reread verse 25: "Ye shall serve [Me—The LORD your God], and *he* [your angel] shall BLESS thy bread, and thy water; and I [God] will take sickness away from the midst of thee."

Are you seeing this?

God has given us *ministering spirits,* or angels, and their sole responsibility is to guard us, get us to places, speak to us, guide us—AND—to BLESS our bread and water, to watch over our food and drink.

I realized years ago that reading those verses out loud, by Faith, in prayer, activates my Covenant with Almighty God. So, back when I was twenty, forty or sixty pounds overweight, back when I was *not* "in shape," I began doing it. I began activating my Covenant where my health and fitness were concerned.

Understand, I still had to do my part *physically* and eat healthy food, live a healthy lifestyle—and yes, that meant plenty of exercise and sweat. But to me, knowing I had a personal angel (like a trainer!) who was available to "BLESS my bread and my water" meant 99 percent of the work I had to do was *done!*

My "heavy lifting" was simply to take God's Covenant promise by Faith, and then, while I was at it: "Be attentive to him [my angel] and obey his voice; do not be rebellious" (verse 21, *New American Standard Bible)*. Get into the exercise room and work out hard before breakfast.

Like a lot of believers, I've always spoken THE BLESSING over what I was about to eat and drink. But once I caught the revelation of *who* was doing *what* in this scripture—and what my responsibility was in the process—I've BLESSED my food and drink accordingly by speaking these Covenant words over my meal, and I've kept my angel busy ever since.

You have an angel too. Every human being born into the earth has an angel. As your life and ministry increases, that angel is the boss angel of your life and ministry. If he needs help, because your life and ministry is growing, God will assign other angels to help. This is the power made available to us when we activate our Blood Covenant with God!

GOD'S COVENANT WITH DAVID

CHAPTER SEVEN

GOD'S COVENANT WITH DAVID

Behold, the days come, saith The LORD, that I will perform that good thing which I have promised unto the house of Israel and to the house of Judah. In those days, and at that time, will I cause the *Branch of righteousness* to grow up unto David; and he shall execute judgment and righteousness in the land. In those days shall Judah be saved, and Jerusalem shall dwell safely: and this is the name wherewith she shall be called, The LORD our righteousness. For thus saith The LORD; David shall never want a man to *sit upon the throne* of the house of Israel (Jeremiah 33:14-17).

God's covenant with David is the last of the Old Testament seed covenants. As we've seen, those covenants began when God promised that Eve's Seed would crush the head of the serpent (Genesis 3). Through the David covenant, God raised up the king whose royal lineage would produce the promised Seed and ultimate King of Israel, who would be the Deliverer of mankind.

The Israelites had long known they would eventually have kings. God had told them so in the Law of Moses and had given specific instructions about how Israel's kings were to conduct their personal and public lives. (See Deuteronomy 17:14-20:20.) During the Israelites' trek through the wilderness, even the ungodly prophet Balaam had foreseen the emergence of Israelite royalty. "The shout of a king is among them," he said (Numbers 23:21).

Centuries before that, Jacob, (Israel) had declared the nation's kings would come through his son Judah. Just before he died, he had prophesied, "The scepter or leadership shall not depart from Judah, nor the ruler's staff from between his feet, until Shiloh [the Messiah, the Peaceful One] comes to Whom it belongs, and to Him shall be the obedience of the people" (Genesis 49:10, *Amplified Bible, Classic Edition*). With the David covenant that prophecy began to be fulfilled.

The David covenant also brought God's Covenant focus full circle. God has always been about redeeming all mankind, but His initial covenants were with individuals, Adam and Noah, who represented all the people of the earth. With Abraham, He had expanded His covenant to include a family that would eventually become a nation. Then, through the Moses covenant, God had taught the people of that nation how to govern themselves in a way that honored both God and the earth, while at the same time bringing His covenant people face to face with their fallen nature.

With the David covenant, however, God went back to focusing on one *family* in one *tribe* of His chosen nation. From that one tribe and family, he chose and anointed as Israel's king one young man from the town of Bethlehem.

Today, when someone mentions Bethlehem, we as believers think of it as the town where Jesus was born. We think of our Savior when we read the words of the prophet Micah: "Thou, Bethlehem Ephratah, though thou be little among the thousands of Judah, yet out of thee shall he come forth unto me that is to be ruler in Israel; whose goings forth have been from of old, from everlasting" (Micah 5:2).

But while that verse is indeed referring to the birth of Jesus, Bethlehem is also where David's covenant story begins. That's the reason it is called "the city of David" (2 Chronicles 33:14). Both in their birthplace and through God's covenant promises, the lives of David and Jesus are eternally intertwined. In fact, many facets of the life and ministry of Jesus were foreshadowed through David.

In addition to being born in the same town of the same tribe and family, they both spent their lives serving God in the same region—Galilee, Judea and Samaria. During Jesus' earthly ministry, people could even be heard calling Him by David's name. *"Son of David,"* they cried, "have mercy *(hesed*—Covenant lovingkindness) on me!"* (Mark 10:47, *New King James Version).*

David's life so foreshadowed Jesus' that it even caught satan's attention. He feared that David might be the seed God had said would crush his head. So, he did everything he could to stop this seed of Abraham, Israel (Jacob) and Judah from taking the throne. He even incited Saul, the king of Israel who preceded David, to try to kill David. But Saul failed.

In the end, so did satan. Despite his efforts to end David's life, David did indeed take the throne. He stood in authority as God's chosen king, and in addition took on the role of a priest before The LORD. He instituted a new form of worship and helped the entire nation access the presence of God.

David did have moral failings. But nevertheless, David remained a man after God's own heart (1 Samuel 13:14; Acts 13:22). He learned and exhibited God's Covenant lovingkindness, and above all he was a man of Faith. A man whose rock-solid belief in the character and nature of the Father became the stabilizing anchor of his soul in the darkest of days.

THE DAVID COVENANT PROMISE

God's covenant with David was an extension of His covenant with Abraham, just as the Moses covenant had been. In it, God confirmed His major promises to Abraham and expounded on them. He also added some significant promises. Those promises, however, did not come all at once as they had with God's earliest covenants. They were revealed to David much like God's covenant promises were revealed to Abraham—progressively over time, as David's relationship with God developed.

Even God's promise that David would become king unfolded progressively. Although he was God's choice from the beginning, he ascended to the throne in three stages, which required him to be anointed as king *three* times.

First, he was anointed at his father's house by the prophet Samuel. At the time, Saul was still king. So that anointing was kept secret. Samuel, having been told by The LORD that one of Jesse's sons was to be Saul's replacement, went to see the family, and when he got there, The LORD showed him David was the one. "Then Samuel took the horn of oil, and *anointed him* in the midst of his brethren: and the Spirit of The LORD *came upon David from that day* forward" (1 Samuel 16:13).

Notice, Samuel used a *horn* of oil to anoint David. That was significant. Previously, when Samuel had anointed Saul to be king, he had used a vial or flask of oil, which was typical (1 Samuel 10:1). The vial of oil served as an early clue from God that Saul, who was from the tribe of Benjamin, was not His first choice for king of Israel (1 Samuel 9:18-27).

In Scripture, vials are associated with God's judgment against man (Revelation 16:1); and God had only agreed to make Saul Israel's king because of man's insistence. God wasn't yet ready to give the Israelites a king. The timing wasn't right. But the Israelites kept pressing God to provide them with a king to lead them in their fight against the Philistines, so He had allowed it (1 Samuel 9:16). As a result King Saul, who came from the tribe of Benjamin, became a contradiction to God's plan for Israel's Messiah King to come from the tribe of Judah.

This is another reason Samuel's use of a horn of oil, rather than a vial, in anointing David is important. Remember now, God is King of the universe. So, He was highlighting David's role as a type and shadow of the coming Messiah King. The horn that held the oil at David's anointing, unlike a vial, came from an animal. Before its horn could be used as a vessel, that animal had to be sacrificed. In other words, blood had to be spilled; a life was required, which pointed to the sacrifice of Jesus on the cross.

Although David's first anointing did take place in secret, the anointing of God on him could not remain hidden for long. Soon, King Saul's son Jonathan recognized it. Not long afterward, King Saul did too. He even admitted openly that David was God's chosen king (1 Samuel 24:20). Yet out of jealousy and rage, Saul sought to destroy him.

During the years David spent being persecuted by Saul, he proved himself to be a man of Faith. He waited for the time to be right for him to ascend to the throne, while living in submission under the Law (and under a disobedient king). He also developed in his worship of The LORD. In this season of David's life, when it appeared he would never fulfill his God-ordained destiny, he learned to function as a king and priest and host the presence of God.

The second time David was anointed was when he became ruler over Israel's southern tribe of Judah. Because King Saul was no longer alive, this event was more public. Rather than Samuel anointing David in the presence of just his family, he did it in the city of Hebron where David was living: "And the men of Judah came, and there *they anointed David king* over the house of Judah" (2 Samuel 2:3-4).

The fact that Samuel anointed David twice pointed to the first and second coming of Jesus. It also foreshadowed the eventual splitting of Israel into two kingdoms.

The third time David was anointed he became ruler not just over Judah but over the entire nation of Israel. In this instance:

All the tribes of Israel came to David at Hebron and said, Behold, we are your bone and your flesh. In times past, when Saul was king over us, it was you who led out and brought in Israel. And The LORD told you, You shall feed My people Israel and be prince over [them]. So all the elders of Israel came to the king at Hebron, and King David made a covenant with them [there] before The LORD, and they anointed [him] king over Israel (2 Samuel 5:1-3, *Amplified Bible, Classic Edition*).

Ten generations after Jacob prophesied that through the bloodline of his son Judah would come a lineage of kings, David, the first king from the tribe of Judah, was anointed king of all Israel. With that kingship came the promise of BLESSING—that he and his descendants would live in the Promised Land, that he would have victory over every enemy, that God would abide with him, and that Christ the Messiah would come from his seed.

By the time David began to reign over Israel, he had walked with God by Faith for decades. Over that time, they had become close covenant Friends. We see just how much they had one another on their minds in 2 Samuel 7. There King David, having gained immeasurable success because of the grace and favor of The LORD, told the Prophet Nathan he wanted to build The LORD a permanent temple.

In response, The LORD told Nathan to tell David that He did not require this, that He had never asked any of His people to build Him a house. Then, as covenant partners do, God reaffirmed His commitment to David and instructed Nathan to tell him:

> Thus says The LORD of hosts: I took you from the pasture, from following the sheep, to be prince over My people Israel. And I was with you wherever you went, and have cut off all your enemies from before you; and I will make you a great name, like [that] of the great men of the earth. And I will appoint a place for My people Israel and will plant them, that they may dwell in a place of their own and be moved no more. And wicked men shall afflict them no more, as formerly and as from the time that I appointed judges over My people Israel; and I will cause you to rest from all your enemies. Also The LORD declares to you that He will make for you a house: And when your days are fulfilled and you sleep with your fathers, I will set up after you your offspring who shall be born to you, and I will establish his kingdom. He shall build a house for My Name [and My Presence], and I will establish the throne of his kingdom forever.... And your house and your kingdom shall be made sure forever before you; your throne shall be established forever (verses 8-13, 16, *Amplified Bible, Classic Edition*).

When Nathan relayed those words to him, David was humbled and overwhelmed with gratitude. He went in and sat before The LORD, and said:

Who am I, O LORD God, and what is my house, that You have brought me this far? Then as if this were a little thing in Your eyes, O LORD God, You have spoken also of Your servant's house in the far distant future…. O LORD God! What more can David say to You? For You know Your servant, O LORD God. Because of Your promise and as Your own heart dictates, You have done all these astounding things to make Your servant know and understand. Therefore You are great, O LORD God; for none is like You, nor is there any God besides You, according to all [You have made] our ears to hear (verses 18-22, *Amplified Bible, Classic Edition*).

Nearly 1,000 years (or only one day to God) after this covenant conversation took place between God and David, the final fulfillment of God's promises to David began to unfold: A Child was born in Bethlehem. A Child about whom the angel Gabriel said, "He shall be great, and shall be called the Son of the Highest: and The LORD God shall give unto him the throne of his father David: And he shall reign over the house of Jacob for ever; and of his kingdom there shall be no end" (Luke 1:32-33).

CUTTING THE DAVID COVENANT

Under the Moses covenant, the Levitical priesthood offered blood sacrifices to God on behalf of the Israelites, because under God's covenant, blood atoned for and covered the sin of the people. The blood of those sacrifices, which continued to be offered in David's day, constituted the blood of the David covenant.

Under David's rule as king, however, some unexpected "sacrifices" were added. He not only followed the instructions of Moses pertaining to blood sacrifices, at times he seemingly took his offerings to The LORD to the extreme. David knew no limits when it came to expressing his passion for God, especially when it came to *giving* to Him.

The day David officially announced, for instance, that his son Solomon would become king and build the Temple, he called together his military leaders and government officials and said:

> Because I have set my affection on the house of my God, in addition to all I have prepared for the holy house, I have a private treasure of *gold and silver* which I give for the house of my God: It is 3,000 talents of gold, gold of Ophir, 7,000 talents of refined silver for overlaying the walls of the house, gold for the uses of gold, silver for the uses of silver, and for every work to be done by craftsmen. Now *who will offer willingly to fill his hand [and consecrate it] today* to The LORD...? (1 Chronicles 29:3–5, *Amplified Bible, Classic Edition*).

The assembly of the Israelites responded to David's question and his extravagant giving with their own offerings and personal commitments to The LORD. Then, they all rejoiced and worshipped The LORD. But the party—and the giving—was not over! After giving of their financial wealth...

> They sacrificed sacrifices unto The LORD, and offered burnt offerings unto The LORD, on the morrow after that day, even a thousand bullocks, a thousand rams, and a thousand lambs, with their drink offerings, and sacrifices in abundance for all Israel: and did eat and drink before The LORD on that day with great gladness. And they made Solomon the son of David king the second time, and anointed him unto The LORD to be the chief governor, and Zadok to be priest (verses 21-22).

More than a decade later, when Solomon completed construction of the Temple, he followed in his father's footsteps. He called together another gathering of the nation's officials; the priests brought into the Temple the Ark of the Covenant of The LORD and the holy vessels of worship; and—like father, like son—King Solomon and all the congregation of Israel sacrificed "sheep and oxen, *that could not be told nor numbered for multitude*" (1 Kings 8:5).

How did God respond to their countless, over-the-top sacrifices?

It came to pass, when the priests were come out of the holy place, that the cloud filled the house of The LORD, so that the priests could not stand to minister because of the cloud: for the glory of The LORD had filled the house of The LORD (verses 10–11).

The result of the extravagant David-like worship and giving that took place that day was the glory of The LORD!

After the glory manifested, Solomon prayed a marvelous prayer. In it, he asked The LORD to have mercy when drought and trouble hit the nation because of the people's sin. "If they pray toward this place, and confess thy name, and turn from their sin, when thou afflictest them: then hear thou in heaven, and forgive the sin of thy servants, and of thy people Israel, that thou teach them the good way wherein they should walk, and give rain upon thy land, which thou hast given to thy people for an inheritance" (verses 35–36).

At the end of his prayer, Solomon, thanking The LORD for His faithfulness said, "BLESSED be The LORD, that hath given rest unto his people Israel, according to all that he promised: there hath not failed one word of all his good promise, which he promised by the hand of Moses his servant" (verse 56).

This still applies to us today! It applies to us as individuals and to our nations. God has not changed. He said, "I am The LORD, I change not" (Malachi 3:6). He still hears us from heaven when we pray. He still forgives. And He still responds to our extravagant worship by manifesting His glory.

How powerful is God's glory? His glory raised Christ from the dead! His glory penetrated the pit of hell after Jesus had fully paid the price for our sin there and resurrected Him, forever defeating every spiritual foe.

The same glory of God that filled the First Covenant Temple in Solomon's day made us new creations in Christ Jesus the instant we were born again. God's glory made us the righteousness of God in Him and set us free from the bondage of sin. As the Apostle Paul said in Romans 6, those of us who have been "baptized into Jesus Christ were baptized into his death…. that like as Christ was raised up from the dead *by the glory of the Father,* even so we also should walk in *newness of life"* (Romans 6:3-4).

The Apostle Paul first experienced God's glory before he was born again, when he was still Saul of Tarsus. On his way to Damascus to imprison Christians, he had an encounter with the resurrected LORD Jesus Christ. Giving his testimony later, he said that when it happened, "I could not see for the glory of that light" (Acts 22:11). Jesus spoke to him in that glory, and it changed him forever. Why? Because it's the glory of The LORD, and He changes not.

The Apostle Paul spent the rest of His life preaching "the *riches of the glory* of this mystery among the Gentiles; which is Christ in you, the *hope of glory"* (Colossians 1:27).

My mentor, Kenneth E. Hagin, searched out every verse in the Bible about the glory of God. He knew a lot about it, and he said, "When we praise God long enough, the spirit of worship will come. In the spirit of worship, the glory will fall. That's when healing and miracles will fill the place of worship just like it did in the Temple."

THE DAVID COVENANT SEAL

This connection between praise, worship and the manifestation of God's glory highlights the awesome power of the David covenant seal. The seal of that covenant was different from those of the Noah and the Abrahamic covenants. God gave Noah the rainbow as a natural reminder of His covenant promises. With Abraham, God pointed to the stars of the sky and dust of the ground to help him grasp the expanse and reality of His great and precious promises. To David, however, God gave the songs of heaven and a revelation of Himself.

I've already said this, but it bears repeating: Without Faith it is impossible to please God, so David was obviously a man of Faith. And because Faith comes by hearing The WORD of God, David used the songs and revelations God gave him to strengthen his Faith in the darkest, most challenging times of his life.

One of those dark times was when David was confronted by

the Prophet Nathan for committing adultery with Bathsheba and having her husband Uriah murdered. Heartbroken over the sin he had committed, and knowing that no matter how many sacrifices he offered to God, it truly would never be enough, David wrote this Psalm: "O LORD, open thou my lips; and my mouth shall show forth thy praise. For thou *desirest not sacrifice;* else would I give it: thou *delightest not in burnt offering.* The sacrifices of God are *a broken spirit: a broken and a contrite heart,* O God, thou wilt not despise" (Psalm 51:15-17).

With those words, David owned up to the truth. That was one of the things that set him apart in God's eyes. It is one of the ways he differed from King Saul who reigned before him. Saul failed to make this vital connection between obedience and sacrifice.

The heavenly songs and revelations God gave to the psalmists in David's day were filled with reminders of God's promise that he would be king and that his Heir would inherit the throne forever. Time and again, God affirmed those covenant promises through words like these in Psalm 89:

Verses 3-4: *I have made a covenant with my chosen,* I have sworn unto David my servant, Thy seed will I establish for ever, and build up thy throne to all generations.

Verses 19-29: Then thou [God] spakest in vision to thy holy one, and saidst, "I have laid help upon one that is mighty; I have exalted one chosen out of the people. I have found David my servant; with my holy oil have I anointed him: with whom my hand shall be established: mine arm also shall strengthen him. The enemy shall not exact upon him; nor the son of wickedness afflict him. And I will beat down his foes before his face, and plague them that hate him. But my faithfulness and my mercy shall be with him: and in my name shall his horn be exalted. I will set his hand also in the sea, and his right hand in the rivers. He shall cry unto me, Thou art my father, my God, and the rock of my salvation. Also I will make him my firstborn, higher than the kings of the earth. My *mercy will I keep for him for evermore,* and my *covenant shall stand fast with him.* His seed also will I make to *endure for ever,* and *his throne* as the days of heaven.

Verses 33-37: Nevertheless *my lovingkindness will I not utterly take from him,* nor suffer my faithfulness to fail. *My covenant will I not break,* nor alter the thing that is gone out of my lips. Once have I sworn by my holiness that I will not lie unto David. His seed shall endure for ever, and *his throne as the sun before me.* It shall be *established for ever as the moon,* and as a *faithful witness in heaven.*

Notice how often The LORD, in recounting His covenant with David, refers to *Love*—"My unfailing love," "I will love him forever," "I will be kind to him forever," "I will never stop loving him."

David, just as we are, was often challenged to trust God's WORD and promises above circumstances that appeared to contradict them. And in the face of those challenges, he focused on God's Covenant lovingkindness. David had such Faith in God's Love that even though he lived under the Law of Moses, he operated with a high level of Faith as Abraham did.

What was different about David, though, was his method of hearing from God. David was a singer. "The sweet psalmist of Israel" (2 Samuel 23:1), he was a musician, head and shoulders above all Israel. When his Faith was challenged, he sang words to The LORD like these in Psalm 17:15: "As for me, I will continue beholding Your face in righteousness (rightness, justice, and right standing with You); I shall be fully satisfied, when I awake [to find myself] beholding Your form [and having sweet communion with You]" *(Amplified Bible, Classic Edition).*

David could have sweet communion with God because he had a revelation of His Love. Love is the key to understanding covenant. It is the motive behind covenant. It is the heart and soul of covenant.

That's why for us to receive the fulfillment of God's Covenant promises, we—like David—must receive the *Love* God has for us. It might seem that receiving should just come naturally to us—and really, it should—but it doesn't. Why? Because, as with any relationship, there's trust involved.

How can we have trust in God? The Apostle John gives us the answer: We can trust God because "we have *known* and *believed* the love that God hath to us" (1 John 4:16).

This great apostle is telling us that we first come to know about God's Love and experience it in some form or fashion and then *believe it*. The word *know* is the Greek word *ginosko*.[26] It means "to have intimate relationship with."

When did we get to know God?

When we accepted Jesus as our LORD and Savior.

John's co-apostle, Peter, used the word *ginosko* in this context in 1 Peter 1:18-19, where he wrote: "Forasmuch as ye *know [ginosko]* that ye were not redeemed with corruptible things, as silver and gold, from your vain conversation received by tradition from your fathers; but with the *precious blood of Christ*, as of a lamb without blemish and without spot."

Both the knowing and believing part of this come to us through the revelation of the Love of God that has been shed abroad in our hearts by the Holy Ghost (Romans 5:5). The revelation of God's never-ending Covenant Love is the reason the Apostle Paul could say: "I am *persuaded*, that neither death, nor life, nor angels, nor principalities, nor powers, nor things present, nor things to come, nor height, nor depth, nor any other creature, shall be able to sepa-rate us from the love of God, which is in Christ Jesus our LORD" (Romans 8:38-39).

Years ago, I had very low self-esteem and dealt with depression. Although I covered it pretty well with pride and ego, inside I was hurting. I also had been hardened by bitterness and anger. The day I met Gloria Jean Neece and fell in love with her, however, the bit-terness and anger left me. Her love made it easy to understand the Love of God.

Six months later, in April of 1962, we were married. Six months

---

26 *The New Strong's Exhaustive Concordance of the Bible* (Nashville: Thomas Nelson Publishers, 1996) G1097.

after that, we were both born again. The next month after that we were baptized in the Holy Ghost. Now we were not only in love with one another, we were both in love with Jesus. Suddenly, we wanted to know what was under every church steeple we saw.

Only four years later, on January 24, 1967, I enrolled at Oral Roberts University. I was thirty years old at that time and was unaware of the significance of that age. With a wife and two small children, we moved to Tulsa, Oklahoma. Oral Roberts became my father in the Faith, Kenneth E. Hagin became my mentor, and from them I learned the laws of Faith and how they work.

While I was a student at ORU, I read John 17 one day. I saw that it was Jesus' prayer to the Father, and because I had learned the power of agreement from hearing Brother Hagin teach from Matthew 18, I prayed all the words in red out loud. As I did, my spirit within me began to come alive, especially over verses 20-21.

Then I came to verses 22 and 23 where Jesus, praying for all who would ever believe on Him, said to the Father, "The glory which thou gavest me I have given them; that they may be one, even as we are one: I in them, and thou in me, that they may be made perfect in one; and that the world may know that thou hast sent me, and hast loved them, as thou hast loved me."

I stuttered a little bit on the *glory* part of those verses. But the words of the Master in verse 23 floored me. I said to myself out loud, "God loves me as much as He loves Jesus? No, no! That can't be true." *But it has to be. It's written in red!*

By that point, my body was trembling. So, I raised my hand and started walking around the room, worshipping God. Finally, I dared to say it out loud: "God loves me as much as He loves Jesus… God loves me as much as He loves Jesus."

Still trembling I kept saying it, and the more I did, the stronger I became, until I was shouting it…"God loves *Kenneth* as much as He loves *Jesus!*"

What happened?

I became totally *convinced* of God's Love for me, just like the Apostle Paul did (Romans 8:37).

That was an important first step toward my victory over depression. From time to time however, the enemy would start in on me again. He would begin accusing me, condemning me, trying to beat me down…and it would build and build and build.

One day, when Gloria and I were at home, I was sitting in a chair in her study and I could sense that depression trying to come back on me, but I wasn't yielding to it. Just ever so gently, Gloria walked over and stood behind me and put her hands on my shoulders. "Kenneth," she said, "I'm quite sure Jesus finds *no fault* in you, and neither do I."

With that, the depression I had struggled with for years was finally gone from me, and it never came back. Why? Because I had come to *know* and *believe* the Love God had for me (1 John 4:16). I had Faith in His *hesed*, Covenant lovingkindness, just as King David did.

A LEGACY OF FAITH AND COVENANT LOVE

David's revelation of God's covenant Love enabled him to step out with exceptionally bold Faith in three areas. In those three areas, David stopped acting like a king and started acting like a priest.

The first of these was the area of sacrifice. David obviously knew the Law forbade him from offering sacrifices to God in the tabernacle. That was the God-ordained role of consecrated priests. Yet because of his passion for The LORD, David desired to offer sacrifices himself.

So, what did he do?

He began offering sacrifices of *praise* and *thanksgiving*. Legally, he was allowed to do that, so he did!

We see this in Psalm 135 where he said: "Praise ye The LORD. Praise ye the name of The LORD; praise him, O ye *servants* of The LORD. Ye that *stand in the house* of The LORD, in the courts of the house of our God" (verses 1-2).

Praise and thanksgiving became a tool in David's hand, just as real and supernatural as the rod was in Moses' hand (Exodus 4:2-4). Moses cast down that rod and it became a serpent. He picked it up, and it became a rod again. David did this through praise, thanksgiving and worship. As he said in Psalm 9:2-3: "I will be glad and rejoice in thee: I will sing praise to thy name, O thou most High. When mine enemies are turned back, they shall fall and perish at thy presence."

David understood the glory and power of hosting God's presence. So, he was insistent about offering spiritual sacrifices as well as physical. And we can be grateful that he was! His insistence on and innovation in the area of praise and worship became a major part of the New Covenant. Think of the impact he has had on God's people through the book of Psalms alone. Think of Hebrews 13:15 that says, "...let us offer the *sacrifice of praise* to God continually, that is, the fruit of our lips *giving thanks* to his name."

The second area in which David stopped acting like a king and started acting like a priest was in establishing a place of worship. While he did not disrespect the tabernacle of Moses at Gibeon (1 Chronicles 21:29), he established his own tabernacle in Jerusalem at Mount Zion (2 Samuel 6:17). In this also, David affirmed his adherence to the Moses covenant, but revealed his love for God by going beyond what the Law required to do something more.

The tabernacle at Jerusalem was a place of continual worship. It was also the hub around which Israel's government operated, making Israel the model of a Spirit-led nation. But perhaps the greatest legacy David left us in setting up his own tabernacle was its breaking of religious barriers.

David allowed Jews, gentiles and women access to the tabernacle. He established it to be a place of worship and praise where all people could experience the Spirit of God. This made the presence of God available to *everyone,* not just to the priesthood—foreshadowing the New Covenant.

After David died and Solomon built the more permanent Temple, these innovative features of access and worship were disbanded. But generations later they were reestablished by the apostles of Jesus. Seeing that God had poured out the Holy Spirit on both

Jews and Gentiles, the Apostle Peter said, "With this the predictions of the prophets agree, as it is written, After this I will come back, and will rebuild the house of David, which has fallen; I will rebuild its [very] ruins, and I will set it up again" (Acts 15:15-16, *Amplified Bible, Classic Edition*).

We now live in the time of that rebuilding.

The third way David acted more as a priest than a king was by doing the unthinkable: He ate the tabernacle bread that only the priests were allowed to eat (Leviticus 24). The tabernacle bread was placed each day on a pure golden table before The LORD. Consecrated and set apart unto God, it was called the *Bread of the Presence*. When the new daily bread was made, the previous day-old bread was given to the priests as a symbol of the bread of life and the daily manna provided by God for the Israelites in the wilderness.

Remember the example prayer that our LORD prayed? It says, "Give us this day our daily bread." That's bread from heaven. It's the bread of God's WORD and His presence that brings tremendous prosperity in every area of the Christian life regardless of the circumstances.

One time when David was running from Saul, who was trying to kill him, David asked the priest, Ahimelech, to allow him and his hungry men to eat the tabernacle bread. Ahimelech allowed them, and he was right to do so. David was simply receiving good from God's house. Many years later, Jesus used this bold act of David's to answer the Pharisees when they criticized Him and his disciples for eating grain from a field on the Sabbath (Matthew 12:3-8).

In this, we see again how David foreshadowed Jesus: Both were born in Bethlehem, which means *house of bread*. Both were of the tribe of Judah, which means *to praise*. David operated as a king and priest under the First Covenant, Jesus became the King and High Priest of our better Covenant, and both stretched the mindsets of the people in their day with their passionate pursuit of God. Both revealed the heart of the Father and the intent of His Blood Covenant, which was a meaningful and personal relationship with mankind.

CONTRADICTIONS TO THE DAVID COVENANT

The natural obstacles to God's promise that David's seed would remain on the throne were compounded over three generations—by the sins of David, by the sins of his son Solomon, and by the sins of a grandson more than 300 years later, who would end up dethroned.

The sins of David that became covenant contradictions centered on his adultery with Bathsheba and subsequent murder of her husband. Those two acts cost David by ravaging his household with violence, rebellion, shame, and then the death of his and Bathsheba's first child (2 Samuel 12:10-11, 14). David was quick to repent, and God was quick to forgive, which spared David his life. Still, David ended up suffering the consequences of violating God's commandments (verses 13-14).

Solomon, in his sins as in his achievements, followed in his father's footsteps. Despite God's warnings, Solomon took 700 wives and 300 concubines and let them turn his heart away from God. As a result, although he took David's success as king to a much higher level with his God-given wisdom, leadership and the construction of the Temple, Solomon ended up with this judgment:

> The LORD said unto Solomon, Forasmuch as this is done of thee, and thou hast not kept my covenant and my statutes, which I have commanded thee, I will surely *rend the kingdom from thee*, and will give it to thy servant. Notwithstanding in thy days I will not do it for David thy father's sake: but *I will rend it out of the hand of thy son*. Howbeit I will not rend away all the kingdom; but will give *one tribe* to thy son for David my servant's sake, and for Jerusalem's sake which I have chosen (1 Kings 11:11-13).

The dividing of Israel into two opposing kingdoms after Solomon's reign became a significant contradiction to the David covenant. Although God did allow Solomon's descendants to rule the Southern Kingdom called *Judah*, with Jerusalem as its capital, they were not allowed to rule the Northern Kingdom which kept the name *Israel*, and its capital, *Samaria*.

Generations later, these geographical-political changes influenced even the ministry of Jesus and His disciples and their movements throughout the land and among the people. Historically, Israel would not reunite as a nation again until 1948, and would not have control of Jerusalem until 1967.

The sins of Jeconiah, King Solomon's 18-year-old descendant who reigned over Judah for only about three months, resulted in yet another serious contradiction to the David covenant. Because of his corruption, God declared over him: "Write ye this man [Jeconiah] childless, a man that shall not prosper in his days: for no man of his seed shall prosper, sitting upon the throne of David, and ruling any more in Judah" (Jeremiah 22:30).

That judgement, pronounced by God on Jeconiah, created an obstacle to the David covenant because Messiah had to come from the royal line of David. Now that bloodline was cursed, threatening the legitimacy of Jesus as the Son of David and royal Heir.

The devil thought he had finally found a way to cut off the Messiah bloodline God had been working on since the day He promised Eve that a Seed would come through her. But as always, God had a plan. We see it revealed in the New Covenant (Testament) records of the *two* genealogies of Jesus. One, in Matthew, tracks The LORD's *kingly* line from Abraham through David, to Solomon, to His earthly father, Joseph. The other, in Luke, focuses on the *humanity* of Jesus, following His lineage from Adam to Abraham to David, then to Nathan (youngest son of David and Bathsheba), down to Heli, the father of Mary, the mother of Jesus.

Mary, probably because she had no brothers, married within her tribe of Judah. So, Jesus' virgin birth gave Him legal right to the throne of David through his mother's side, which was not connected to the curse of Solomon's bloodline. Either way, either bloodline, God had it worked out, and over thousands of years. Jesus truly was, is and always will be the Covenant Son of David *and* Son of Man... Messiah, the Seed of salvation.

David held onto God's covenant and covenant promises his entire life. Even in death...

He charged Solomon his son, saying, I go the way of all the earth: be thou strong therefore, and show thyself a man; and keep the charge of The LORD thy God, to walk in his ways, to keep his statutes, and his commandments, and his judgments, and his testimonies, as it is written in the law of Moses, that thou mayest prosper in all that thou doest, and whithersoever thou turnest thyself: that The LORD may continue his WORD which he spake concerning me, saying, If thy children take heed to their way, to walk before me in truth with all their heart and with all their soul, there shall not fail thee (said he) a man on the throne of Israel.... So David slept with his fathers, and was buried in the city of David (1 Kings 2:1-4, 10).

Even with his last words David commanded his son to keep God's commandments and reminded him of God's covenant promises. He told Solomon that if he walked in God's ways he would prosper as David did. As a result, King Solomon turned out to be the richest man in history, surpassing even his father who had previously held that place.

What's more, because of David, we have as part of the exceeding precious promises of God, and I quote from Psalm 150:6, "Let every thing that hath breath praise The LORD. Praise ye The LORD." Because Solomon was also a Psalm writer just like his father David, we also have the book of Proverbs, Ecclesiastes and the Song of Solomon.

In those sacred writings and in the lives of those who penned them we see how attentive God is to the details of His covenants! He continually watches over His WORD to perform it (Jeremiah 1:12). So, let's be more like King David and abandon ourselves to worship and God's WORD. As children of our heavenly Father, let's give honor and glory to the Son of the living God, the One who brought us into equal standing with Him through His covenants.

GO DEEPER
WITH GREG

HONORING COVENANT:
A STORY OF COVENANT BROTHERS

Even as a young boy, David was covenant minded. His covenant with Almighty God was the filter through which he saw and experienced much of life. We can see that in the account of David's famous encounter with Goliath.

When he heard Goliath taunting Israel's army, David didn't respond as just a shepherd. He didn't act like just a teenager taking supplies to his military-age brothers on the front lines. Nor did he focus on the massive frame and military fame of the Philistines' champion soldier.

Those things weren't what mattered to David. All that mattered to him was that as the circumcised seed of Abraham, he had a covenant with God...and Goliath did not. So, rather than shrinking back with fear, David responded to the giant's threats with a Faith-charged question: "Who is this *uncircumcised* Philistine, that he should defy the armies of the living God?" (1 Samuel 17:26, *New King James Version*).

That bold question created such a stir among the Israelite soldiers that King Saul got wind of it. He sent for David, who asked the king for permission to take out Goliath. Skeptical, King Saul reminded the seemingly over-confident David of his youth, lack of fighting skills and experience. But rather than backing down, David recounted for the king the *combat* experience that, as a shepherd, he did have.

"Your servant has killed both the lion and the bear;" he said, "and this *uncircumcised* Philistine [Goliath] will be like one of them, since he has defied the armies of the living God.... The LORD who saved me from the paw of the lion and the paw of the bear, He will save me from the hand of this Philistine" (1 Samuel 17:36-37, *New American Standard Bible*).

Persuaded, King Saul sent David off to fight. Not with state-of-the-art Israeli body armor and weaponry, but with only his slingshot, five smooth stones, and Faith in his covenant with God. Once face to face with the massive Goliath, David said:

You come to me with a sword, a spear, and a javelin, but I come to you in the name of The LORD of hosts, the God of the ranks of Israel, Whom you have defied. This day The LORD will deliver you into my hand, and I will smite you and cut off your head (1 Samuel 17:45–46, *Amplified Bible, Classic Edition*).

Sure enough, that's exactly what happened. Because of his covenant mindset and boldness, David's covenant passion secured his victory—against all odds. He felled Goliath and became a national hero.

Afterward, King Saul made David a commander of Israel's army. He also brought him into the royal household where David met Saul's son Jonathan. As the two became close friends, "the soul of Jonathan was knit to the soul of David, and Jonathan loved him as his own soul.... Then Jonathan and David made a *covenant*, because he loved him as his own soul. And Jonathan took off the *robe* that was on him and gave it to David, with his *armor*, even to his *sword* and his *bow* and his *belt*" (1 Samuel 18:1, 3-4, *New King James Version*).

Because of covenant, David was now *dressed* as a king, or at least, as the son of a king. As David won more military victories and his popularity among the Israelites increased, however, so did Saul's jealousy. His resentment mounted until he erupted in violent outbursts against David, eventually ordering Jonathan and some of his servants to kill him.

Of course, Jonathan wouldn't kill his covenant brother, and interceded with Saul to spare David. But when Saul resumed his attempts on David's life, David was forced to distance himself from the king and his covenant friend, Jonathan, and live life on the run as a fugitive.

In the end, King Saul and his sons, including Jonathan, died tragically in a losing battle against the Philistines. After a period of national mourning, God cut covenant with David, and David was crowned king. It was then that *King* David asked the question only a truly covenant-minded brother would ask: "Is there still anyone who is left of the house of Saul, that I may show him *[covenant loving] kindness* for Jonathan's sake?" (2 Samuel 9:1, *New King James Version*).

After much searching, Jonathan's one surviving son was located. His name was *Mephibosheth,* which in Hebrew means "from the mouth of shame." Crippled in both feet due to having been accidently dropped by his nurse as a child, he was living in a dry place called *Lodebar,* which means "pastureless"[27] (verses 4-5). With most of his family dead, Mephibosheth's prospects had been bleak until he met his covenant uncle, King David.

When David found him, he ordered Mephibosheth be brought to the palace. He didn't bring him there just to visit, either. He said to the frightened Mephibosheth, who prostrated himself before him:

"Don't be afraid!... I intend to show kindness to you because of my promise to your father, Jonathan. I will give you all the property that once belonged to your grandfather Saul, and you will eat here with me at the king's table!" Mephibosheth bowed respectfully and exclaimed, "Who is your servant, that you should show such kindness to a dead dog like me?" Then the king summoned Saul's servant Ziba and said, "I have given your master's grandson everything that belonged to Saul and his family. You and your sons and servants are to farm the land for him to produce food for your master's household. But Mephibosheth, your master's grandson, will eat here at my table" (2 Samuel 9:7–10, *New Living Translation*).

27 *Strong's,* H3810.

Why did David do all that? Because of the Blood covenant of strong friendship between him and Jonathan. It produced in David a burning desire to BLESS Jonathan's son. Whether Mephibosheth was worthy of that BLESSING or not made no difference. He had a right to it by blood because David had sworn an oath.

David's heart toward Mephibosheth is a type and shadow of our heavenly Father's heart toward us. It's a picture of God's *hesed* (Covenant lovingkindness) toward us. As the Apostle Paul wrote:

God, who is rich in mercy, for his *great love* wherewith he loved us, *even when we were dead* in sins, hath quickened [made us alive] together with Christ, (by grace ye are saved;) and hath *raised us up* together, and *made us sit* together in heavenly places in Christ Jesus: that in the ages to come he might show *the exceeding riches of his grace in his kindness toward us* through Christ Jesus. For by grace are ye saved through faith; and that not of yourselves: it is the gift of God: not of works, lest any man should boast (Ephesians 2:4-9).

While we were in the same condition as Mephibosheth, living in the pastureless land of sin, in due time Christ died for us (Romans 5:6). And because of His Blood Covenant with the Father, Almighty God sent Jesus, the promised Seed, to bring us out of that barren land of sin to the Palace—seating us together with Him in heavenly places.

- He was *made to be sin* for us (2 Corinthians 5:21)
- He died in our place on Calvary's Cross so we could become sons and daughters of Almighty God (2 Corinthians 5:21)
- He paid the sin price for us all and has defeated death, hell and the grave (Colossians 2:15; Ephesians 4:9-10; Matthew 12:40; Revelation 1:18)
- He was raised from the dead by the power of Almighty God (Romans 6:4, *Amplified Bible, Classic Edition*)
- He has made us joint heirs with the King of kings—the King's own Son (Romans 8:17)

- We are invited to sit at the table prepared for us in the presence of our enemies (Psalm 23:5)
- Like the King's Son, our head is anointed with the oil of gladness (Psalm 23:5; Hebrews 1:9).

So, like Mephibosheth in the house of King David, we can say, "Surely goodness and mercy [covenant *hesed*] shall follow me all the days of my life; and I will dwell in the house of The LORD forever" (Psalm 23:6, *New King James Version*).

PART 2

WHEN COVENANT PROMISES WERE FULFILLED

THE
NEW
COVENANT

CHAPTER EIGHT

THE NEW COVENANT

When Jesus began His earthly ministry, He went to the synagogue on the Sabbath, stood up and read from the Book of Isaiah: "The Spirit of The LORD is upon me, because he hath anointed me to preach the gospel to the poor; he hath sent me to heal the brokenhearted, to preach deliverance to the captives, and recovering of sight to the blind, to set at liberty them that are bruised, to preach the acceptable year of The LORD" (Luke 4:18–19).

Why did He read those particular verses?

Jesus found Himself in The BOOK! After reading to the people in the synagogue what it said about Him, He gave the scroll back to the attendant, sat down—and all eyes were fixed on Him "And he began to say unto them, This day is this scripture fulfilled in your ears" (verse 21).

It is obvious what those people were thinking. Nazareth was a very small town of 120 to 150 people. They had known Him all of His life. So how could this be? Our hometown boy could not be the Messiah. They knew the old covenants. They knew their history. They knew there would come *a* Messiah who would *fulfill* it all. Now, here was Jesus, declaring that He was Messiah, the One who was promised.

Later in Jesus' ministry, He said: "Think not that I am come to destroy the law, or the prophets: I am not come to destroy, but to fulfil" (Matthew 5:17). He fulfilled the promises and prophecies

of Scripture throughout His life. The Gospel of Matthew reveals it
happened over and over again:

- When Jesus was born: "So all this was done that it might
  be *fulfilled* which was spoken by The LORD through the
  prophet, saying: 'Behold, the virgin shall be with child,
  and bear a Son, and they shall call His name Immanuel,'
  which is translated, 'God with us'" (Matthew 1:22-23,
  New King James Version).

- When Jesus' parents fled to Egypt with Him: "That it
  might be *fulfilled* which was spoken by The LORD
  through the prophet, saying, 'Out of Egypt I called My
  Son'" (Matthew 2:14-15, *New King James Version*).

- When Herod ordered every male child under two put
  to death: "Then was *fulfilled* what was spoken by Jeremiah the prophet, saying: 'A voice was heard in Ramah,
  lamentation, weeping, and great mourning, Rachel
  weeping for her children, refusing to be comforted, because they are no more'" (Matthew 2:17-18, *New King
  James Version*).

- When it was said Jesus would be called a Nazarene:
  "And he came and dwelt in a city called Nazareth, that it
  might be *fulfilled* which was spoken by the prophets, 'He
  shall be called a Nazarene'" (Matthew 2:23, *New King
  James Version*).

- When Jesus was baptized: "For thus it is fitting for us
  to *fulfill* all righteousness" (Matthew 3:15, *New King
  James Version*).

- When Jesus came and dwelt in Capernaum, which is by
  the sea, in the regions of Zebulun and Naphtali: "That it
  might be *fulfilled* which was spoken by Isaiah the prophet,
  saying: 'The land of Zebulun and the land of Naphtali,
  by the way of the sea, beyond the Jordan, Galilee of the
  Gentiles: The people who sat in darkness have seen a great
  light, and upon those who sat in the region and shadow
  of death Light has dawned'" (Matthew 4:14-16, *New
  King James Version*).

- When Jesus healed ALL who were sick: "That it might be *fulfilled* which was spoken by Isaiah the prophet, saying: 'He Himself took our infirmities and bore our sicknesses'" (Matthew 8:17, *New King James Version*).
- When Jesus healed them ALL again: "But when Jesus knew it, He withdrew from there. And great multitudes followed Him, and He healed them all. Yet He warned them not to make Him known, that it might be *fulfilled* which was spoken by Isaiah the prophet" (Matthew 12:15-17, *New King James Version*).
- When Jesus spoke one parable after another: "That it might be *fulfilled* which was spoken by the prophet, saying: "'I will open My mouth in parables; I will utter things kept secret from the foundation of the world'" (Matthew 13:35, *New King James Version*).
- When Jesus entered Jerusalem on the back of a donkey: "All this was done that it might be *fulfilled* which was spoken by the prophet" (Matthew 21:4, *New King James Version*).
- When the woman anointed Him for His burial.
- When Judas betrayed Him.
- When He celebrated Passover with His disciples.
- When He instituted The LORD's Supper.
- When He predicted Peter's denial.
- When He went to the Garden of Gethsemane where He was betrayed and arrested.
- When Jesus was handed over to Pontius Pilate and Judas hung himself: "All this was done that the Scriptures of the prophets might be fulfilled" (Matthew 26:56, 27:9, *New King James Version*).

After all, Jesus fulfilled more than 300 Old Covenant prophecies.

We can biblically trace thousands of years. The Apostle James said in James 5:7-8, "Be patient therefore, brethren, unto the coming of The LORD. Behold, the husbandman waiteth for the precious fruit of the earth, and hath long patience for it, until he receive the early and latter rain. Be ye also patient; stablish your hearts: for the coming of The LORD draweth nigh."

This man, being the half-brother of Jesus and raised in the household with Him, had powerful insight. This man's teaching on Faith is unique to everyone except his older brother. For example, he brought it up in James 1:6, "Let him ask in faith, nothing wavering."

His book is the one that points out that Faith without corresponding actions is dead, being alone (James 2:14-22). Then in James 1:22, *Amplified Bible, Classic Edition,* he explained how this is done:

But be doers of The WORD [obey the message], and not merely listeners to it, betraying yourselves [into deception by reasoning contrary to the Truth].

The pitfall here is outlined in the Apostle Paul's letter to the Ephesians. He exhorts them to remember in Ephesians 2:12-13, "That at that time ye were without Christ, being aliens from the commonwealth of Israel, and strangers from the covenants of promise, having no hope, and without God in the world: But now in Christ Jesus ye who sometimes were far off are made nigh by the blood of Christ." A covenant-minded stranger does not have the working knowledge of the Bible fact that he or she is guaranteed freedom: spirit, soul, body and the entire spectrum of human existence. To the Covenant-promise believer, who is a faithful doer of The WORD and not a hearer only, this Covenant BOOK is the perfect law of liberty (James 1:25). What kind of law? The Greek word *perfect* in this verse is *teleios*. It means, "perfect, complete, full grown, of full age, developed into a consummating completion by fulfilling the necessary process."

It is a perfect law, by a perfect God. All of that is the truth. Jesus said it will make you free (John 8:32). The key word in the book of James is *Faith*. Even though it is truth, Hebrews 4:2 states, "For unto us was the gospel preached, as well as unto them: but The WORD preached did not profit them, not being mixed with faith in them that heard it." We have come full circle; Faith is acting on The WORD.

Jesus fulfilled ALL the Law and ALL the words spoken by God through the prophets. He *fulfilled*, through His birth, life, death, Resurrection and Ascension to the right hand of God, all the previous covenants God ever made with man. Every one of those covenants— from Adam to Noah, to Abraham, Moses and David—pointed to the one moment in history when Jesus, the promised Seed, would fulfill them all. And you can fulfill all of the promises in your life by being constantly aware of the statement, "The just shall live by faith." We walk by Faith and not by sight.

THE NEW-COVENANT PROMISE

This is why we've had to study all those previous covenants. The promises of the New Covenant can only be fully understood in the light of the covenants recorded in the first part of the Bible. Notice I didn't say the Old Testament. Although there's nothing wrong with defining the Bible as the Old Testament and the New Testament, it really is one story. It's all about covenant, and all about the coming Messiah who would fulfill every Covenant promise—and provide for us an ultimate, everlasting Covenant that can never be broken or surpassed.

In Professor Stephen's Bible, on the page between the Old Testament and the New Testament, he's drawn a large arrow. The tip of the arrow points toward the New Testament and away from the Old. It means a lot to him because he has spent years studying the history, culture and language of the *First Testament* (his words for the Old Testament).

At one point he even considered converting to Judaism. Back then he thought nothing could surpass the glorious crossing of the Red Sea, the fire and smoke on Mount Sinai, and the glory that filled the Temple. But then, he received a revelation of the glorious New Covenant. That's when he drew the arrow in his Bible. It reminds him that he lives on *this side* of The BOOK, in a *"better covenant... established upon better [Covenant] promises"* (Hebrews 8:6).

He discovered what you and I have been learning together in

this study: "On this side of The BOOK," we have it all! Although some of the temporal elements of the Moses covenant have passed away, the everlasting elements of all the previous covenants remain. In fact, they've come to life through Jesus, the One who is alive forevermore. Therefore, Moses is alive forevermore.

All these find their expression in Jesus:

- The everlasting BLESSING of Adam and Noah
- The everlasting inheritance of Abraham, Isaac and Jacob
- The everlasting priesthood of Moses
- The everlasting kingdom and throne of David.

Jesus also fulfilled all the "seed" covenants we've studied:

- He was the Seed of the Adam covenant; the One who would be born of woman
- He was the Seed of the Abraham covenant; the One God would provide Himself
- He was the Seed of the David covenant; the One who would be King and High Priest forever.

What's more, Jesus didn't fulfill those seed covenants just on behalf of the natural seed of Abraham. He became the Seed and the Covenant sacrifice that provided salvation for "the whole world" (John 12:24; 1 John 2:2).

Remember, in the First Testament, God cut covenant primarily with the chosen Hebrew people. The Gentiles had for the most part been left out. Although God did offer glimpses of hope for them from time to time, there was always a wall that separated Gentiles from Hebrews. Why? Because the Hebrews had a covenant with God and the Gentiles did not.

That, however, changed in Acts, after the resurrection of Jesus and His seating at the right hand of power. Jesus, the Waymaker, brought salvation to all—to the Jews first, and then to the Gentiles (Romans 1:16). In Him, the wall that had separated God from man since the days of Adam, and Jews from Gentiles since the days of

Moses, was torn down. El Shaddai chose Abraham; Jesus of Nazareth chose Cornelius.

The gospel of the Kingdom is good news for everybody—and it's especially good news for us non-Jewish believers. Let's go back to Ephesians 2:11-14 where he pointed out that we were strangers from the covenants:

> Remember, that ye being in time past Gentiles in the flesh, who are called Uncircumcision by that which is called the Circumcision in the flesh made by hands; that at that time ye were without Christ, being aliens from the commonwealth of Israel, and strangers from the covenants of promise, having no hope, and without God in the world: *But now in Christ Jesus ye who sometimes were far off are made nigh by the blood of Christ. For he is our peace, who hath made both one, and hath broken down the middle wall of partition between us.*

CUTTING THE NEW COVENANT

The blood that brought us near is the blood of the New Covenant. It's the precious, sinless blood of the Second Adam, Jesus. His sacrifice was an everlasting, once-and-for-all sacrifice that brought an end to all others. Because of what He did for us, there will never again be a need for the blood sacrifices of Moses.

> For if the blood of bulls and of goats, and the ashes of an heifer sprinkling the unclean, sanctifieth to the purifying of the flesh: how much more shall the blood of Christ, who through the eternal Spirit offered himself without spot to God, purge your conscience from dead works to serve the living God? And for this cause he [Jesus] is the mediator of the new testament, that by means of death, for the redemption of the transgressions that were under the first testament, they which are called might receive the promise of eternal inheritance (Hebrews 9:13-15).

Jesus' blood is forever before the Father on the Mercy Seat, interceding on our behalf. It continually cleanses us from sin and *speaks* for us just as Abel's blood did for him when he was killed by his brother Cain. Only, Jesus' blood *"speaketh better things* than that of Abel" (Hebrews 12:24). Instead of crying out for vengeance, Jesus' blood cries out mercy and Redemption.

Every verse in the New Covenant that speaks of Jesus' blood is connected to our redemption—and that redemption is complete. Now and forever—

- We are cleansed by His blood (1 John 1:7)
- We are justified by His blood (Romans 5:9)
- We are redeemed by His blood (Ephesians 1:7)
- We are reconciled by His blood (Romans 3:25)
- We are sanctified by His blood (Hebrews 13:12)
- We are completed by His blood (Hebrews 13:20-21)
- We overcome by His blood (Revelation 12:11).

Through Jesus' blood, we've also been given His Name, the "name which is above every name." The Name at which, as Philippians 2 says, "every knee should bow, of things [or names] in heaven, and things [or names] in earth, and things [or names] under the earth; and…every tongue should confess that Jesus Christ is LORD, to the glory of God the Father" (verses 10-11).

Just think of the power and authority Jesus has given to us in His Name:

- We are saved when we call upon His Name (Romans 10:13)
- We are justified by His Name (1 Corinthians 6:11)
- We are baptized in His Name (Matthew 28:19)
- We cast out devils in His Name (Mark 16:17-18)
- We pray in His Name (1 John 5:14)
- We ask in His Name (John 14:13-14, 16:23-24)
- We bring healing in His Name (Acts 3:6, 3:16, 4:10)

- *Everything* we do and say is to be done in His Name (Colossians 3:17).

Jesus' Name guarantees not only the validity, but the absoluteness of the New Blood Covenant. There is no need for any more sacrifice. Innocent blood no longer needs to be repeatedly shed on our behalf and applied again and again, as it was during the Moses covenant. Every benefit of Redemption is ours permanently and irrevocably in the blood-backed Name of Jesus.

This is the revelation the Apostle Paul so desired for us to receive. It's the reason he prayed—

That the God of our LORD Jesus Christ, the Father of glory, may give unto you the spirit of wisdom and revelation in the knowledge of him: the eyes of your understanding being enlightened; that ye may know what is the hope of his calling, and what the riches of the glory of his inheritance in the saints, and what is the exceeding greatness of his power to us-ward who believe, according to the working of his mighty power, which he wrought in Christ, when he raised him from the dead, and set him at his own right hand in the heavenly places, far above all principality, and power, and might, and dominion, and every name that is named, not only in this world, but also in that which is to come: and hath put all things under his feet, and gave him to be the head over all things to the church, which is his body, the fulness of him that filleth all in all (Ephesians 1:17–23).

THE NEW COVENANT SEAL
AND THE CONTRADICTION

As we've seen, God always set seals in place to remind His covenant partners of His commitment to them. In the First Testament, He used physical or natural things as covenant seals. He used a tree, a Sabbath day off, animal skins and circumcised foreskins, rainbows, the sun, moon, and stars to affirm to His people the promises He made to them.

God's New Covenant seal, however, is different. It's unlike any other because the New Covenant is unlike any other. The significance of its seal is *twofold.*

First, instead of being natural or temporal, the New Covenant seal is supernatural and eternal. Instead of being some*thing,* it is Some*one.* It is "the holy Spirit of God, whereby ye are *sealed* unto the day of redemption" (Ephesians 4:30).

The seal of the Holy Spirit is your assurance of salvation. He came to live in you the moment you made Jesus The LORD of your life. In that instant, you exchanged your unrighteousness for Jesus' righteousness. Your spirit was born again by the power of the Holy Spirit, who now bears witness with your own spirit that you are a child of God. The Covenant word for *salvation* is far more than going to heaven when you die. It is the Greek word *sōzō* in James 5:16. This word means "to save, deliver, protect, heal, preserve, do well, be made whole, to deliver from the perils of judgment." The Holy Spirit is the agent sent to represent the Savior. The coming of the Holy Spirit into the earth was an exceeding great and precious promise. In John 14:13-18 *(Amplified Bible, Classic Edition):*

And I will do [I Myself will grant] whatever you ask in My Name [as presenting all that I AM], so that the Father may be glorified and extolled in (through) the Son. [Yes] I will grant [I Myself will do for you] whatever you shall ask in My Name [as presenting all that I AM]. If you [really] love Me, you will keep (obey) My commands. And I will ask the Father, and He will give you another Comforter (Counselor, Helper, Intercessor, Advocate, Strengthener, and Standby), that He may remain with you forever—The Spirit of Truth, Whom the world cannot receive (welcome, take to its heart), because it does not see Him or know and recognize Him. But you know and recognize Him, for He lives with you [constantly] and will be in you. I will not leave you as orphans [comfortless, desolate, bereaved, forlorn, helpless]; I will come [back] to you.

He came back on the Day of Pentecost.

Second, in addition to assuring you of what you have now, the seal of the New Covenant is your assurance of the glory to come. As Ephesians 1:13-14 explains, you can look forward to the future with confidence because you've been "stamped with the seal of the long-promised Holy Spirit," and "that [Spirit] is the guarantee of our inheritance [the firstfruits...the down payment on our heritage] in anticipation of its full redemption..." *(Amplified Bible, Classic Edition).*

What part of our full redemption are we, as believers, anticipating? The glorification of our physical bodies! There's coming a time when our natural, temporal frames will be transformed into supernatural, eternal bodies that are just like Jesus' body is now (Romans 8:23).

In other words, the seal of the Holy Spirit gives us hope—not just in the now, but for the future. He's our proof that one of these days, "we shall all be changed, in a moment, in the twinkling of an eye, at the last trump: for the trumpet shall sound, and the dead shall be raised incorruptible.... this mortal shall have put on immortality, then shall be brought to pass the saying that is written, Death is swallowed up in victory" (1 Corinthians 15:51–54).

Herein lies the contradiction to the New Covenant: We have a re-created spirit, yet we're still living in the same body we had before we were born again. We were instantly transformed in our spirits into the image of Jesus through the new birth, but we weren't instantly transformed physically into His image. We've been delivered out of the kingdom of darkness and translated into the kingdom of the Son of God's Love in the spirit realm, but in the natural we're still living in a fallen world.

How do we operate in the face of these contradictions? How do we lay hold of the fulfillment of God's Covenant promises when everything around us in the natural tells us they can never come to pass? We do what Abraham did.

When God promised him that he and his wife were going to have a baby, he believed it. No matter that he was ninety-nine and she was ninety. To Abraham, what mattered was what God said. So, "he staggered not at the promise of God through unbelief; but was strong in faith, giving glory to God" (Romans 4:20).

Abraham's covenant with God was one of relationship, mutual

Friendship and Faith. So when faced with a covenant contradiction, he responded with Faith, and it was counted to him as righteousness. As New Covenant believers, it's the same for us. Unlike the people who lived under the Moses covenant—the Law—we don't try to earn our righteousness by rigorously keeping religious rules. We don't try to qualify for God's promises of BLESSING by working hard to be good enough. No, we are saved and made righteous "by grace...through faith" (Ephesians 2:8). So, the New Covenant frees us up to walk with God by Faith in His grace instead of human effort and works!

I can't tell you how liberating this realization was for me. It opened my eyes to the fact that the same Holy Spirit who sealed us and dwells within us will also empower us to operate according to our Covenant. He will bring God's WORD to our remembrance and teach us how to live in THE BLESSING. As a result, sin no longer has dominion over us, for we "are not under the law, but under grace" (Romans 6:14).

How much of God's grace we experience, however, is up to us. We determine by our believing the degree to which we walk in God's New Covenant promises. To walk in them in their fullness, we must live by Faith—daily. Or as James said, "Be doers of The WORD." We must believe God's WORD and trust in Jesus' perfect sacrifice on our behalf, instead of our old performance-driven works.

I've often heard Greg say, *"Jesus* plus *nothing* is *everything!"*

I've also heard him say, "You can't be *married* to Jesus and *date* Moses!" What does he mean by that? You can see an example in Paul's letter to the believers in Galatia. After getting born again, they fell back in love with the Law of Moses. They started slipping away from grace and Faith and trying to earn their right-standing with God through works. So, Paul wrote them and said:

This only would I learn of you, Received ye the Spirit by the works of the law, or by the hearing of faith? Are ye so foolish? Having begun in the Spirit, are ye now made perfect by the flesh? Have ye suffered so many things in vain? If it be yet in vain. He therefore that ministereth to you the Spirit, and worketh miracles among you, doeth he it by the works of the law, or by the hearing of faith? Even as Abraham believed God, and it was accounted to him for righteousness. Know ye therefore that they which are of faith, the same are the children of Abraham. And the scripture, foreseeing that God would justify the heathen through faith, preached before the gospel unto Abraham, saying, In thee shall all nations be BLESSED (Galatians 3:2-8).

You and I can never operate in the fullness of THE BLESSING by trying to combine elements of the Law of Moses with the fulfillment provided by Jesus. We can only do it, as Galatians 5:6 says by, "faith which worketh by love."

Why does Faith work by Love? Because as we've seen over and over, Love is God's motive for everything He does. It's the basis for all the covenants He's ever made with mankind.

I had an experience years ago that opened my eyes to this as never before. Really, it was an encounter I had with *Love*. An encounter with *hesed*, God's Covenant lovingkindness. I was driving my car one afternoon and I said, "LORD, You spoke face to face with Moses. I need that. I need You to speak face to face with me."

He said: *That Book laying there in the seat is everything I said to Moses, everything I said to all the prophets, it is all in My covenants. Everything I said to Jesus, everything I did through Him, is all inside you, because I live on the inside of you.*

Everything He said to Abraham, Isaac, Jacob, Moses and all of the prophets, is all in that BOOK.

Now you live by every word that proceeds out of My mouth. And then He said, *I am the Almighty God, I could speak a new word every second throughout eternity and never say the same thing twice.* It shook me to my core.

I am speaking to you also, for in Me you are a new creation. I'm not looking at what you did in the past. It has been wiped out by the blood of My Covenant, and it's gone. You are not only My Friend, but you are also My child. I'll talk with you, too—face to face—when you get your face in My WORD.

I was so overcome by emotion, I had to pull the car over to the side of the road. I sat there and wept and shouted and cried out with joy!

Scriptures in the New Testament began to stand out to me. I was thrilled to find Galatians 4:7: "Wherefore thou art no more a servant, but a son; and if a son, then an heir of God through Christ."

And 2 Corinthians 5:17: "If any man be in Christ, he is a new creature: old things are passed away; behold, all things are become new."

That's what Jesus' blood of the New Covenant bought for you and me.

Any man or woman, boy or girl who has accepted the New Covenant moves into Him, and He into them by His Spirit, and becomes the very seed of Abraham—an heir according to the promise (Galatians 3:29).

Through Abraham, the Gentiles (or heathen) have been brought into the same Covenant of strong Friendship with God by the sacrifice and shed blood of Jesus, the Lamb of God.

God's Covenant lovingkindness justifies all who will live by Faith, believe His Love and accept His gift of grace.

THE BLESSING FOREVER SECURED

As we close our study of this New Covenant, I want to come full circle and look again at THE BLESSING. Remember, the motive behind God's method always goes back to relationship. He desires more than anything to be in constant fellowship with you. When you enter in Covenant agreement with God, you are obligating yourself by Faith to a relationship with Him. You are binding yourself to Almighty God, which has been His intention and hope all along. Once you make that connection and commitment, God can release His purpose and desire for you, your life, and all creation, through the promises and BLESSINGS of the Covenant.

It was THE BLESSING God bestowed on Adam in the Garden

of Eden that enabled him to fulfill his divine mandate. THE BLESS-ING empowered him with all of heaven's resources so that he could fill the earth with God's goodness and mercy. It crowned Adam with glory and with the anointing or divine ability to carry out his destiny (Psalm 103:5, 8:5; Hebrews 2:7).

You'll also remember that when Adam disobeyed God and handed his authority over to the devil, he lost it all. He lost his fellowship with God and had to hide from His presence. He traded THE BLESSING for the curse, not only for himself but for all mankind.

But now, thank God, through the New Covenant THE BLESS-ING has been restored to us. Instead of hiding from God, through Jesus we can come into God's presence and call Him *Father!* Jesus has made the way for us to "come boldly unto the throne of grace, that we may obtain mercy, and find grace to help in time of need" (Hebrews 4:16).

What's more, Jesus has made us heirs of God's glory that Adam lost (Romans 8:15-17). He's restored our dominion, and when we deposit His words of dominion into our heart they produce the Faith of Jesus Himself to—

- Move mountains (Mark 11:22-23)
- Subdue kingdoms (2 Samuel 8:1, 11-15, 5:7-10, 23:20)
- Bring peace, quietness and confidence (Isaiah 32:17)
- Quench violent fires (Daniel 3:26-28)
- Close the mouths of lions (Daniel 6:16, 22)
- Raise the dead (1 Kings 17:22; 2 Kings 13:21; Luke 8:53-55)
- Cast out devils (Matthew 8:16, 10:8, 12:28; Mark 1:25, 5:8, 9:25)
- And anything else His overcoming power can do (Hebrews 11:33-35).

Through the New Covenant, Jesus has equipped us with everything we need to do what God originally told Adam to do with THE BLESSING. He's equipped and empowered us to "be fruitful and multiply, fill the earth and subdue it." He's given us the divine ability to fulfill our assignment and be BLESSED and be a BLESSING.

Our BLESSING, which is ours through Jesus, covers every area of life—spirit, soul, body, socially and financially. It also encompasses all realms of influence, including:

- Government (Exodus 8:21, 23:6; Leviticus 19:6; Deuteronomy 1:17, 16:18; Psalm 105:22; Isaiah 1:26, 9:6)
- Business, economics and commerce (Exodus 20:15; Deuteronomy 5:19, 28:1-14; Joshua 1:8; 1 Kings 9:26-28, 10:28-29; Proverbs 4:7-8, 10:4, 31:10-31)
- Education (Genesis 18:19; Deuteronomy 6:5-9, 11:19, 31:11-13; Proverbs 1:7, 22:6, 6:20; 2 Timothy 3:16)
- Communication and technology (1 Kings 8:60; Psalm 19:1-4, 48:2; Mark 16:15; Romans 10:18; Revelation 14:6)
- And everything involving and affecting mankind and the rest of God's creation on this planet (Genesis 1:26-28; Romans 8:19-22).

Proverbs 10:22 says, "THE BLESSING of The LORD—it makes [truly] rich, and He adds no sorrow with it [neither does toiling increase it]" *(Amplified Bible, Classic Edition)*. That verse means exactly what it says: The fullness of God's BLESSING provides for total success, prosperity and fullness. David wrote about this in Psalm 112:3, "Wealth and riches shall be in his house: and his righteousness endureth for ever." Wealth and riches can also be in our houses because we have been made the righteousness of God in Christ.

Does total success include financial and material prosperity? Certainly. We see that confirmed in the life of Abraham. THE BLESSING of God made him "very rich" (Genesis 13:2). What's more, his riches didn't bring any harm to him, because unlike worldly riches, the riches produced by THE BLESSING have no downside. They don't come by painful toil (which is what the Hebrew word translated *sorrow* means).

Pain and sorrow are part of the curse that came on mankind through Adam's high treason. That curse produced the threefold results of spiritual death (separation from God), sickness and poverty.

THE BLESSING produces just the opposite. It brings spiritual life (the new birth), health and prosperity.

It's no wonder the Apostle Paul described the New Covenant as a "better covenant"! Not only does it have better promises. Not only is it unbreakable because it was cut between God the Father and His resurrected Son. There is no curse attached to the New Covenant as there was with other covenants!

The moment Jesus cried out from the cross, "It is finished!" (John 19:30, *New Living Translation*), He ended the claim that sin and its curse and separation had on us. He "redeemed us from the curse of the law, being made a curse for us: for it is written, Cursed is every one that hangeth on a tree" (Galatians 3:13).

The New Covenant is curse-free and irrevocable; however, it is not unconditional. It's like the Abrahamic covenant. The condition of this Covenant is *Faith*. That's how the new birth is received; Jesus gives "the right to become children of God, to those who *believe in His name*" (John 1:12, *New King James Version*). It's how answers to prayer are received; you *"believe that ye receive* them, when ye pray" (Mark 11:24).

Every Covenant BLESSING comes by Faith. As the Bible says, "Now the just shall live by faith." "For we have known and believed the love that God hath to us" (Hebrews 10:38; 1 John 4:16).

Knowing God loves us is one thing. Having faith in His Love is another. To receive the New Covenant promises that are ours by the blood of Jesus, we must *believe* God's Love. We must have Faith in it, because it's the foundation upon which our Covenant with Him rests. His motivation in establishing the New Covenant was to redeem us. He wanted to restore His family back. He wanted to get His hands on us and BLESS us.

He loves us that much!

In fact, when Jesus was praying for us on His way to the cross, He made this request of the Father: "May they experience such perfect unity that the world will know that you sent me and that *you love them as much as you love me*" (John 17:22-23, *New Living Translation*).

What's our testimony to the world?

That God loves us as much as He loves Jesus!

I'm telling you, when anyone fully realizes that our Covenant with God is based on *His* Love for us, rather than *our* love for Him—like Abraham who said in Romans 4:21, "And being fully persuaded that, what he had promised, he was able also to perform," we'll never doubt His WORD to save, heal, provide, prosper, answer, restore, break through, show up, be present, move, reveal, deliver, fill, overflow or meet with us right where we are. We won't doubt—we'll only believe, and *freely* receive ALL He has *freely* given.

GO DEEPER
WITH GREG

THE PARALLELS
OF JOSEPH AND JESUS

Whenever we read key passages in Scripture that include the word *Messiah,* we immediately think of Jesus, don't we? When we read Isaiah 11:1-16, it's the coming Savior who comes to mind, particularly as we read the first several verses:

And there shall come forth a rod out of the stem of Jesse, and a Branch shall grow out of his roots: And the spirit of The LORD shall rest upon him, the spirit of wisdom and understanding, the spirit of counsel and might, the spirit of knowledge and of the fear of The LORD; and shall make him of quick understanding in the fear of The LORD: and he shall not judge after the sight of his eyes, neither reprove after the hearing of his ears: But with righteousness shall he judge the poor, and reprove with equity for the meek of the earth: and he shall smite the earth: with the rod of his mouth, and with the breath of his lips shall he slay the wicked. And righteousness shall be the girdle of his loins, and faithfulness the girdle of his reins. The wolf also shall dwell with the lamb, and the leopard shall lie down with the kid; and the calf and the young lion and the fatling together; and a little child shall lead them.

While we often think of Jesus as *the* Messiah—and rightfully so—for generations, Jewish tradition has often referred to two messiahs: Joseph and Jesus. Referred to as Messiah Son of Joseph (Mashiach

Ben Yoself), which is Joseph, and Messiah Son of David (Mashiach Ben David), which is Jesus; they are both recognized as redeemers who will usher in an age of the kingdom of God and Israel.

Historic rabbis identify the Messiah Son of Joseph from their exegesis of Obadiah 1:18: "And the house of Jacob shall be a fire, and the house of Joseph a flame, and the house of Esau for stubble, and they shall kindle in them, and devour them; and there shall not be any remaining of the house of Esau; for The LORD hath spoken it."

They also teach that Messiah Son of Joseph will be killed in the battle against evil which is described in the prophecy of Zechariah 12:10: "And I will pour upon the house of David, and upon the inhabitants of Jerusalem, the spirit of grace and of supplications: and they shall look upon me whom they have pierced, and they shall mourn for him, as one mourneth for his only son, and shall be in bitterness for him, as one that is in bitterness for his firstborn."

It is taught that after the death of Messiah Son of Joseph, there will be a period of tragedy and tribulation until Messiah Son of David comes and avenges him, fighting the enemies of Israel, and establishing an everlasting kingdom.

Many Jewish sages have written on this concept of the two messiahs, most notably Rabbi Saadiah Gaon (1720-1797) and Rabbi Rambam (1138-1204), both towering figures in the history of the Jewish people. Rabbi Gaon said that if Jewish people repent, they may be redeemed immediately, even before the appearance of Messiah Son of David.[28]

According to Rabbi Rambam, "It is said that He (Messiah Son of David) will restore the temple, regather the exiles of Israel, cause all the nations of the Earth to be subjected, put an end to sin and evil, raise the dead, and set up a blissful utopia headquartered in Jerusalem."[29]

When I read such context from their writings, I always recall

---

28 "Sanhedrin 97b," The William Davidson Talmud (Koren-Steinsaltz), Sefaria.org, https://www.sefaria.org/Sanhedrin.97b.1?lang=bi&with=Talmud&lang2=en (accessed 6-2023).

29 "The Rambam," Nissen Mangel, Kehol Publication Society, Jewish History, Chabad.org, https://www.chabad.org/library/article_cdo/aid/107769/jewish/The-Rambam.htm (accessed 6-2023).

Jesus' cousin John the Baptist asking if Jesus is truly the Messiah. When Jesus hears about this from people listening to Him speak, he says, "Tell John what things ye have seen and heard; how that the blind see, the lame walk, the lepers are cleansed, the deaf hear, the dead are raised, to the poor the gospel is preached" (Luke 7:22).

Although God did not make a formal covenant with Joseph, and Jesus is the true Messiah, there are markers or commonalities between Joseph and Jesus that are worth examining.

Joseph was the beloved of his father (Genesis 37:3).
Jesus is the beloved of the Father (Matthew 3:17).

Joseph was stripped of his coat (Genesis 37:23).
Jesus was stripped of His coat, covered with a scarlet robe (Matthew 27:28).

Joseph was sold into Egypt at the proposal of Judah (Genesis 37:26–27).
Jesus was betrayed and handed over to the Jews by Judas (Matthew 27:3).

Joseph was sold for the price of redemption (Genesis 37:28).
Jesus was sold for thirty pieces of silver (the price of a slave) (Matthew 26:15).

Joseph's blood-sprinkled coat (goat's blood) was presented to his father (Genesis 37:31).
Jesus is our scapegoat, and His blood was presented to the Father as a sin offering (Hebrews 13:12; Leviticus 16:8-10).

Joseph became a servant (Genesis 39:1).
Jesus became a servant (Philippians 2:6-7; Luke 22:27; John 13:1-17).

Joseph was sorely tempted by Potiphar's wife and did not sin (Genesis 39:7-12).

Jesus was tempted and did not sin (Matthew 4:1-11; Hebrews 2:18, 4:15).

Joseph was falsely accused (Genesis 39:16-18).
Jesus was falsely accused (Matthew 26:59-61).

Joseph attempted no defense (Genesis 39:19).
Jesus gave no defense at His trials (Isaiah 53:7).

BLESSED
TO BE A
BLESSING

CHAPTER NINE

BLESSED TO BE A BLESSING

My dad was discussing the challenges involved with a doctor once about the healing of the human body. He and I both laughed when we heard this doctor's simple solution: "It's very easy to get a man healed," he said. "Take his head off, put it on a shelf, heal his body, then put his head back on."

That doctor's point being: The biggest battles you and I face in this life are in our heads—in our minds. If only we could take our heads off at times and set them on a shelf, we could win those battles far more easily. We could fix whatever needs to be fixed—and maybe discipline our flesh while we're at it—then put our heads back on. We could save ourselves years of fighting contradictions to our Covenant, because most of these contradictions are based in our minds.

In the Apostle Paul's second letter to the church at Corinth he stated:

For though we walk (live) in the flesh, we are not carrying on our warfare according to the flesh and using mere human weapons. For the weapons of our warfare are not physical [weapons of flesh and blood], but they are mighty before God for the overthrow and destruction of strongholds, [Inasmuch as we] refute arguments and theories and reasonings and every proud and lofty thing that sets itself up against the

[true] knowledge of God; and we lead every thought and purpose away captive into the obedience of Christ (the Messiah, the Anointed One) (2 Corinthians 10:3-5, *Amplified Bible, Classic Edition*).

Every thought must be taken captive, not just a thought here or a thought there. In his letter to the church in Rome he said:

I beseech you therefore, brethren, by the mercies of God, that ye present your bodies a living sacrifice, holy, acceptable unto God, which is your reasonable service. And be not conformed to this world: but be ye transformed by the renewing of your mind, that ye may prove what is that good, and acceptable, and perfect, will of God. For I say, through the grace given unto me, to every man that is among you, not to think of himself more highly than he ought to think; but to think soberly, according as God hath dealt to every man the measure of faith (Romans 12:1-3).

So the mind must be renewed to the Covenant. How is this done? Jesus said in Matthew 6:31, "Take no thought, saying." The words of the Covenant become our thoughts and therefore we do what is said in Proverbs 4:20-22: "My son, attend to my words; incline thine ear unto my sayings. Let them not depart from thine eyes; keep them in the midst of thine heart. For they are life unto those that find them, and health [*medicine*] to all their flesh."

In order to renew our minds to His Covenant promises, we must be attentive, inclining our ears to them, letting them not depart from our eyes, and keeping them in the midst of our hearts. What are we to be attentive to? What are we to keep hearing? What are we to keep looking at? What are we to keep in our hearts? His Covenant WORD. It is only then that we FIND His promises, and in finding them, His WORD becomes *medicine* to ALL our flesh. Therefore, His WORD becomes final authority in our lives. His WORD will always answer the contradictions in our lives. He stands in back of every word, "…watching over His WORD to perform it"! (Jeremiah 1:12, *Amplified Bible, Classic Edition*).

As I mentioned in the previous chapter, we see this in Abraham's life. When God told him that he and Sarah would conceive a child, Abraham was ninety-nine and Sarah was ninety. Yet, The WORD tells us that "he considered not his own body now dead, when he was about an hundred years old, neither yet the deadness of Sarah's womb" (Romans 4:19).

He considered not. Those three words tell us exactly how Abraham faced and overcame the contradiction that came against him and Sarah. He *considered not* what they were up against. Instead, he gave more consideration to the promises of God. He *considered more* what God said than what the circumstances said. As a result, he was "strengthened in faith" (verse 20, *New King James Version*).

"Considering" happens in the mind. So let me ask you:

What is it you're *considering not?*

Who is it you're *considering more?*

To walk in all the promises and provision of the New Covenant, you must *consider not* the contradictions and *consider more the Covenant.* How do you *consider more* the Covenant? Hebrews 12:2-3 tells us. It says:

Looking unto Jesus the author and finisher of our faith; who for the joy that was set before him endured the cross, despising the shame, and is set down at the right hand of the throne of God. ...consider him that endured such contradiction of sinners against himself, lest ye be wearied and faint in your minds.

Consider Jesus!

Consider the One whom God sent and anointed to be the High Priest of your confession of healing, prosperity, deliverance and victory.

Consider Him who bore your sicknesses and carried your diseases, poverty and debt into hell itself (Acts 2:31; Colossians 2:15).

Consider the One who was made to be the curse and redeemed you from it (Galatians 3:13).

Consider everything Jesus is and everything He has provided for you over whatever it is you might be facing. Consider more than anything else the fact that you have a Covenant of victory in the One who provided all your needs (Isaiah 53:4-5; 1 Peter 2:24; Philippians 4:19).

At the time of this writing, I am eighty-six years old, and I consider not my body and its age. I consider only that which God promised, and in Genesis 6:3 He promised me 120 years. I have a Covenant with *El Shaddai,* Almighty God, the One who made a covenant with Abraham, and *El Shaddai* asked me to live to be 120 years old. So, that's become a command and mandate to me. I will preach this Word of Faith until December 2056, or Jesus will come before that time, because I am fully persuaded of the truth of His promise.

Why am I fully persuaded of it? Because it's impossible for God to lie (Hebrews 6:18). He is Light, absolute Light. In Him is no darkness at all (1 John 1:5), and a lie is of darkness. Satan is the father of lies and all liars (John 8:44), and Jesus said that satan, "the prince of this world...hath nothing in me" (John 14:30).

Therefore, I *consider not* any symptoms in my body. They are a contradiction! They are contrary to God's WORD, and like Abraham, I consider only what God has promised in His WORD. I believe the eternal, Blood-sworn, Covenant WORD. I look to Him, the Author and Finisher (or Developer) of my Faith. I consider *Him!*

Again, what are you facing?

Is it sickness? Give no consideration to any symptoms that attack your mind or body. Is it lack? Give no consideration to the debt that is threatening your finances. Don't walk by sight if your bank account looks empty. Instead, give consideration to your Covenant-keeping God. Consider Him who is the Author, Provider, Finisher and Developer of your Faith. For He is faithful!

START WITH YOUR HEAD

In every covenant we have studied, there was at least one major contradiction. There was always something that opposed the rights and privileges guaranteed by the covenant, something that tried to keep God's covenant promises from coming to pass.

For Adam, it was sin itself, which was separation from God and from fellowship with Him.

For Noah, it was that evil would once again prevail, despite God wiping the earth clean with the Flood.

For Abraham, it was his and Sarah's age, as they were well beyond their childbearing years.

For Moses, it was the four Faith failures that became the obstacles to the relationships God sought with the children of Israel.

For David, it was the fallout from his own sins, the sins of his son Solomon, and the sins of his grandson.

For us, it's everything that happens to us that's contrary to our Covenant with God. It's everything that's not part of THE BLESSING. It's every thought that is contrary to God's WORD. And there's only one way for us to overcome those contradictions and defeat the enemy of our souls. We must lay hold of everything provided by our Covenant with Almighty God by *considering more* His WORD—both His written WORD and the living WORD who is Jesus.

We've read this scripture before, but it bears repeating. The Gospel of John, revealing that Jesus and The WORD are One, says:

In the beginning was The WORD, and The WORD was with God, and The WORD was God.... And The WORD was made flesh, and dwelt among us, (and we beheld his glory, the glory as of the only begotten of the Father,) full of grace and truth.... And of his fulness we have all received, and grace for grace. For the law was given by Moses, but grace and truth came by Jesus Christ (John 1:1, 14, 16-17).

The WORD was made flesh! He fulfilled The WORD of the Law given through Moses that had condemned mankind. Then

He turned it around for our good and turned it into a Covenant tool for us to use. He became the victor for those born with a covenant (the Jews) and those born without one (the gentiles). For in Him, there is neither Jew nor Greek but, as believers, we are one in Christ Jesus (Galatians 3:28).

Because The WORD was made flesh, Jesus and The WORD are One and the same. And The WORD is as alive today as it was when The WORD was walking the shores of Galilee healing the sick, casting out devils, restoring sight and cleansing lepers.

The WORD is as bold as He was the day the wind and the waves obeyed The WORD, yet as tender as when The WORD spoke to a child or restored a broken woman.

The WORD comforts the brokenhearted and challenges the self-righteous at the same time. The WORD has power in three realms—heaven, earth and under the earth (Philippians 2:10).

The WORD is as effective as it was when Jesus answered the devil, saying, "It is written…" (Matthew 4:1-10).

The WORD is the meeting place where God's Faith and our Faith come together. It is The WORD that prevails when a believer speaks it in Faith, confident in his or her Covenant (John 8:31).

In the kingdom of God, The WORD of His power is the only foundation fit to undergird and empower believers to walk in the God kind of Faith (Mark 11:22). The WORD is the only way we can overcome the contradictions to the Covenant and walk in THE BLESSING.

"But Brother Copeland," somebody might say, "how do we get The WORD to work in our lives? In our families? In our bodies? In our finances?"

As the doctor told my dad when they were talking that day, it all starts with our heads. That doctor had learned from experience that what's going on in people's heads often gets in the way of their health. It affects their healing. Why would the thoughts in our heads govern our bodies? Because what we believe is a result of our thinking. If our thinking is wrong, our believing will be wrong. The WORD of God is given to us to straighten out our thinking. If our believing is wrong, our confession will be wrong. Whatever is in our heads is going to affect what comes out our mouths, and whatever comes out our mouths will steer our lives. Proverbs 23:7 says, "For as he thinketh in his heart, so is he...."

IN CONSISTENCY LIES THE POWER

It's a spiritual principle revealed through the Bible: The way we release Faith and cause it to work on our behalf is by speaking it. Romans 10:8 says, "The WORD is nigh thee, even in thy mouth, and in thy heart: that is, The WORD of faith, which we preach."

Faith speaks, but it cannot say The WORD of God if The WORD does not first reside in our minds. Why? Because we speak what we think. We say what's in our hearts. When we're squeezed by pressure, what's inside us automatically comes out of our mouths. If we have God's WORD inside us in abundance, Faith words come out. If we don't have His WORD abiding in us, then fear and everything that goes with it comes out. The Bible says in Luke 6:45, "A good man out of the good treasure of his heart bringeth forth that which is good; and an evil man out of the evil treasure of his heart bringeth forth that which is evil: for of the abundance of the heart his mouth speaketh."

David praised God saying, "Your WORD I have hidden in my heart, that I might not sin against You" (Psalm 119:11, *New King James Version*). To hide God's WORD in our hearts is to read it, meditate it, study it, memorize it and speak it. We call this *renewing our minds* because that's the phrase the Apostle Paul used in Romans 12:2 where he wrote: "Do not be conformed to this world (this age), [fashioned after and adapted to its external, superficial customs], but be transformed (changed) by the [entire] renewal of your mind [by its new ideals and its new attitude], so that you may prove [for yourselves] what is the good and acceptable and perfect will of God, even the thing which is good and acceptable and perfect [in His sight for you]" (Romans 12:2, *Amplified Bible, Classic Edition*).

In the Apostle Paul's second letter to the church at Corinth, we find the answer to the renewing of the mind. The bottom line of all this is to put God's Covenant words from The BOOK into your heart and mind, and build a Covenant stronghold that will hold you strong in your spirit and in your soul (or your will, mind and emotions), and the results will be divine health. In John 10:10 (*Amplified Bible, Classic Edition*), Jesus said, "The thief comes only in order to steal and kill and destroy. I came that they may have and enjoy life, and have it in abundance (to the full, till it overflows)." He is the Good Shepherd; renew your mind to that.

A man stopped me in a parking lot and said, "Brother Copeland, God only promised to meet our needs, not our wants." Let's look at that. Small pieces of verses bring up small pieces of the truth. The truth that will make you free is found in the Apostle Paul's partner letter in Philippians 4:18-19 which says, "But I have all, and abound: I am full, having received of Epaphroditus the things which were sent from you, an odour of a sweet smell, a sacrifice acceptable, wellpleasing to God. But my God shall supply all your need according to his riches in glory by Christ Jesus." All my need covers what I want. Shall we go to the First Covenant and see what the Prophet David said? "The LORD is my shepherd; I shall not want" (Psalm 23:1). I reminded him of that scripture, and he just looked a little sad and walked away.

The LORD spoke to Gloria many years ago about this very issue and said to her, *In consistency lies the power.* If we want to walk in all our Covenant rights and privileges, we must *keep* the words of THE BLESSING in our hearts and in our mouths all the time. We must *consistently* speak The WORD only. Nothing else. Because in consistency lies the power. Being consistent is another way of saying "diligent."

When the centurion Cornelius wanted Jesus to heal his servant, he said, "I am not worthy that thou shouldest come under my roof: but speak The WORD only, and my servant shall be healed" (Matthew 8:8). Speak The WORD only. That's what Gloria and I have been teaching people to do for years. It's the key to receiving all that God has for us.

The WORD contains God's own creative ability. It carries within it the power to bring itself to pass. Therefore, when we believe and speak The WORD of THE BLESSING over our lives, we release its power and experience its life-changing manifestations. As we are diligent to activate it by speaking it in Faith, it empowers us to prosper and succeed. That's why there are pages of scriptures at the end of this book that you can personalize and pray over your own life.

I've asked you twice, but I'll ask once more: What are you facing? And what are you saying to what you are facing?

When Joshua and the children of Israel first entered the Promised Land, they faced the walls of Jericho. Those walls presented them with an impossible situation—a contradiction to God's WORD. He'd said that He'd given Jericho into their hand (Joshua 6:2). But the walls around the city were more than eleven feet high and almost six feet thick.

What did Joshua do in the face of that contradiction?

He believed and acted on what God had said to him: "This Book of the Law shall not depart from your mouth, but you shall meditate in it day and night, that you may observe to do according to all that is written in it. For then you will make your way prosperous, and then you will have good success" (Joshua 1:8, *New King James Version*).

To observe to do all that is written in it, is seeing it in the spirit, or revealed knowledge from The BOOK. If it is Western movies, that's what will come out of your mouth. If it is constantly reading novels, that is what will come forth. If it is meditating on your problems, your problems will come forth in your speech. If you meditate on The WORD only 10 percent, you will have 10 percent results. If you meditate on The WORD 50 percent, you will have 50 percent results. Heart and mind full of the Covenant, 100 percent results: spirit, soul, financially and socially!

Joshua followed that divine formula for success, and under his leadership the Israelites fulfilled their assignment. Joshua's words activated the vast power and might of heaven's armies to fight for Israel and they delivered a decisive victory over the heavily fortified city.

What's in your mind? And what's coming out of your mouth? Is your mind renewed with The WORD of God? The answer to that, according to Jesus, is that it's what is in your heart in abundance that will come out of your mouth.

To walk in all that God has for us, we must be speaking The WORD only. Yet oftentimes we waffle between speaking The WORD and speaking everything else *but* The WORD. We act like the people James was correcting when he wrote:

> Out of the same mouth proceed BLESSING and cursing. My brethren, these things ought not to be so. Does a spring send forth fresh water and bitter from the same opening? Can a fig tree, my brethren, bear olives, or a grapevine bear figs? Thus no spring yields both salt water and fresh (James 3:10-12, *New King James Version*).

God's words, the bedrock of the Covenant, are alive and filled with Himself, with His very nature, with Jesus. They are filled with His *hesed*—life, health, prosperity and BLESSING (John 6:63; Proverbs 4:22; Deuteronomy 29:9). They are the expression of His thoughts and innermost being, bringing the essence of Himself into human thought and language. You and I are to meditate on, know and learn them so that we speak them only, all the time.

HAVING THE FAITH OF GOD

A number of years ago I was in one of Brother Jerry Savelle's meetings. We had a single-engine airplane that was due to have the engine overhauled. Brother Savelle said, "Write down your need, then sow a seed." Gloria and I did that. We began to call things that be not as though they were. Each time the cost of the engine overhaul crossed my mind, I said in Faith, "Engine, (and I called it by its manufacturer's name), I call you overhauled. Father, I thank You and I see myself according to Proverbs 4, flying that airplane."

After that, we just praised God. Then we took the petition that we wrote down according to what Jesus said, "It is written." It was truly amazing how rapidly the money needed came. To me, that became a Covenant promise from the God who is more than enough. Our ministry has sown a number of planes into other ministers and ministries to help them further the gospel. It's something that's a privilege for Gloria and me. It's seed we get to sow, and because it's seed, we make sure every plane we give away is in mint condition. I make sure we never give damaged seed—and not just with airplanes but with anything we sow to anyone.

What was I doing? I was considering not what I didn't have. I was calling things "which be not as though they were" (Romans 4:17). I was using my Faith in The WORD to speak to the contradiction that was trying to keep me from doing what God had told me to do—sow another airplane. Since that time, The LORD has directed this ministry to sow many airplanes and seed money to other ministries for *their* airplanes and *their* engine overhauls.

This is what Jesus told us to do in Mark 11:22-23:

Have faith in God [literally: have the faith of God]. For verily I say unto you, That whosoever shall say unto this mountain, Be thou removed, and be thou cast into the sea; and shall not doubt in his heart, but shall believe that those things which he saith shall come to pass; he shall have whatsoever he saith.

God's promise to us is: "So shall my WORD be that goeth forth out of my mouth: it shall not return unto me void, but it shall accomplish that which I please, and it shall prosper in the thing whereto I sent it" (Isaiah 55:11). He always sees to it that His WORD comes to pass. For, as He told the prophet Jeremiah, "I am alert and active, watching over My WORD to perform it" (Jeremiah 1:12, *Amplified Bible, Classic Edition*).

What is it that God has impressed upon you to do? What do you need that you don't have? *Consider not* the contradiction before you. *Consider more* what God has said. Value The WORD. Renew your mind according to The WORD. Speak The WORD only—and watch it work!

ONE MORE THING...

When I spoke to that airplane and said, "I call you overhauled now!" I actually added one more phrase. I said, "I call you overhauled now in the NAME OF JESUS." I spoke with all the power and authority Jesus has given to me, by His blood, death, burial and resurrection. The same power that raised Him from the dead now lives in me (Romans 8:11). So, I use that power when I release my Faith, speaking to whatever mountain I face—and I use it in the NAME OF JESUS when I do it.

His Name is above every name. It's backed by His blood. That's why we end our praying by saying, "In the Name of Jesus. Amen." It's in His NAME that we pray and believe we receive.

We're not just to believe and receive in His Name for our own benefit, either. We're to go beyond accessing God's New Covenant BLESSINGS for our own life, family, health and finances. In Jesus' Name, we're to take the good news and the power of THE BLESSING to the world.

That's the last thing Jesus told us to do before He left the earth. After He rose from the dead, He said to His disciples:

All authority (all power of rule) in heaven and on earth has been given to Me. Go then and make disciples of all the nations, baptizing them into the name of the Father and of the Son and of the Holy Spirit, teaching them to observe everything that I have commanded you, and behold, I am with you all the days (perpetually, uniformly, and on every occasion), to the [very] close and consummation of the age. Amen (so let it be) (Matthew 28:18-20, *Amplified Bible, Classic Edition*).

Go ye into all the world, and preach the gospel to every creature. He that believeth and is baptized shall be saved; but he that believeth not shall be damned. And these signs shall follow them that believe; In my name shall they cast out devils; they shall speak with new tongues; they shall take up serpents; and if they drink any deadly thing, it shall not hurt them; they shall lay hands on the sick, and they shall recover (Mark 16:15-18).

That's what we call the Great Commission. Jesus commanded it be carried out *in His Name*, then ascended into heaven and sat down at the right hand of the Father. Those who heard Him took Him at His WORD and acted on it. "They went forth, and preached every where, The LORD working with *them*, and confirming The WORD with signs following" (Mark 16:20).

"Yes, but that verse is talking about the apostles!" somebody might say. "I'm not an apostle."

Maybe not, but you're a believer.

And because you are a believer, you are equipped to fulfill the Great Commission.

Look at it again and you'll see what I mean. Jesus didn't say when He delivered that Commission, "These signs shall follow *apostles*." He didn't say, "In My Name, *apostles* shall cast out devils and lay hands on the sick." No, He said, signs will follow *"them that believe."* He said, *those who believe* will do works in His Name.

In John 14:12 *(New King James Version),* He put it this way: "Most assuredly, I say to you, he who believes in Me, the works that I do he will do also; and greater works than these he will do, because I go to My Father." Let's qualify that by first reading John 14:10: Jesus said, "Believest thou not that I am in the Father, and the Father in me? the words that I speak unto you I speak not of myself: but the Father that dwelleth in me, he doeth the works."

Jesus said in John 14:21, "He that hath my commandments, and keepeth them, he it is that loveth me: and he that loveth me shall be loved of my Father, and I will love him, and will manifest myself to him." What is the commandment he is referring to? The new commandment of Love. "A new commandment I give unto you, That ye love one another; as I have loved you, that ye also love one another" (John 13:34).

What good news! It's the Father that dwells within us who does the work. It's the same Holy Spirit that came on the day of Pentecost who dwells in us.

All of us as believers are called to go and tell others about Jesus. We're all called to disciple others in His Name. It's why we don't keep all this good news to ourselves. But in our going and telling and discipling, there will also be some *doing*—the same kind of *doing* we see in the Gospels that Jesus did. The same kind of doing the first apostles did.

Actually, if you look closely at Mark 16:20, you'll see it doesn't say about the apostles that The LORD worked with "them." In the *King James Version* the word *them* is italicized. That indicates it was added by the translators. If you leave that word out, you can see the original text says that The LORD worked with and confirmed *The WORD* with signs following. What is a sign? In this case it is Jesus' signature. If it is done in His Name, then He will sign for it.

Jesus and The WORD are One! The WORD is His written Covenant bond. It's our license to walk like Him, think like Him, talk like Him and do what He did in this earthly realm. It's our guarantee of living out the victorious, empowering life of THE BLESSING that the Father had planned for mankind all along.

God's Covenant WORD is truth, sworn in His own blood, a rock-solid foundation for Faith. He means what He says on every page: "For The WORD of The LORD is right; and all his works are done in truth" (Psalm 33:4). "Then said Jesus to those Jews which believed on him, If ye continue in my WORD, then are ye my disciples indeed; and ye shall know the truth, and the truth shall make you free" (John 8:31-32).

His WORD is the Truth about salvation and the Holy Spirit.

His WORD is the Truth about healing.

His WORD is the Truth about money and relationships.

His WORD is the Truth about dealing wisely in all the affairs of life.

His WORD is the Truth about all the works He's planned for us to do from the beginning.

When we accept the Great Commission and take The WORD of God's truth to the world, Jesus will work with and confirm that WORD. When we share with others the good news that THE

BLESSING has been restored to all who will put their Faith in Jesus, signs shall follow. In the Name of Jesus we can do the works that He did and greater works than these because He said so, and because—

All authority in heaven and earth has been given to Him.

He is seated today at the right hand of the Father.

Through Him, we have an everlasting, irrevocable Blood Covenant with Almighty God.

For we are God's [own] handiwork (His workmanship), re-created in Christ Jesus, [born anew] that we may do those good works which God predestined (planned beforehand) for us [taking paths which He prepared ahead of time], that we should walk in them [living the good life which He prearranged and made ready for us to live] (Ephesians 2:10; *Amplified Bible, Classic Edition*).

GO DEEPER
WITH KENNETH

THE POWERFUL
PASSOVER-COMMUNION LINK

When God initiated the first Passover, the Israelites had been enslaved to Egypt for 400 years. He commanded Israel to observe Passover as an eternal ordinance, commemorating their deliverance and His covenant promise to protect them as His chosen people. This Passover rite also served as a vivid reminder of the tenth plague—the death of every firstborn in all Egyptian households—which forced Pharaoh to grant the Israelites their freedom (Exodus 12:14, 17).

On that first Passover night, God instructed the members of every Hebrew household to do the following things: Kill an unblemished, year-old male lamb. Put some of its blood on the doorposts and lintel of their houses and remain inside until morning (Exodus 12:7, 22). Roast the lamb and eat it with unleavened bread and bitter herbs, hurriedly, with each person dressed and ready to go—believing to be released from their bondage that night.

"When I see the blood [over the doorposts]," The LORD said, "I will pass over you; and the plague shall not be on you to destroy you when I strike the land of Egypt" (Exodus 12:13, *New King James Version).*

In light of all we've studied, it is clear that the covenant lamb for each household was a type and shadow of Jesus. He is the true Lamb of God without spot or blemish, slain from the foundation of the world (Revelation 13:8). In the end, it would be His blood that delivered us from all symptoms of the curse, as the lamb's blood delivered the Hebrew people that night thousands of years ago.

What a deliverance that was! After centuries of being mistreated and held in captivity, many of the Hebrews were likely weak, bedridden, lame, diseased, dealing with natural aging, and more. But that night, young and old alike were supernaturally healed, strengthened and enabled to make a desert journey on foot. There was not one feeble person among them—and we're talking about anywhere from one to two million people, or more (Psalm 105:37).

In addition, The LORD gave the Hebrews such favor with the Egyptians that they were more than willing to give these former slaves articles of gold, silver and clothing—anything just to get them to leave! So, these oppressed Israelites, the chosen people of God, literally became a free, healthy and wealthy nation overnight (Exodus 12:35-36).

They were supernaturally compensated for all the free labor. By God's power and covenant relationship, they left that wicked place more than equal to the former slave masters.

Think about it: How much more is God's Covenant power available to us today as we sit in remembrance around our New Covenant Communion tables?

Jesus, our Lamb of God, shed His blood that we might enjoy the same deliverance, favor, healing, strength and wealth the Israelites did.

On the night of Jesus' final *Seder* (Passover covenant meal) with the men who had been with Him before His crucifixion, He demonstrated that He was indeed the Passover Lamb. He "took bread, gave thanks and broke it, and gave it to them, saying, 'This is My body which is given for you; this do in remembrance of Me. Likewise He also took the cup after supper, saying, 'This cup is the new covenant in My blood, which is shed for you'" (Luke 22:19, *New King James Version*).

Notice, particularly, Jesus' instructions to His disciples when He served the cup: "And he took the cup, and gave thanks, and gave it to them, saying, Drink ye all of it" (Matthew 26:27).

God gave the same instructions, in type and shadow, to the

Hebrew people who ate the first Passover meal: they were to eat *all* of it and leave *nothing* behind. They were to even burn the bones (Exodus 12:10). God wanted the entire sacrifice consumed, one way or another. Also, as I said, they were to eat their meal *prepared* to leave at a moment's notice. The LORD even required them to stand as they ate (Exodus 12:11).

For us today that means when we approach the Communion table, we are to consume *all the fullness* of God's promises. We're to partake of the Communion elements in Faith, *expecting, anticipating, believing* for the fulfillment of those promises—ready to receive our deliverance at any moment!

Can you see how, no matter what you may be facing—sin, sickness, addictions, worry, strife, old habits—you can be delivered through properly receiving The LORD's Supper?

The New Covenant word for salvation is *sōzō*. We have mistakenly thought it applied only to our being saved from sin, but it has a far greater application. *Sōzō* means "to save, deliver, protect, heal, preserve, be (make) whole."[30] It is used 110 times throughout the New Testament.

In the same way, the body and blood of Jesus covers *every* area of our existence. It is our full and complete salvation, or deliverance, spirit, soul and body. All we have to do to receive any facet of that "so great a salvation," as Paul refers to it (Hebrews 2:3, *New King James Version),* is go before God and receive Communion as the children of Israel did, fully prepared to receive the full range of our deliverance.

What's more, the beauty of Communion is that we don't have to wait until we go to church to receive it, once a week or once a quarter. No, we can receive it at home, in our car, in our hotel room— wherever we are and whenever we want.

Anywhere, anyplace, anytime, the body and blood of Jesus is a powerful point of contact for us, as believers, to release our Faith and receive deliverance from sin, sickness, disease, weakness, pain, infirmity, poverty—any part of the curse that came on mankind through Adam's sin. Communion itself declares we are free from

---

30 *The New Strong's Exhaustive Concordance of the Bible* (Nashville: Thomas Nelson Publishers, 1996) G4982.

that curse because Jesus, the spotless Lamb of God, took it all upon Himself, *becoming* the curse for us (Galatians 3:13).

TAKING COMMUNION

If you aren't sure how to take Communion on your own, let us walk you through it.

First, get your Communion elements—preferably grape juice, a small piece of bread, crackers or whatever you have. The elements are important, but they are not the most important. Releasing your Faith in the power of Jesus' finished work on the cross is vital to our lives.

Once you've done your physical preparations for Communion, then begin preparing your spirit and soul. On the night Jesus instituted this Communion meal, He began by praying over the physical elements, as well as giving practical instructions to the disciples as He served them. This set the tone and atmosphere for the rest of their time together, allowing the Holy Spirit to minister freely among them. Again, notice what Jesus said and did:

And as they were eating, Jesus took bread, and BLESSED it, and brake it, and gave it to the disciples, and said, Take, eat; this is my body. And he took the cup, and gave thanks, and gave it to them, saying, Drink ye all of it; for this is my blood of the new testament [Covenant], which is shed for many for the remission of sins (Matthew 26:26-28).

Communion is an opportunity to engage our whole being in this precious and personal time before The LORD. That total engagement is important because, as Isaiah prophesied, Jesus' body and blood sacrifice covers every part of our being. He bore *spiritual torment* for our sins; *mental distress* for our worry, care and fear; and *physical pain* for our sickness and disease.

God gave His all to redeem us from every aspect, every manifestation, every symptom of the curse. In turn, we need to give our all in receiving the full measure of His sacrifice. Part of giving our all involves properly preparing ourselves to take Communion. It includes us checking up on ourselves to make sure we're not approaching the Communion table in a way that's not worthy of The LORD. The Apostle Paul received direct instruction from The LORD about this. He said:

> Whoever eats this bread or drinks this cup of The LORD in an unworthy manner will be guilty of the body and blood of The LORD. But let a man *examine himself,* and so let him eat of the bread and drink of the cup. For he who eats and drinks in an unworthy manner eats and drinks judgment to himself, not *discerning* The LORD's body (1 Corinthians 11:27-29, *New King James Version).*

If we don't examine and judge ourselves *completely,* we will miss the full meaning of Communion, as well as its benefits. How exactly do we *judge* and *examine* ourselves? In the light of the two elements of Communion: the *bread* and the *cup,* or the body and the blood.

The blood was shed for our sin. It provides us with forgiveness for sin, cleansing of sin, and freedom from bondage to it. So, we examine ourselves in light of the blood to make sure we're walking accordingly. In our years of ministry, we've found most believers are quick to do this. They readily judge themselves where *sin* is concerned, receive conviction, confess their sin and repent, which is good. That's what Jesus expects us to do, and it's definitely part of examining ourselves in preparation for Communion. That's what the *cup* represents, especially in the area of forgiving others. Jesus said in Mark 11:25, "And when ye stand praying, forgive, if ye have ought against any: that your Father also which is in heaven may forgive you your trespasses."

But the cup is only half of the Communion meal. What about the *bread?* What about Jesus' body? His body was broken for us. It was bruised for us. Ultimately, it was buried, then resurrected for us. How quick are we to judge ourselves in light of all that?

The LORD once addressed this very issue with Greg by telling him:

If you'll judge yourself, judgment won't come on you. You've been judging yourself where the blood was concerned. You

are ready to judge yourself where sin is concerned and re-
pent and get rid of it every time you take Communion. You
say, "LORD, I've done this wrong, and I've been wrong about
that. I am not going to partake of that blood until I'm right
before You. I repent of that, and I judge myself of it, and Your
WORD said judgment won't come on me."

Why didn't you take the same judgment, look at your body and
say to Me, "LORD, it's not right that this disease and this pain
are in my body. This body was bought with a price, and it is
not right that it's sick. And I am judging this thing, and I repent
of that sin in my body. I repent of that sickness and disease in
my body, and I reject it right along with the sin. And in Jesus'
Name, I receive my healing, I receive my forgiveness, and I par-
take of that precious body and the blood!"

The brokenness, the bruising, the stripes on Jesus' back—it was
all for our healing, all for the physical part of our being. And that's
the half of the Communion table we tend to overlook or neglect.

At Communion, we should judge ourselves where our physical
health is concerned, because Jesus purchased healing for us at Calvary the same as He purchased our spiritual salvation and prosperity for our souls (3 John 2).

So, always make it a point when you approach Communion to
judge yourself to the fullest extent. Don't judge or examine yourself
halfway, and don't receive Communion halfway. If you do, it will
become for you just a religious ritual, and you'll partake of it in an
"unworthy manner." Paul referred to this as "not discerning The
LORD's body" and warned—

Anyone who eats and drinks without discriminating and
recognizing with due appreciation that [it is Christ's] body,
eats and drinks a sentence (a verdict of judgment) upon himself. That [careless and unworthy participation] is the reason
many of you are weak and sickly, and quite enough of you
have fallen into the sleep of death (1 Corinthians 11:29-30,
Amplified Bible, Classic Edition).

Yes, Communion is that serious, and that powerful.

COMMUNION PRAYER

Are you ready to take Communion?

Here is a prayer that you can use as a guide when you pray before breaking the bread:

Father God, in the Name of Jesus, I recognize that I have a Covenant with You—a Covenant that was ratified by the shed blood of Jesus. Because His body was broken for me and His blood was shed on my behalf, I acknowledge that He bore sin, sickness, disease, sorrow, grief, fear, torment, unforgiveness, strife and lack for me. Through His substitutionary sacrifice, I have complete redemption, total deliverance from the works of satan. As a new creation in Christ Jesus, I realize my freedom has been bought and paid for. I am forgiven. I am redeemed. I give thanks for it all. In Jesus' Name I pray. Amen.

As you break the bread and eat it, examine yourself—*spirit, soul* and *body*—in the light of The WORD. Repent of anything The LORD shows you. He is faithful and just to forgive us when we confess our sins, and He cleanses us from all unrighteousness.

Next, take the cup in the same manner and make a confession like this:

Father, I give You thanks for all You have provided for us in Christ Jesus. I confess this day that I am BLESSED of The LORD. This Covenant I entered into at the new birth is a Covenant filled with Your exceeding, great and precious promises, and I am a partaker of those promises now.

I am the healed. I am the redeemed. I am delivered from the authority of darkness. I am translated into the kingdom of Your dear Son, Jesus. I am the head and not the tail. I am above and not beneath. All that I set my hands to prospers. I praise You, Father, for the newness of life I now enjoy. In Jesus' Name I pray. Amen.

Now do this every time The LORD leads you. Each time I receive Communion in remembrance of Him, I remember the outstanding miracles I have witnessed in the ministry of Oral Roberts. Gloria and I remember, as we take Communion together, the Faith seminars as we sat under the teaching of Kenneth E. Hagin. Not only that, but the miracles and healings in Healing School since 1979 and the testimonies from all over the world that have come because Jesus is still the Healer! We take Communion over ourselves, our children, our grandchildren and our great-grandchildren. We take Communion over our ministry, our Partners, and decisions that are before us. We never miss an opportunity to judge ourselves rightly and receive *all* Jesus made possible through our New Covenant.

CONCLUSION

I wrote the book *The BLESSING of The LORD Makes Rich and He Adds No Sorrow With It* more than a decade ago. If you haven't read it, I encourage you to do so. If you have read it, I recommend picking it up again and going through it with refreshed *Covenant-minded* eyes and revelation. It will mean even more to you now that you have a greater understanding of Covenant and all it means to your relationship with your heavenly Father.

Hebrews 11:6 says, "But without faith it is impossible to please him: for he that cometh to God must believe that he is, and that he is a rewarder of them that diligently seek him." Faith begins where the will of God is known. God has always been the Healer and Good Health of His Covenant people. There is no sickness in heaven! Jesus prayed, "Thy will be done in earth *as it is* in heaven (Matthew 6:10). There was no sickness in the Garden of Eden. Adam lived 130 years and begat Seth, "and all the days of Adam were nine hundred and thirty years: and he died" (Genesis 5:3-5). He did not know how to die! It's obvious he continued to say the things the Creator taught him to say. God's covenant Friend Abraham, whose body was "dead," married again after Sarah died and had six more sons—and lived to be 175 years old. Faith in God works!

Professor Stephens and I don't want you to go another day without walking in *all* that God has for you as His Covenant son or daughter. We know what it is to live a life of Covenant, so intimately connected to God, to His WORD, to His promises, to His Son, to His Spirit—as much as one can this side of heaven—and we want that for *you*. Greg and Michelle, Gloria and I know Him as LORD and Savior. We have experienced His Love and the baptism in the Holy Spirit with evidence of speaking in other tongues. In

Matthew 24:14, the Master said, "And this gospel of the kingdom shall be preached in all the world for a witness unto all nations; and then shall the end come." There are 195 nations in the world today, and the VICTORY Channel™ is reaching people all over the world.

The Apostle John recalled in John 11:25-26, "Jesus said unto her, I am the resurrection, and the life: he that believeth in me, though he were dead, yet shall he live: And whosoever liveth and believeth in me shall never die. Believest thou this?" Yes, we do.

The next great event in heaven is the Marriage Supper of the Lamb. The next great event in the earth is the great Resurrection. Jesus, prophesying of the end times said:

And there shall be signs in the sun, and in the moon, and in the stars; and upon the earth distress of nations, with perplexity; the sea and the waves roaring; men's hearts failing them for fear, and for looking after those things which are coming on the earth: for the powers of heaven shall be shaken. And then shall they see the Son of man coming in a cloud with power and great glory. And when these things begin to come to pass, then look up, and lift up your heads; for your redemption draweth nigh. And he spake to them a parable; Behold the fig tree, and all the trees; when they now shoot forth, ye see and know of your own selves that summer is now nigh at hand. So likewise ye, when ye see these things come to pass, know ye that the kingdom of God is nigh at hand. Verily I say unto you, This generation shall not pass away, till all be fulfilled. Heaven and earth shall pass away: but my words shall not pass away (Luke 21:25-33).

Behold the fig tree, and all the trees. That's referring to the state of Israel, and was fulfilled in 1948. We, as believers, are about to experience Jesus as the Great Resurrection. Every day we live is one day closer.

Here's the question: When did your life begin? It began today, and it begins every day, the moment you wake up. Your place in the plan of the Almighty God, in His Covenant Name *El Shaddai,* the God who is more than enough, was determined before the foundation of the world (Ephesians 1:3-6; 1 Peter 1:20).

Do these three things and success will always be yours:

1. Find the will of God for your life.
2. Confer no longer with flesh and blood. Why? People will always tell you that you can't do it.
3. Then get your job done at any cost.

We know God's WORD is His will. I'm convinced, and so is Professor Stephens, that that's the reason the translators used the word *testament*. Jesus is the one and only Man who wrote His will in the New Covenant, then died and was raised from the dead to probate His own will by His Spirit in the earth. Therefore, and I say this with a smile, we are joint heirs in the Last Will and Testament of the Almighty God.

I leave you with these precious Covenant words from the writings of the Apostle Paul, given by the Holy Spirit, in Galatians:

No man is justified by the law in the sight of God, it is evident; for, The just shall live by faith. [This is the mandate of this ministry—to teach God's people Faith.] ...Christ hath redeemed us from the curse of the law, being made a curse for us: for it is written, Cursed is every one that hangeth on a tree: that THE BLESSING of Abraham might come on the Gentiles through Jesus Christ; that we might receive the promise of the Spirit through faith. Brethren, I speak after the manner of men; Though it be but a man's covenant, yet if it be confirmed, no man disannuls or adds thereto.

Now to Abraham and his seed were the promises made. He saith not, And to seeds, as of many; but as of one, And to thy seed, which is Christ. And this I say, that the covenant, that was confirmed before of God in Christ, the law, which was four hundred and thirty years after, cannot disannul, that it should make the promise of none effect. For if the inheritance be of the law, it is no more of promise: but God gave it to Abraham by promise....

For ye are all the children of God by faith in Christ Jesus. For as many of you as have been baptized into Christ have put on Christ. There is neither Jew nor Greek, neither bond or free, neither male nor female; for ye are all one in Christ Jesus. And if ye be Christ's [if you be in Christ!], then are ye Abraham's seed, and heirs according to the promise (Galatians 3:11-18, 26-29).

We close with this: *God loves you, we love you, and Jesus is Lord!*

THE
COVENANT
NAMES
OF
GOD

THE COVENANT NAMES OF GOD

Throughout Scripture, God is called by different Names. Because each Name reveals something about His nature and His character, through His Names we find out who God is.

The two primary Hebrew Names by which God is called are *Elohim* and *YHWH*. The first to appear in the Bible is *Elohim*. A plural term, *Elohim* speaks of God's triune nature that includes God' the Father, God the Son and God the Holy Spirit. This is the Name of God used in Genesis 1:1: "In the beginning God *[Elohim]* created the heaven and the earth." *Elohim*, which is translated *God*, means *the powerful Creator.* It is the Name by which all people know Him or know *of* Him.

The second primary Hebrew Name by which God identifies Himself in Scripture, *YHWH* (pronounced *Yahweh* or *Jehovah*), is God's personal Covenant Name. Translated *LORD*, it is the Name God uses with His Friends—those who are in covenant with Him. While others may only know Him as *Elohim*, to us, His Covenant people to whom He reveals Himself intimately, He is our LORD.

This is why here at Kenneth Copeland Ministries we close our *Believer's Voice of Victory* broadcasts and believers' meetings not by saying, "Goodbye," or "See you next time," but by saying, "Jesus Is LORD!" We don't do that just because Gloria and I thought would be a catchy phrase for our ministry. No, that's a declaration of Faith in our Covenant with God and in THE BLESSING of that Covenant that's ours in the Name of our resurrected LORD Jesus. By declaring in Faith that "Jesus is LORD" over our own lives, our Partners, and everyone else who hears the voice of victory through our ministry, we're activating our Covenant. We're declaring THE BLESSING over people.

In addition to *YHWH* and *Elohim*, there are two other Names of God in the Bible that, like *Elohim*, begin with *El*. They include *El Shaddai* and *El Elyon*. All three of God's *El* Names reference His creative nature, His majesty, excellence and mighty work. They speak of the vast power of the One who created the heavens and the earth, the One who dwells in us. We see God called by these Names in Genesis 1:1; Deuteronomy 8:15, 5:23; Psalm 68:7; Isaiah 54:5, 45:18; and Jeremiah 32:27.

El Shaddai speaks of *the breasty one, the nurse, the provider, the all-sufficient One, the more-than-enough God who supplies BLESSING and nourishment to His people.* This Name first appears in Genesis 17:1 where The LORD appeared to Abram and said to him, "I am the Almighty God *[El Shaddai]*; walk before me, and be thou perfect." Other verses that refer to God as *El Shaddai* include Genesis 28:3; Exodus 6:1; and Psalm 91:1-2.

El Elyon, translated the *Most High God*, speaks of *the supreme sovereignty, power, authority and majesty of God and His total preeminence above all.* Psalm 57:2 says, "I will cry unto God most high *[El Elyon]*; unto God that performeth all things for me."

This is the Name used in Genesis 14:19-20 where the High Priest Melchizedek said, "BLESSED be Abram of the most high God *[El Elyon]*, possessor of heaven and earth; and BLESSED be the most high God *[El Elyon]*, which hath delivered thine enemies into thy hand."

Yet another Name of God that, like *YHWH*, speaks of Covenant is *"I AM."* This is the Name God told Moses to give the Israelites when He instructed him to go back to Egypt to deliver them from bondage. As Exodus 3 records:

Moses said unto God, Behold, when I come unto the children

of Israel, and shall say unto them, The God of your fathers hath sent me unto you; and they shall say to me, What is his name? what shall I say unto them?" And God *[Elohim]* said unto Moses, I AM THAT I AM: and he said, Thus shalt thou say unto the children of Israel, I AM hath sent me unto you. And God said moreover unto Moses, Thus shalt thou say unto the children of Israel, The LORD God of your fathers, the God of Abraham, the God of Isaac, and the God of Jacob, hath sent me unto you: this is my name for ever, and this is my memorial unto all generations (verses 13-15).

The Hebrew phrase translated *"I AM WHO I AM,"* literally means, "I WILL BE WHAT I WILL BE." Through this Name, God is saying to us He will be whatever we need Him to be. We see an example of this in Exodus 15:26. There, when the thirsty Israelites complained that the water at Marah was bitter and would make them sick, God responded by saying. "I AM The LORD that healeth thee." He didn't just say that He is *the* Healer. He said, "I AM *your* Healer."

I AM is a Covenant Name of God. By putting that Name in His WORD, He has given us access to everything in Him. He's given us access to everything His WORD says He is and everything it promises He will do and be for us. God and His eternal WORD are One. His WORD is filled with Himself, His life, His power and His presence. God's WORD is where *His* Faith and *our* Faith converge. It manifests in our lives when we understand and have Faith in our Covenant.

Jesus, the Messiah, embodies God's WORD. So, just as in the Old Covenant God revealed Himself as the great I AM, Jesus revealed Himself as the fulfillment of that Name in the New Covenant. We see this particularly in the Gospel of John, where Jesus said:

- I am the bread of life (John 6:35, 41, 48, 51)
- I am the light of the world (John 8:12)
- I am the gate/door of the sheep/sheepfold (John 10:7, 9)
- I am the good shepherd (John 10:11, 14)
- I am the resurrection and the life (John 11:25)
- I am the way, the truth and the life (John 14:6).
- I am the true vine (John 15:1, 5).

What do you need God to be in your life today? Whatever it is, He is I AM THAT I AM. He will be whatever you need Him to be.

THE COMPOUND COVENANT NAMES OF GOD

Often in Scripture, the Name *Yaweh* or *Jehovah* is linked with a second word to form a compound Covenant Name of God. These compound Names are sometimes referred to as the *Jehovah* Names of God, and all of them reveal His redemptive nature. They include: *Jehovah Jireh, Jehovah Rapha, Jehovah Nissi, Jehovah M'Kaddesh, Jehovah Shalom, Jehovah Rohi, Jehovah Tsidkenu, Jehovah Shammah* and *Jehovah Sabaoth.*

Taking them in that order, since that is the order in which these compound redemptive Names are introduced to us in the Bible, let's examine each one to see—

- when God first revealed this part of Himself
- to whom He revealed it
- why He revealed it
- And how we because of our Blood Covenant with Jesus can call on these Names in Faith and receive that aspect of God's character and nature in our lives.

JEHOVAH JIREH

God revealed Himself as *Jehovah Jireh* to Abraham when he was about to sacrifice his son Isaac on Mount Moriah. While it may be hard for us to understand why God asked His covenant partner to do this, Abraham lived in a culture where such sacrifices were common. The gentile nations at that time sacrificed their firstborn sons as the highest appeasement to their false and unholy gods. So, for God to ask Abraham to sacrifice Isaac wasn't a foreign idea— Abraham saw this practice taking place all around him.

As we saw in our study of the Abraham covenant however, Isaac was never actually sacrificed. At the last moment, God intervened, providing a substitute for Isaac in the form of a ram, while at the same time revealing Himself more fully to Abraham.

And Abraham lifted up his eyes, and looked, and behold behind him a ram caught in a thicket by his horns: and Abraham went and took the ram, and offered him up for a burnt offering in the stead of his son. And Abraham called the name of that place *Jehovahjireh*: as it is said to this day, *In the mount of The LORD it shall be seen.* And the angel of The LORD called unto Abraham out of heaven the second time, and said, By myself have I sworn, saith The LORD, for because thou hast done this thing, and hast not withheld thy son, thine only son: that in BLESSING I will BLESS thee, and in multiplying I will multiply thy seed as the stars of the heaven, and as the sand which is upon the sea shore; and thy seed shall possess the gate of his enemies; and in thy seed shall all the nations of the earth be BLESSED; because thou hast obeyed my voice (Genesis 22:13-18).

Abraham was the first man to call God *Jehovah Jireh,* "The LORD will provide." He was not, however, to be the last. Today, we believers can call God by that Name as well. In fact, this entire scene was a foreshadowing of the New Covenant. It was a prophetic picture of Jesus our Substitute going to the cross as the sacrificial Lamb of God and providing the payment necessary for our sins.

In addition to its big, eternal context, this particular Name of God also tells us what we do when in our own lives we need something we don't have: We look to *Jehovah Jireh* to supply it. We call in Faith upon that part of His character and nature. We stand on The WORD in the First and Second Covenants and say that God is *Jehovah Jireh,* our Provider.

In Philippians, the Apostle Paul said it clearly: "My God shall supply all your need according to his riches in glory by Christ Jesus" (Philippians 4:19).

Is there lack in some area of your life? Call upon the Covenant Name of *Jehovah Jireh,* The LORD who provides.

JEHOVAH RAPHA

Jehovah Rapha is The LORD who heals. As we've already seen, this compound Name of God first makes its appearance in Scripture when the Israelites, after traveling three days into the wilderness, reached Marah. Upon finding the water there was bitter, they murmured against Moses and said, "What shall we drink?"

> And he cried unto The LORD; and The LORD showed him a tree, which when he had cast into the waters, the waters were made sweet: there he made for them a statute and an ordinance, and there he proved them, and he said, If thou wilt diligently hearken to the voice of The LORD thy God, and wilt do that which is right in his sight, and wilt give ear to his commandments, and keep all his statutes, I will put none of these diseases upon thee, which I have brought upon the Egyptians: for I am *[Jehovah Rapha]* The LORD that healeth thee (Exodus 15:25- 26).

In this context, God revealed Himself as *Jehovah Rapha* by healing the waters at Marah. But previously He revealed Himself as their Healer by healing the Israelites themselves. He so thoroughly healed them before they left Egypt that when they went out *"there was* not one feeble *person* among their tribes" (Psalm 105:37). They all had been made whole!

This is the revelation Gloria has taught time and again in her Healing School: healing is included in our Covenant with God. He is The LORD our Healer, and as His New Covenant people, we are the healed. We have been made whole.

We aren't the sick trying to get healed; we were created to walk in divine health. Yes, we do live in a fallen world and sickness does come against us at times. But when it does, we fight the good fight of Faith. We stand against it. We speak The WORD of God for our healing. We call on the Name of *Jehovah Rapha*, The LORD who heals, The LORD who made us whole. There's power in the NAME(s) of God!

JEHOVAH NISSI

The Name *Jehovah Nissi* is introduced in Exodus 17 in the context of the Israelites' battle with the Amalekites. At the beginning of that battle Moses told Joshua, "Choose us out men, and go out, fight with Amalek: to morrow I will stand on the top of the hill with the rod of God in mine hand" (verse 9). Joshua did as Moses said, and while he fought the Amalekites, Moses, Aaron and Hur went up to the top of a hill overlooking the fight.

> And it came to pass, when Moses held up his hand, that Israel prevailed: and when he let down his hand, Amalek prevailed. But Moses hands were heavy; and they took a stone, and put it under him, and he sat thereon; and Aaron and Hur stayed up his hands, the one on the one side, and the other on the other side; and his hands were steady until the going down of the sun. And Joshua discomfited Amalek and his people with the edge of the sword. And The LORD said unto Moses, Write this for a memorial in a book, and rehearse it in the ears of Joshua: for I will utterly put out the remembrance of Amalek from under heaven. And Moses built an altar, and called the name of it Jehovah-Nissi: (verses 11-15).

The Septuagint translates *Jehovah Nissi* as "The LORD my refuge." Just as Joshua and his men fought a flesh-and-blood enemy, we as believers fight against principalities, powers, and rulers of the darkness (Ephesians 6:12). In our fight, just like Joshua in his fight, The LORD is our banner; He is our refuge.

Are you in a fight? A fight for your life, your finances, your marriage, your children, your job or anything else? Not a fight *with*, but a fight *for*. Then call upon *Jehovah Nissi*, The LORD your banner, The LORD your refuge.

JEHOVAH M'KADDESH

This compound Name of God first appears in connection with the Moses covenant. In Exodus 31:13, while giving instruction to Moses about the tabernacle, The LORD said, "Speak thou also unto the children of Israel, saying, Verily my sabbaths ye shall keep: for it is a sign between me and you throughout your generations; that ye may know that I am *[Jehovah M'Kaddesh]* The LORD that doth sanctify you."

God used that Name again in Leviticus 20:7-8, where He said to the Israelites, "Consecrate yourselves therefore, and be holy; for I am The LORD your God. And you shall keep My statutes and do them. I am *[Jehovah M'Kaddesh]* The LORD Who sanctifies you" *(Amplified Bible, Classic Edition)*.

The LORD desired for His people to be holy so He could dwell among them. They were to be different from all nations of the earth as a holy people unto Himself (Deuteronomy 14:2, 28:9). Under the Moses covenant, God's people were sanctified, set apart, made holy before God by keeping the Law, which was hard to do. But under the New Covenant, we are sanctified by Faith in The LORD Jesus and The WORD.

Jesus, in His prayer to the Father just before He went to the cross, said, "Sanctify them [make holy, consecrate[31] (set apart)] through thy truth: thy WORD is truth" (John 17:17).

Hebrews 10:10 assures us that "we are sanctified through the offering of the body of Jesus Christ once *for all.*"

First Peter 2:9 says of us "who believe" on Jesus: "are a chosen generation, a royal priesthood, an holy nation, a peculiar people; that ye should show forth the praises of him who hath called you out of darkness into his marvellous light."

Through Jesus, our Covenant God is to us *Jehovah M'Kaddesh*. So, despite what we may have done or what battles we may be facing, we can call upon that Covenant Name and know that in Him we have been made holy.

---

31 *The New Strong's Exhaustive Concordance of the Bible* (Nashville: Thomas Nelson Publishers, 1996), G37.

JEHOVAH SHALOM

Jehovah Shalom occurs only once in the Old Covenant, in Judges 6, where the angel of The LORD appeared to Gideon and called him a mighty man of valor. At the time, Gideon appeared to be anything but courageous. Hiding in a winepress, He was already afraid of the Midianites and the appearance of the angel of The LORD frightened him even more. Certain that if the former didn't kill him the latter would, Gideon cried out:

> Alas, O LORD God! for because I have seen an angel of The LORD face to face. And The LORD said unto him, Peace be unto thee; fear not: thou shalt not die. Then Gideon built an altar there unto The LORD, and called it *Jehovah-shalom* (verses 22–24).

Jehovah Shalom means "The LORD is Peace." It's the Covenant Name of God we need when fear comes against us. In Gloria's teachings, she has often said that the meaning of *peace* is "nothing missing and nothing broken."

While the Name *Jehovah Shalom* is mentioned in the Bible only once, peace *(shalom)* is seen more than 200 times in Scripture. Isaiah 26:3 says, "Thou wilt keep him in perfect peace, whose mind is stayed on thee: because he trusteth in thee." Psalm 29:11 says, "The LORD will give strength unto his people; The LORD will BLESS his people with peace."

Jesus referenced peace in Mark 5 when speaking to the woman with the issue of blood, who was a daughter of Abraham. A Hebrew-Aramaic-speaking Man, Jesus' words, written in Greek, are translated, "Daughter, thy faith hath made thee whole; go in peace, and be whole of thy plague" (verse 34).

Part of the Greek definition[32] of the word *peace* includes "prosperity." So, I believe the woman who had the issue of blood received even more than healing from Jesus. Because she had spent all the money she had on physicians (verse 26), I believe her Faith in Jesus also brought in the prosperity necessary to make her whole

---

32 *Strong's*, G1515.

financially. After all, *peace* means "nothing missing and nothing broken."

Do you need peace in any area of your life? Is something missing from your life? Is something broken on the inside of you or in your world? Is fear trying to consume you? Has it taken on one of its many forms, like worry or anxiety? Is it affecting your physical body? Are you living through sleepless nights? Call on the Covenant Name of God *Jehovah Shalom.*

JEHOVAH ROHI

It was King David, "the sweet psalmist of Israel" (2 Samuel 23:1) who gave us the beautiful picture of *Jehovah Rohi*. He said in Psalm 23:

The LORD is my shepherd *[Jehovah Rohi]*; I shall not want. He maketh me to lie down in green pastures: he leadeth me beside the still waters. He restoreth my soul: he leadeth me in the paths of righteousness for his name's sake. Yea, though I walk through the valley of the shadow of death, I will fear no evil: for thou art with me; thy rod and thy staff they comfort me. Thou preparest a table before me in the presence of mine enemies: thou anointest my head with oil; my cup runneth over. Surely goodness and mercy shall follow me all the days of my life: and I will dwell in the house of The LORD for ever (verses 1-6).

Those are Covenant words that David spoke. And they are the Covenant words God wants us to speak. He wants us to call on *Jehovah Rohi*, The LORD our Shepherd because Psalm 23 is where we as believers live today. In Christ, we are seated at God's table, in the presence of our enemies, with our heads anointed with oil, and our cup running over. Goodness and mercy, the *hesed* Love of God, follows us all the days of our lives.

Jesus said, "I am the good shepherd: the good shepherd giveth his life for the sheep" (John 10:11). The Good Shepherd tenderly leads His flock and feeds them in green pastures (Ezekiel 34:11-15). He watches over His sheep. He knows each one and cares deeply for them, risking His life to rescue them from predators. He picks them up when they fall, and cares for them when they are injured.

Are you unsure which way to go? Do you need the protection and direction of the Good Shepherd? Then call upon the Covenant Name *Jehovah Rohi* and follow Him.

JEHOVAH TSIDKENU

The foundation Name for all the other compound Covenant Names of God is *Jehovah Tsidkenu,* "The LORD, Our Righteousness." The first two times it is mentioned are both in the book of Jeremiah:

Behold, the days come, saith The LORD, that I will raise unto David a righteous Branch, and a King shall reign and prosper, and shall execute judgment and justice in the earth. In his days Judah shall be saved, and Israel shall dwell safely: and this is his name whereby he shall be called, THE LORD OUR RIGHTEOUSNESS (Jeremiah 23:5-6).

In those days shall Judah be saved, and Jerusalem shall dwell safely: and this is the name wherewith she shall be called, The LORD our righteousness (Jeremiah 33:16).

Clearly, those verses foreshadow the redemptive work Jesus came to do on our behalf. He is the Righteous Branch who brought restoration and destroyed all the works of the adversary. He became the Scapegoat (Leviticus 16:21-22), the Lamb of God (John 1:29, impaled on Calvary's Cross to restore our righteousness. We have been made the righteousness of God in Him (2 Corinthians 5:21).

Jesus committed no sin, just as we committed no righteousness. But through Jesus, Almighty God, who is always faithful to His promise, restored the Covenant of righteousness that had been cut with faithful Abraham, His Friend, 430 years before the Law was given through Moses.

In the early days of my ministry, I got into more trouble for preaching this Covenant of righteousness than for anything else I preached. When I released an album with a song entitled, "I Am the Righteousness of God in Him," there were Christian disc jockeys who refused to play it. "Who does he think he is, saying he is righteous?" they huffed.

That's not what I said! I didn't say I am righteous. I said, "I am the righteousness of God *in Christ*. Jesus has *made* me righteous with *His* righteousness. I am in Blood Covenant with Him."

Apart from that Blood Covenant, I could never be righteous. Neither could any other human being. For, as Romans 5 says:

> By one man [Adam] sin entered into the world, and death by sin; and so death passed upon all men, for that all have sinned…. (Nevertheless death reigned from Adam to Moses, even over them that had not sinned after the similitude of Adam's transgression, who is the figure of him that was to come. But not as the offence, so also is the free gift. For if through the offence of one many be dead, much more the grace of God, and the gift by grace, which is by one man, Jesus Christ, hath abounded unto many)…. That as sin hath reigned unto death, even so might grace reign through righteousness unto eternal life by Jesus Christ our LORD (verses 12, 14-15, 21).

The kingdom of God is "righteousness, peace, and joy in the Holy Ghost" (Romans 14:17). Righteousness is God's nature: "A sceptre of righteousness is the sceptre of thy kingdom" (Hebrews 1:8).

Adam was clothed with God's righteousness until the light of the glory of that righteousness went out because of his treason. Now, through the Blood of the New Covenant, God's righteousness has been restored to us. As believers, we are clothed in His righteousness. We have "put on the new man, which after God is created in righteousness and true holiness" (Ephesians 4:24).

JEHOVAH SHAMMAH

In Ezekiel's vision of the Holy City, The LORD said to him, "The city shall be *Jehovah Shammah*, 'The LORD is there'" (see Ezekiel 48:35). Although used only this one time in the First Covenant, this compound Name of God is a powerful reminder that The LORD will never leave nor forsake *any* of His Covenant people (Hebrews 13:5).

His *hesed* presence, represented by the Ark of the Covenant in the First Covenant and by the indwelling of the Holy Spirit in the Second Covenant, has always been with His people—and it always will be (Psalm 46:11). God has covenanted, in His own blood—sworn by Himself, because He could swear by no greater—that He will never leave nor forsake us.

Jesus said that the Holy Spirit, the Comforter, the Spirit of Truth, will not only be *with* us but *in* us forever (John 14:17). He also said, "Lo, I am with you always, even unto the end of the world" (Matthew 28:20).

It's easy to feel alone at times, to think we're alone, and to believe it. But nothing could be further from the truth. The character and nature of God is *Jehovah Shammah*, The LORD is there.

JEHOVAH SABAOTH

Jehovah Sabaoth is The LORD of the angelic forces (armies) of heaven and earth. He is called by that Name for the first time in 1 Samuel 1:3, which tells about a godly man (Hannah's husband, Elkanah) who "went up out of his city yearly to worship and to sacrifice unto The LORD of hosts in Shiloh."

God's role as LORD of the angelic armies is revealed in Scripture however as early as Exodus 14:14. There, Moses told the fearful Israelites who were caught between Pharaoh's approaching army and the Red Sea, "The LORD shall fight for you."

A second early reference to God as The LORD of the angelic forces is found in Joshua 5:15 where an angel appeared to Joshua before the battle of Jericho and identified himself as "the captain of The LORD's host."

Jehovah Sabaoth is the Covenant Name David used when confronting Goliath. In answer to Goliath's claim that he was going to feed David's carcass to the birds and the beasts, David said to him, "Thou comest to me with a sword, and with a spear, and with a shield: but I come to thee in the name of The LORD of hosts *[Jehovah Sabaoth]*, the God of the armies of Israel, whom thou hast defied" (1 Samuel 17:45).

This aspect of The LORD's identity is also seen in 2 Kings 6. Although the Name *Jehovah Sabaoth* is not referenced there, His presence as The LORD of the angelic forces is made known when the prophet Elisha and his servant are surrounded by the Assyrian army. Comforting his panicked servant, Elisha prayed, "LORD... open his eyes, that he may see. And The LORD opened the eyes of the young man; and he saw: and, behold, the mountain was full of horses and chariots of fire round about Elisha" (verse 17).

Additional scriptures that serve as reminders of *Jehovah Sabaoth's* promise to deliver His people include:

- Psalm 34:8: "O taste and see that The LORD is good: BLESSED is the man that trusteth in him" (verse 8).
- Psalm 91:11-12: "For he shall give his angels charge over thee, to keep thee in all thy ways. They shall bear thee up in their hands, lest thou dash thy foot against a stone."
- Malachi 3:10-11: "Bring ye all the tithes into the storehouse...And prove me now herewith, saith *The LORD of hosts,* if I will not open you the windows of heaven, and pour you out a BLESSING, that there shall not be room enough to receive it. And I will rebuke the devourer for your sakes...." *(Jehovah Sabaoth* is mentioned twenty-two times in Malachi.)
- Romans 9:28-29: "For he will finish the work, and cut it short in righteousness: because a short work will The LORD make upon the earth. And as Esaias said before, Except The LORD of Sabaoth had left us a seed, we had been as Sodoma, and been made like unto Gomorrha."
- James 5:4: "Behold, the hire of the labourers who have reaped down your fields, which is of you kept back by

fraud, crieth: and the cries of them which have reaped
are entered into the ears of The LORD of sabaoth."

Jehovah Sabaoth is not just the God of David and Joshua and
Elisha. Because of Covenant, He is *your* God and Father. His angels
surround and watch over *you*. As the writer of Hebrews says, "Are
they not all *ministering spirits* sent forth to minister for them who
shall be heirs of salvation?" (Hebrews 1:14).

THE NAME OF JESUS

Proverbs 18:10 says, "The name of The LORD is a *strong tower:*
the righteous runneth into it, and is safe." What is the Name of
The LORD? All the Covenant Names we've been studying. Those
Covenant Names of God belong not only to Israel, the natural
seed of Abraham but also to those of us who are the seed of Abraham through Faith in Christ Jesus (Romans 4:16; Galatians 3:29).

In fact, all God's Covenant Names are summed up in the Name
of Jesus. As Philippians 2:9-11 says:

God…hath highly exalted him, and given him a name which
is above every name: that at the name of Jesus every knee
should bow, of things in heaven, and things in earth, and
things under the earth; and that every tongue should confess
that Jesus Christ is LORD, to the glory of God the Father.

A person's name in the natural world can be measured by what
that person owns or how much worldly influence and power they
have. But no natural name measures up to that of Almighty God,
from whom Jesus inherited His Name. He created the entire universe. He is the ultimate power. There is none greater in any realm.
Therefore, the very mention of Jesus' Name causes principalities,
powers, rulers of the darkness and every name that is named to
tremble (Isaiah 64:2; Psalm 60:2).

What's more, the Body of Christ is called by that Name (Daniel
9:19; Ephesians 3:15).

We as born-again believers have been given the legal right to use it. In the Name of Jesus we can exercise His authority, power and dominion. His Name can do everything Jesus Himself can do (Matthew 28:18-20; Mark 16:17-20).

Jesus is our LORD. He is the King of kings, and we are the kings over which He has Lordship. Through Him we are in Blood Covenant with God and have power of attorney to use His Name as a weapon against the forces of darkness and to lay claim to THE BLESSING that belongs to us in Him. THE BLESSING is the bottom line. Both Covenants, and the power of the Name given to us, were to make it available so God's people could walk in it— BLESSED, spirit, soul, body, financially and socially, with power over all the works of the enemy.

Call upon the Name. And you shall be saved, not just *from* spending eternity apart from God but *into* a life of eternal BLESS-ING and everlasting fellowship with Him (Romans 10:13)!

COVENANT
HEALING
SCRIPTURES

COVENANT HEALING SCRIPTURES

For more than forty years, at every one of our meetings, Gloria and I have taught Healing School. For an hour, sometimes more, she would read through the Scripture, teaching believers what The WORD of God promises us...healing, wholeness, soundness, divine health. She read one after the other, shared testimonies, and expounded on the truth of The WORD of God. She did this purposely to help the people build their Faith and get ready to receive their healing. She invited people to come up to the front and testify how they were healed while she taught. And then, for as many hours as it took, she laid hands on everyone who came to receive, so they could receive healing. It was marvelous to behold the power of God healing His people.

Gloria wrote in her book *God's Prescription for Divine Health*:

There's a medicine so powerful it can cure every sickness and disease known to man. It has no dangerous side effects. It is safe even in massive doses. And when taken daily according to directions, it can prevent illness altogether and keep you in vibrant divine health.

Does that sound too good to be true? It's not. I can testify to you by the Word of God and by my own experience that such a supernatural medicine exists. Even more important, it is available to you every moment of every day.

You don't have to call your doctor to get it. You don't even have to drive to the pharmacy. All you must do is reach for your Bible, open to Proverbs 4:20-24, and follow the instructions you find there:

"My son, attend to my words, incline thine ear unto my sayings. Let them not depart from thine eyes; keep them in the midst of thine heart. For they are life unto those that find them, and health *[Hebrew: medicine]* to all their flesh. Keep thy heart with all diligence; for out of it are the issues of life. Put away from thee a froward mouth, and perverse lips put far from thee."[33]

She called those four verses the supernatural prescription for divine health. You could also call them instructions for how to receive our Covenant rights and promises, believing them, speaking them, declaring them and standing on them until they come to pass.

Do you need to be healed? Are you in covenant with God? Then you are the healed (1 Peter 2:24). Take in His WORD, believing it and receiving it, and He will do what He promised (Hebrews 10:23).

EXODUS 15:26

If thou wilt diligently hearken to the voice of The LORD thy God, and wilt do that which is right in his sight, and wilt give ear to his commandments, and keep all his statutes, I will put none of these diseases upon thee, which I have brought upon the Egyptians: for I am The LORD that healeth thee.

EXODUS 23:25-26

And ye shall serve The LORD your God, and he shall BLESS thy bread, and thy water; and I will take sickness away from the midst of thee. There shall nothing cast their young, nor be barren, in thy land: the number of thy days I will fulfil.

---

33 *God's Prescription for Divine Health,* Gloria Copeland (Fort Worth: Kenneth Copeland Publications, 1995) p. 5-7.

DEUTERONOMY 7:14-15

Thou shalt be BLESSED above all people: there shall not be male or female barren among you, or among your cattle. And The LORD will take away from thee all sickness, and will put none of the evil diseases of Egypt, which thou knowest, upon thee; but will lay them upon all them that hate thee.

DEUTERONOMY 30:19-20

I call heaven and earth to record this day against you, that I have set before you life and death, BLESSING and cursing: therefore choose life, that both thou and thy seed may live: That thou mayest love The LORD thy God, and that thou mayest obey his voice, and that thou mayest cleave unto him: for he is thy life, and the length of thy days: that thou mayest dwell in the land which The LORD sware unto thy fathers, to Abraham, to Isaac, and to Jacob, to give them.

1 KINGS 8:56

Blessed be The LORD, that hath given rest unto his people Israel, according to all that he promised: there hath not failed one word of all his good promise, which he promised by the hand of Moses his servant.

PSALM 91:9-10, 14-16

Because thou hast made The LORD, which is my refuge, even the most High, thy habitation; there shall no evil befall thee, neither shall any plague come nigh thy dwelling.

Because he hath set his love upon me, therefore will I deliver him: I will set him on high, because he hath known my name. He shall call upon me, and I will answer him: I will be with him in trouble; I will deliver him, and honour him. With long life will I satisfy him, and show him my salvation.

PSALM 103:1-5

BLESS The LORD, O my soul: and all that is within me, bless his holy name. BLESS The LORD, O my soul, and forget not all his benefits: who forgiveth all thine iniquities; who healeth all thy diseases; who redeemeth thy life from destruction; who crowneth thee with lovingkindness and tender mercies; who satisfieth thy mouth with good things; so that thy youth is renewed like the eagle's.

PSALM 107:17, 19-21

Fools because of their transgression, and because of their iniquities, are afflicted.

Then they cry unto The LORD in their trouble, and he saveth them out of their distresses. He sent his WORD, and healed them, and delivered them from their destructions. Oh that men would praise The LORD for his goodness, and for his wonderful works to the children of men!

PSALM 118:17

I shall not die, but live, and declare the works of The LORD.

PROVERBS 4:20-24

My son, attend to my words; incline thine ear unto my sayings. Let them not depart from thine eyes; keep them in the midst of thine heart. For they are life unto those that find them, and health to all their flesh. Keep thy heart with all diligence; for out of it are the issues of life. Put away from thee a froward mouth, and perverse lips put far from thee.

ISAIAH 41:10

Fear thou not; for I am with thee: be not dismayed; for I am thy God: I will strengthen thee; yea, I will help thee; yea, I will uphold thee with the right hand of my righteousness.

ISAIAH 53:4-5

Surely he hath borne our griefs, and carried our sorrows: yet we did esteem him stricken, smitten of God, and afflicted. But he was wounded for our transgressions, he was bruised for our iniquities: the chastisement of our peace was upon him; and with his stripes we are healed.

JEREMIAH 1:12

Then said The LORD unto me, Thou hast well seen: for I will hasten my WORD to perform it.

JEREMIAH 17:14

Heal me, O LORD, and I shall be healed; save me, and I shall be saved: for thou art my praise.

JEREMIAH 30:17

For I will restore health unto thee, and I will heal thee of thy wounds, saith The LORD....

JOEL 3:10

Beat your plowshares into swords and your pruninghooks into spears: let the weak say, I am strong.

NAHUM 1:9

What do ye imagine against The LORD? he will make an utter end: affliction shall not rise up the second time.

MATTHEW 8:2-3

And, behold, there came a leper and worshipped him, saying, LORD, if thou wilt, thou canst make me clean. And Jesus put forth his hand, and touched him, saying, I will; be thou clean. And immediately his leprosy was cleansed.

MATTHEW 8:16-17

When the even was come, they brought unto him many that were possessed with devils: and he cast out the spirits with his WORD, and healed all that were sick: that it might be fulfilled which was spoken by Esaias the prophet, saying, Himself took our infirmities, and bare our sicknesses.

MATTHEW 15:30-31

And great multitudes came unto him, having with them those that were lame, blind, dumb, maimed, and many others, and cast them down at Jesus' feet; and he healed them: insomuch that the multitude wondered, when they saw the dumb to speak, the maimed to be whole, the lame to walk, and the blind to see: and they glorified the God of Israel.

MATTHEW 18:18-19

Verily I say unto you, Whatsoever ye shall bind on earth shall be bound in heaven: and whatsoever ye shall loose on earth shall be loosed in heaven. Again I say unto you, That if two of you shall agree on earth as touching any thing that they shall ask, it shall be done for them of my Father which is in heaven.

MATTHEW 21:21-22

Jesus answered and said unto them, Verily I say unto you, If ye have faith, and doubt not, ye shall not only do this which is done to the fig tree, but also if ye shall say unto this mountain, Be thou removed, and be thou cast into the sea; it shall be done. And all things, whatsoever ye shall ask in prayer, believing, ye shall receive.

MARK 9:23

Jesus said unto him, If thou canst believe, all things are possible to him that believeth.

MARK 10:27

And Jesus looking upon them saith, With men it is impossible, but not with God: for with God all things are possible.

MARK 11:22-24

And Jesus answering saith unto them, Have faith in God. For verily I say unto you, That whosoever shall say unto this mountain, Be thou removed, and be thou cast into the sea; and shall not doubt in his heart, but shall believe that those things which he saith shall come to pass; he shall have whatsoever he saith. Therefore I say unto you, What things soever ye desire, when ye pray, believe that ye receive them, and ye shall have them.

MARK 16:14-18

Afterward he appeared unto the eleven as they sat at meat, and upbraided them with their unbelief and hardness of heart, because they believed not them which had seen him after he was risen. And he said unto them, Go ye into all the world, and preach the gospel to every creature. He that believeth and is baptized shall be saved; but he that believeth not shall be damned. And these signs shall follow them that believe; In my name shall they cast out devils; they shall speak with new tongues; they shall take up serpents; and if they drink any deadly thing, it shall not hurt them; they shall lay hands on the sick, and they shall recover.

LUKE 6:19

And the whole multitude sought to touch him: for there went virtue out of him, and healed them all.

LUKE 9:2

And he sent them to preach the kingdom of God, and to heal the sick.

LUKE 13:16

And ought not this woman, being a daughter of Abraham, whom satan hath bound, lo, these eighteen years, be loosed from this bond on the sabbath day?

ACTS 5:16

There came also a multitude out of the cities round about unto Jerusalem, bringing sick folks, and them which were vexed with unclean spirits: and they were healed every one.

ACTS 10:38

How God anointed Jesus of Nazareth with the Holy Ghost and with power: who went about doing good, and healing all that were oppressed of the devil; for God was with him.

ROMANS 4:16-21

Therefore it is of faith, that it might be by grace; to the end the promise might be sure to all the seed; not to that only which is of the law, but to that also which is of the faith of Abraham; who is the father of us all, (As it is written, I have made thee a father of many nations,) before him whom he believed, even God, who quickeneth the dead, and calleth those things which be not as though they were. Who against hope believed in hope, that he might become the father of many nations, according to that which was spoken, So shall thy seed be. And being not weak in faith, he considered not his own body now dead, when he was about an hundred years old, neither yet the deadness of Sarah's womb: He staggered not at the promise of God through unbelief; but was strong in faith, giving glory to God; and being fully persuaded that, what he had promised, he was able also to perform.

ROMANS 8:2, 11

For the law of the Spirit of life in Christ Jesus hath made me free from the law of sin and death.

But if the Spirit of him that raised up Jesus from the dead dwell in you, he that raised up Christ from the dead shall also quicken your mortal bodies by his Spirit that dwelleth in you.

2 CORINTHIANS 4:18

While we look not at the things which are seen, but at the things which are not seen: for the things which are seen are temporal; but the things which are not seen are eternal.

2 CORINTHIANS 10:3-5

For though we walk in the flesh, we do not war after the flesh: (For the weapons of our warfare are not carnal, but mighty through God to the pulling down of strong holds;) casting down imaginations, and every high thing that exalteth itself against the knowledge of God, and bringing into captivity every thought to the obedience of Christ.

GALATIANS 3:13-14, 29

Christ hath redeemed us from the curse of the law, being made a curse for us: for it is written, Cursed is every one that hangeth on a tree: that THE BLESSING of Abraham might come on the Gentiles through Jesus Christ; that we might receive the promise of the Spirit through faith.

And if ye be Christ's, then are ye Abraham's seed, and heirs according to the promise.

EPHESIANS 6:10-17

Finally, my brethren, be strong in The LORD, and in the power of his might. Put on the whole armour of God, that ye may be able to stand against the wiles of the devil. For we wrestle not against flesh and blood, but against principalities, against powers, against the rulers of the darkness of this world, against spiritual wickedness in high places. Wherefore take unto you the whole armour of God, that ye may be able to withstand in the evil day, and having done all, to stand. Stand therefore, having your loins girt about with truth, and having on the breastplate of righteousness; and your feet shod with the preparation of the gospel of peace; above all, taking the shield of faith, wherewith ye shall be able to quench all the fiery darts of the wicked. And take the helmet of salvation, and the sword of the Spirit, which is The WORD of God.

PHILIPPIANS 2:13
AMPLIFIED BIBLE, CLASSIC EDITION

[Not in your own strength] for it is God Who is all the while effectually at work in you [energizing and creating in you the power and desire], both to will and to work for His good pleasure and satisfaction and delight.

PHILIPPIANS 4:6-9
AMPLIFIED BIBLE, CLASSIC EDITION

Do not fret or have any anxiety about anything, but in every circumstance and in everything, by prayer and petition (definite requests), with thanksgiving, continue to make your wants known to God. And God's peace [shall be yours, that tranquil state of a soul assured of its salvation through Christ, and so fearing nothing from God and being content with its earthly lot of whatever sort that is, that peace] which transcends all understanding shall garrison and mount guard over your hearts and minds in Christ Jesus. For the rest, brethren, whatever is true, whatever is worthy of reverence and is honorable and seemly, whatever is just, whatever is pure, whatever is lovely and lovable, whatever is kind and winsome and gracious, if there is any virtue and excellence, if there is anything worthy of praise, think on and weigh and take account of these things [fix your minds on them]. Practice what you have learned and received and heard and seen in me, and model your way of living on it, and the God of peace (of untroubled, undisturbed well-being) will be with you.

2 TIMOTHY 1:7

For God hath not given us the spirit of fear; but of power, and of love, and of a sound mind.

HEBREWS 10:23

Let us hold fast the profession of our faith without wavering; (for he is faithful that promised).

HEBREWS 10:35-36

Cast not away therefore your confidence, which hath great recompence of reward. For ye have need of patience, that, after ye have done the will of God, ye might receive the promise.

HEBREWS 11:11

Through faith also Sara herself received strength to conceive seed, and was delivered of a child when she was past age, because she judged him faithful who had promised.

HEBREWS 13:8

Jesus Christ the same yesterday, and to day, and for ever.

JAMES 4:7

Submit yourselves therefore to God. Resist the devil, and he will flee from you.

JAMES 5:14-16

Is any sick among you? let him call for the elders of the church; and let them pray over him, anointing him with oil in the name of The LORD: And the prayer of faith shall save the sick, and The LORD shall raise him up; and if he have committed sins, they shall be forgiven him. Confess your faults one to another, and pray one for another, that ye may be healed. The effectual fervent prayer of a righteous man availeth much.

1 PETER 2:24

Who his own self bare our sins in his own body on the tree, that we, being dead to sins, should live unto righteousness: by whose stripes ye were healed.

1 JOHN 3:21-22

Beloved, if our heart condemn us not, then have we confidence toward God. And whatsoever we ask, we receive of him, because we keep his commandments, and do those things that are pleasing in his sight.

1 JOHN 5:14-15

And this is the confidence that we have in him, that, if we ask any thing according to his will, he heareth us: And if we know that he hear us, whatsoever we ask, we know that we have the petitions that we desired of him.

3 JOHN 2

Beloved, I wish above all things that thou mayest prosper and be in health, even as thy soul prospereth.

REVELATION 12:11

And they overcame him by the blood of the Lamb, and by The WORD of their testimony; and they loved not their lives unto the death.

COVENANT
PROSPERITY
SCRIPTURES

COVENANT
PROSPERITY
SCRIPTURES

"**B**eloved," the Apostle John began, "I wish above all things that thou mayest prosper and be in health, even as thy soul prospereth" (3 John 2). It is the perfect will of God—the Covenant perfect will of God—for you to prosper. The LORD prophesied to us in 2010 that the world was in serious trouble, and that it would grow worse—and it did. It has. But for the believer who stays in the house of Faith, there will be prosperity, and not just financially. It is the will of God that we prosper spiritually, mentally, emotionally, relationally, physically and financially. [34]

To stay in the house of Faith, we're going to have to stay in His WORD. To prosper in every area of our lives, we're going to have to stand on His Covenant promises. Are you dealing with lack? It's not from God, because there is no lack in Him. What do you need? Call on the Covenant Name of God, *Jehovah Jireh*, the God who provides.

In Philippians 4:19, through the Apostle Paul, God promises us, "But my God shall supply all your need according to his riches in glory in Christ Jesus."

That's a Covenant promise. Stand on it and the rest of the following verses and watch your Faith work. Watch God move in your life and bring you not only what you need, but His abundance.

---

34 "Everything Is Going to Be All Right," word from The LORD delivered through Kenneth Copeland, Aug. 6, 2010, Southwest Believers' Convention, © 2010 Eagle Mountain International Church Inc. aka Kenneth Copeland Ministries. All rights reserved

GENESIS 13:2
NEW KING JAMES VERSION

Abram was very rich in livestock, in silver, and in gold.

GENESIS 13:14-17

And The LORD said unto Abram, after that Lot was separated from him, Lift up now thine eyes, and look from the place where thou art northward, and southward, and eastward, and westward: For all the land which thou seest, to thee will I give it, and to thy seed for ever. And I will make thy seed as the dust of the earth: so that if a man can number the dust of the earth, then shall thy seed also be numbered. Arise, walk through the land in the length of it and in the breadth of it; for I will give it unto thee.

GENESIS 17:1-9

And when Abram was ninety years old and nine, The LORD appeared to Abram, and said unto him, I am the Almighty God; walk before me, and be thou perfect. And I will make my covenant between me and thee, and will multiply thee exceedingly. And Abram fell on his face: and God talked with him, saying, As for me, behold, my covenant is with thee, and thou shalt be a father of many nations. Neither shall thy name any more be called Abram, but thy name shall be Abraham; for a father of many nations have I made thee. And I will make thee exceeding fruitful, and I will make nations of thee, and kings shall come out of thee. And I will establish my covenant between me and thee and thy seed after thee in their generations for an everlasting covenant, to be a God unto thee, and to thy seed after thee. And I will give unto thee, and to thy seed after thee, the land wherein thou art a stranger, all the land of Canaan, for an everlasting possession; and I will be their God. And God said unto Abraham, Thou shalt keep my covenant therefore, thou, and thy seed after thee in their generations.

GENESIS 39:21-23

But The LORD was with Joseph, and showed him mercy, and gave him favour in the sight of the keeper of the prison. And the keeper of the prison committed to Joseph's hand all the prisoners that were in the prison; and whatsoever they did there, he was the doer of it. The keeper of the prison looked not to any thing that was under his hand; because The LORD was with him, and that which he did, The LORD made it to prosper.

LEVITICUS 26:3-5

If ye walk in my statutes, and keep my commandments, and do them; then I will give you rain in due season, and the land shall yield her increase, and the trees of the field shall yield their fruit. And your threshing shall reach unto the vintage, and the vintage shall reach unto the sowing time: and ye shall eat your bread to the full, and dwell in your land safely.

LEVITICUS 27:30

All the tithe of the land, whether of the seed of the land, or of the fruit of the tree, is The LORD'S: it is holy unto The LORD.

DEUTERONOMY 2:7

For The LORD thy God hath BLESSED thee in all the works of thy hand: he knoweth thy walking through this great wilderness: these forty years The LORD thy God hath been with thee; thou hast lacked nothing.

DEUTERONOMY 6:1-3

Now these are the commandments, the statutes, and the judgments, which The LORD your God commanded to teach you, that ye might do them in the land whither ye go to possess it: That thou mightest fear The LORD thy God, to keep all his statutes and his commandments, which I command thee, thou, and thy son, and thy son's son, all the days of thy life; and that thy days may be prolonged. Hear therefore, O Israel, and observe to do it; that it may be well with thee, and that ye may increase mightily, as The LORD God of thy fathers hath promised thee, in the land that floweth with milk and honey.

DEUTERONOMY 11:11-15
NEW KING JAMES VERSION

But the land which you cross over to possess is a land of hills and valleys, which drinks water from the rain of heaven, a land for which The LORD your God cares; the eyes of The LORD your God are always on it, from the beginning of the year to the very end of the year. And it shall be that if you earnestly obey My commandments which I command you today, to love The LORD your God and serve Him with all your heart and with all your soul, then I will give you the rain for your land in its season, the early rain and the latter rain, that you may gather in your grain, your new wine, and your oil. And I will send grass in your fields for your livestock, that you may eat and be filled.

DEUTERONOMY 7:13

He will love thee, and BLESS thee, and multiply thee: he will also BLESS the fruit of thy womb, and the fruit of thy land, thy corn, and thy wine, and thine oil, the increase of thy kine, and the flocks of thy sheep, in the land which he sware unto thy fathers to give thee.

DEUTERONOMY 28:1-11

And it shall come to pass, if thou shalt hearken diligently unto the voice of The LORD thy God, to observe and to do all his commandments which I command thee this day, that The LORD thy God will set thee on high above all nations of the earth: and all these BLESSINGS shall come on thee, and overtake thee, if thou shalt hearken unto the voice of The LORD thy God.

BLESSED shalt thou be in the city, and BLESSED shalt thou be in the field. BLESSED shall be the fruit of thy body, and the fruit of thy ground, and the fruit of thy cattle, the increase of thy kine, and the flocks of thy sheep. BLESSED shall be thy basket and thy store. BLESSED shalt thou be when thou comest in, and BLESSED shalt thou be when thou goest out.

The LORD shall cause thine enemies that rise up against thee to be smitten before thy face: they shall come out against thee one way, and flee before thee seven ways. The LORD shall command THE BLESSING upon thee in thy storehouses, and in all that thou settest thine hand unto; and he shall BLESS thee in the land which The LORD thy God giveth thee.

The LORD shall establish thee an holy people unto himself, as he hath sworn unto thee, if thou shalt keep the commandments of The LORD thy God, and walk in his ways. And all people of the earth shall see that thou art called by the name of The LORD; and they shall be afraid of thee. And The LORD shall make thee plenteous in goods, in the fruit of thy body, and in the fruit of thy cattle, and in the fruit of thy ground, in the land which The LORD sware unto thy fathers to give thee.

DEUTERONOMY 28:13

And The LORD shall make thee the head, and not the tail; and thou shalt be above only, and thou shalt not be beneath; if that thou hearken unto the commandments of The LORD thy God, which I command thee this day, to observe and to do them:

DEUTERONOMY 30:15-16

See, I have set before thee this day life and good, and death and evil; in that I command thee this day to love The LORD thy God, to walk in his ways, and to keep his commandments and his statutes and his judgments, that thou mayest live and multiply: and The LORD thy God shall BLESS thee in the land whither thou goest to possess it.

DEUTERONOMY 30:19-20

I call heaven and earth to record this day against you, that I have set before you life and death, BLESSING and cursing: therefore choose life, that both thou and thy seed may live: That thou mayest love The LORD thy God, and that thou mayest obey his voice, and that thou mayest cleave unto him: for he is thy life, and the length of thy days: that thou mayest dwell in the land which The LORD sware unto thy fathers, to Abraham, to Isaac, and to Jacob, to give them.

JOSHUA 1:5, 7-8
NEW KING JAMES VERSION

No man shall be able to stand before you all the days of your life; as I was with Moses, so I will be with you. I will not leave you nor forsake you.

Only be strong and very courageous, that you may observe to do according to all the law which Moses My servant commanded you; do not turn from it to the right hand or to the left, that you may prosper wherever you go. This Book of the Law shall not depart from your mouth, but you shall meditate in it day and night, that you may observe to do according to all that is written in it. For then you will make your way prosperous, and then you will have good success.

1 CHRONICLES 22:13

Then shalt thou prosper, if thou takest heed to fulfil the statutes and judgments which The LORD charged Moses with concerning Israel: be strong, and of good courage; dread not, nor be dismayed.

2 CHRONICLES 20:20

They rose early in the morning, and went forth into the wilderness of Tekoa: and as they went forth, Jehoshaphat stood and said, Hear me, O Judah, and ye inhabitants of Jerusalem; Believe in The LORD your God, so shall ye be established; believe his prophets, so shall ye prosper.

2 CHRONICLES 26:5

And [Uzziah] sought God in the days of Zechariah, who had understanding in the visions of God: and as long as he sought The LORD, God made him to prosper.

1 CHRONICLES 29:11-12

Thine, O LORD is the greatness, and the power, and the glory, and the victory, and the majesty: for all that is in the heaven and in the earth is thine; thine is the kingdom, O LORD, and thou art exalted as head above all. Both riches and honour come of thee, and thou reignest over all; and in thine hand is power and might; and in thine hand it is to make great, and to give strength unto all.

2 CHRONICLES 31:21

In every work that [Hezekiah] began in the service of the house of God, and in the law, and in the commandments, to seek his God, he did it with all his heart, and prospered.

1 KINGS 2:3

Keep the charge of The LORD thy God, to walk in his ways, to keep his statutes, and his commandments, and his judgments, and his testimonies, as it is written in the law of Moses, that thou mayest prosper in all that thou doest, and whithersoever thou turnest thyself.

JOB 36:11

If [the righteous] obey and serve [God], they shall spend their days in prosperity, and their years in pleasures.

PSALM 1:1-3

Blessed is the man that walketh not in the counsel of the ungodly, nor standeth in the way of sinners, nor sitteth in the seat of the scornful. But his delight is in the law of The LORD; and in his law doth he meditate day and night. And he shall be like a tree planted by the rivers of water, that bringeth forth his fruit in his season; his leaf also shall not wither; and whatsoever he doeth shall prosper.

PSALM 23:1

The LORD is my shepherd; I shall not want.

PSALM 34:10

The young lions do lack, and suffer hunger: but they that seek The LORD shall not want any good thing.

PSALM 35:27

Let them shout for joy, and be glad, that favour my righteous cause: yea, let them say continually, Let The LORD be magnified, which hath pleasure in the prosperity of his servant.

PSALM 37:3-11

Trust in The LORD, and do good; so shalt thou dwell in the land, and verily thou shalt be fed. Delight thyself also in The LORD: and he shall give thee the desires of thine heart. Commit thy way unto The LORD; trust also in him; and he shall bring it to pass. And he shall bring forth thy righteousness as the light, and thy judgment as the noonday.

Rest in The LORD, and wait patiently for him: fret not thyself because of him who prospereth in his way, because of the man who bringeth wicked devices to pass. Cease from anger, and forsake wrath: fret not thyself in any wise to do evil. For evildoers shall be cut off: but those that wait upon The LORD, they shall inherit the earth.

For yet a little while, and the wicked shall not be: yea, thou shalt diligently consider his place, and it shall not be. But the meek shall inherit the earth; and shall delight themselves in the abundance of peace.

PSALM 37:25-26

I have been young, and now am old; yet have I not seen the righteous forsaken, nor his seed begging bread. He is ever merciful, and lendeth; and his seed is BLESSED.

PSALM 68:19

BLESSED be The LORD, who daily loadeth us with benefits, even the God of our salvation.

PSALM 84:1-12

How amiable are thy tabernacles, O LORD of hosts! My soul longeth, yea, even fainteth for the courts of The LORD: my heart and my flesh crieth out for the living God. Yea, the sparrow hath found an house, and the swallow a nest for herself, where she may lay her young, even thine altars, O LORD of hosts, my King, and my God.

BLESSED are they that dwell in thy house: they will be still praising thee. Selah. BLESSED is the man whose strength is in thee; in whose heart are the ways of them. Who passing through the valley of Baca make it a well; the rain also filleth the pools. They go from strength to strength, every one of them in Zion appeareth before God.

O LORD God of hosts, hear my prayer: give ear, O God of Jacob. Selah. Behold, O God our shield, and look upon the face of thine anointed. For a day in thy courts is better than a thousand. I had rather be a doorkeeper in the house of my God, than to dwell in the tents of wickedness.

For The LORD God is a sun and shield: The LORD will give grace and glory: no good thing will he withhold from them that walk uprightly. O LORD of hosts, BLESSED is the man that trusteth in thee.

PSALM 85:12

Yea, The LORD shall give that which is good; and our land shall yield her increase.

PSALM 92:12-15

The righteous shall flourish like the palm tree: he shall grow like a cedar in Lebanon. Those that be planted in the house of The LORD shall flourish in the courts of our God. They shall still bring forth fruit in old age; they shall be fat and flourishing; to show that The LORD is upright: he is my rock, and there is no unrighteousness in him.

PSALM 112:1-9

Praise ye The LORD. BLESSED is the man that feareth The LORD, that delighteth greatly in his commandments. His seed shall be mighty upon earth: the generation of the upright shall be BLESSED. Wealth and riches shall be in his house: and his righteousness endureth for ever. Unto the upright there ariseth light in the darkness: he is gracious, and full of compassion, and righteous. A good man showeth favour, and lendeth: he will guide his affairs with discretion. Surely he shall not be moved for ever: the righteous shall be in everlasting remembrance. He shall not be afraid of evil tidings: his heart is fixed, trusting in The LORD. His heart is established, he shall not be afraid, until he see his desire upon his enemies. He hath dispersed, he hath given to the poor; his righteousness endureth for ever; his horn shall be exalted with honour.

PSALM 115:11-16

Ye that fear The LORD, trust in The LORD: he is their help and their shield. The LORD hath been mindful of us: he will BLESS us; he will BLESS the house of Israel; he will BLESS the house of Aaron. He will BLESS them that fear The LORD, both small and great. The LORD shall increase you more and more, you and your children. Ye are BLESSED of The LORD which made heaven and earth. The heaven, even the heavens, are The LORD'S: but the earth hath he given to the children of men.

PSALM 122:6-7
NEW KING JAMES VERSION

Pray for the peace of Jerusalem: "May they prosper who love you. Peace be within your walls, prosperity within your palaces."

PSALM 132:12-18
NEW KING JAMES VERSION

If your sons will keep My covenant and My testimony which I shall teach them, their sons also shall sit upon your throne forevermore. For The LORD has chosen Zion; He has desired it for His dwelling place: "This is My resting place forever; Here I will dwell, for I have desired it. I will abundantly BLESS her provision; I will satisfy her poor with bread. I will also clothe her priests with salvation, and her saints shall shout aloud for joy. There I will make the horn of David grow; I will prepare a lamp for My Anointed. His enemies I will clothe with shame, but upon Himself His crown shall flourish."

PSALM 145:8-9

The LORD is gracious, and full of compassion; slow to anger, and of great mercy. The LORD is good to all: and his tender mercies are over all his works.

PROVERBS 3:9-10
NEW KING JAMES VERSION

Honor The LORD with your possessions, and with the first-fruits of all your increase; so your barns will be filled with plenty, and your vats will overflow with new wine.

PROVERBS 8:17-21
NEW KING JAMES VERSION

I love those who love me, and those who seek me diligently will find me. Riches and honor are with me, enduring riches and righteousness. My fruit is better than gold, yes, than fine gold, and my revenue than choice silver. I traverse the way of righteousness, in the midst of the paths of justice, that I may cause those who love me to inherit wealth, that I may fill their treasuries.

PROVERBS 10:2-6
NEW KING JAMES VERSION

Treasures of wickedness profit nothing, but righteousness delivers from death. The LORD will not allow the righteous soul to famish, but He casts away the desire of the wicked. He who has a slack hand becomes poor, but the hand of the diligent makes rich. He who gathers in summer is a wise son; he who sleeps in harvest is a son who causes shame. BLESS-INGS are on the head of the righteous, but violence covers the mouth of the wicked.

PROVERBS 11:25
NEW KING JAMES VERSION

The generous soul will be made rich, and he who waters will also be watered himself.

PROVERBS 13:4
NEW KING JAMES VERSION

The soul of a lazy man desires, and has nothing; but the soul of the diligent shall be made rich.

PROVERBS 19:17

He that hath pity upon the poor lendeth unto The LORD; and that which he hath given will he pay him again.

PROVERBS 28:13

He that covereth his sins shall not prosper: but whoso confesseth and forsaketh them shall have mercy.

PROVERBS 28:25
NEW KING JAMES VERSION

He who is of a proud heart stirs up strife, but he who trusts in The LORD will be prospered.

PROVERBS 28:27

He that giveth unto the poor shall not lack: but he that hideth his eyes shall have many a curse.

ECCLESIASTES 5:19

Every man also to whom God hath given riches and wealth, and hath given him power to eat thereof, and to take his portion, and to rejoice in his labour; this is the gift of God.

ISAIAH 1:19

If ye be willing and obedient, ye shall eat the good of the land.

ISAIAH 58:10-11
NEW KING JAMES VERSION

If you extend your soul to the hungry and satisfy the afflicted soul, then your light shall dawn in the darkness, and your darkness shall be as the noonday. The LORD will guide you continually, and satisfy your soul in drought, and strengthen your bones; you shall be like a watered garden, and like a spring of water, whose waters do not fail.

JEREMIAH 17:7-8

BLESSED is the man who trusts in The LORD, and whose hope is The LORD. For he shall be like a tree planted by the waters, which spreads out its roots by the river, and will not fear when heat comes; but its leaf will be green, and will not be anxious in the year of drought, nor will cease from yielding fruit.

JEREMIAH 29:11

For I know the thoughts that I think toward you, saith The LORD, thoughts of peace, and not of evil, to give you an expected end.

MALACHI 3:10-12
NEW KING JAMES VERSION

"Bring all the tithes into the storehouse, that there may be food in My house, and try Me now in this," says The LORD of hosts, "if I will not open for you the windows of heaven and pour out for you such BLESSING that there will not be room enough to receive it. And I will rebuke the devourer for your sakes, so that he will not destroy the fruit of your ground, nor shall the vine fail to bear fruit for you in the field," says The LORD of hosts; "and all nations will call you BLESSED, for you will be a delightful land," says The LORD of hosts.

ACTS 14:17

He [God] left not himself without witness, in that he did good, and gave us rain from heaven, and fruitful seasons, filling our hearts with food and gladness.

ROMANS 8:32

He that spared not his own Son, but delivered him up for us all, how shall he not with him also freely give us all things?

1 CORINTHIANS 13:3
NEW KING JAMES VERSION

And though I bestow all my goods to feed the poor, and though I give my body to be burned, but have not love, it profits me nothing.

2 CORINTHIANS 9:6-7

But this I say, He which soweth sparingly shall reap also sparingly; and he which soweth bountifully shall reap also bountifully. Every man according as he purposeth in his heart, so let him give; not grudgingly, or of necessity: for God loveth a cheerful giver.

GALATIANS 6:6-10

Let him that is taught in The WORD communicate unto him that teacheth in all good things. Be not deceived; God is not mocked: for whatsoever a man soweth, that shall he also reap. For he that soweth to his flesh shall of the flesh reap corruption; but he that soweth to the Spirit shall of the Spirit reap life everlasting. And let us not be weary in well doing: for in due season we shall reap, if we faint not. As we have therefore opportunity, let us do good unto all men, especially unto them who are of the household of faith.

PHILIPPIANS 4:19

And my God shall supply all your need according to his riches in glory by Christ Jesus.

TITUS 3:8

This is a faithful saying, and these things I will that thou affirm constantly, that they which have believed in God might be careful to maintain good works. These things are good and profitable unto men.

HEBREWS 7:19-22
NEW KING JAMES VERSION

For the law made nothing perfect; on the other hand, there is the bringing in of a better hope, through which we draw near to God. And inasmuch as He was not made priest without an oath (for they have become priests without an oath, but He with an oath by Him who said to Him: "The LORD has sworn and will not relent, 'You are a priest forever according to the order of Melchizedek'"), by so much more Jesus has become a surety of a better covenant.

HEBREWS 11:6

But without faith it is impossible to please him: for he that cometh to God must believe that he is, and that he is a rewarder of them that diligently seek him.

JAMES 1:17

Every good gift and every perfect gift is from above, and cometh down from the Father of lights, with whom is no variableness, neither shadow of turning.

3 JOHN 2

Beloved, I wish above all things that thou mayest prosper and be in health, even as thy soul prospereth.

Prayer for Salvation
and Baptism in the Holy Spirit

Heavenly Father, I come to You in the Name of Jesus. Your Word says, "Whosoever shall call on the name of the Lord shall be saved" (Acts 2:21). I am calling on You. I pray and ask Jesus to come into my heart and be Lord over my life according to Romans 10:9-10: "If thou shalt confess with thy mouth the Lord Jesus, and shalt believe in thine heart that God hath raised him from the dead, thou shalt be saved. For with the heart man believeth unto righteousness; and with the mouth confession is made unto salvation." I do that now. I confess that Jesus is Lord, and I believe in my heart that God raised Him from the dead. I repent of sin. I renounce it. I renounce the devil and everything he stands for. Jesus is my Lord.

I am now reborn! I am a Christian—a child of Almighty God! I am saved! You also said in Your Word, "If ye then, being evil, know how to give good gifts unto your children: HOW MUCH MORE shall your heavenly Father give the Holy Spirit to them that ask him?" (Luke 11:13). I'm also asking You to fill me with the Holy Spirit. Holy Spirit, rise up within me as I praise God. I fully expect to speak with other tongues as You give me the utterance (Acts 2:4). In Jesus' Name. Amen!

Begin to praise God for filling you with the Holy Spirit. Speak those words and syllables you receive—not in your own language, but the language given to you by the Holy Spirit. You have to use your own voice. God will not force you to speak. Don't be concerned with how it sounds. It is a heavenly language!

Continue with the blessing God has given you and pray in the spirit every day.

You are a born-again, Spirit-filled believer. You'll never be the same!

Find a good church that boldly preaches God's Word and obeys it. Become part of a church family who will love and care for you as you love and care for them.

We need to be connected to each other. It increases our strength in God. It's God's plan for us.

Make it a habit to watch the *Believer's Voice of Victory* broadcast and VICTORY Channel™ and become a doer of the Word, who is blessed in his doing (James 1:22-25).

About the Author

Kenneth Copeland is co-founder and president of Kenneth Copeland Ministries in Fort Worth, Texas, and best-selling author of books that include *Honor—Walking in Honesty, Truth and Integrity,* and *THE BLESSING of The LORD Makes Rich and He Adds No Sorrow With It.*

Since 1967, Kenneth has been a minister of the gospel of Christ and teacher of God's Word. He is also the artist on award-winning albums such as his Grammy-nominated *Only the Redeemed, In His Presence, He Is Jehovah, Just a Closer Walk* and *Big Band Gospel.* He also co-stars as the character Wichita Slim in the children's adventure videos *The Gunslinger, Covenant Rider* and the movie *The Treasure of Eagle Mountain,* and as Daniel Lyon in the *Commander Kellie and the Superkids*TM videos *Armor of Light* and *Judgment: The Trial of Commander Kellie.* Kenneth also co-stars as a Hispanic godfather in the 2009 and 2016 movies *The Rally and The Rally 2: Breaking the Curse.*

With the help of offices and staff in the United States, Canada, England, Australia, South Africa, Ukraine and Latin America, Kenneth is fulfilling his vision to boldly preach the uncompromised Word of God from the top of the world to the bottom and all the way around the middle. His ministry reaches millions of people worldwide through daily and Sunday TV broadcasts, magazines, teaching audios and videos, conventions and campaigns, and the World Wide Web.

Learn more about Kenneth Copeland Ministries
by visiting our website at **kcm.org**

About the Author

Pastor, author, Bible college professor, radio and television personality, Greg Stephens holds a Doctor of Ministry in Theology degree and is known for his extensive knowledge of Jewish culture and God's covenants with His people. He is a certified expert in biblical Hebrew, and has hosted many groups traveling to Israel.

Greg is a U.S. Air Force veteran of Operations Desert Shield and Desert Storm and was a first responder to the Oklahoma City bombing in 1995, for which he received numerous awards for his meritorious service. He has also been a television producer and director, working on a variety of television programs, and has won four Telly Awards for outstanding broadcasting and journalistic achievement.

A graduate of Rhema Bible Training College in Tulsa, Oklahoma, Greg later became a teacher there and traveled with Kenneth E. Hagin for many years before pastoring his own church in La Mesa, California. He is a third-generation pastor who is passionate about helping reveal the living Jesus to wounded and hurting people. He is currently an instructor at Kenneth Copeland Bible College in Fort Worth, Texas; a host of Victory Channel's *VICTORY News* program; and is a regular guest on the *Believer's Voice of Victory* broadcast with Kenneth Copeland.

Greg and Michelle Stephens live in the Fort Worth area and are the parents of three adult children: Madison, Matthew and Mitchell.

We're Here for You!®

Your growth in God's WORD and victory in Jesus are at the very center of our hearts. In every way God has equipped us, we will help you deal with the issues facing you, so you can be the **victorious overcomer** He has planned for you to be.

The mission of Kenneth Copeland Ministries is about all of us growing and going together. Our prayer is that you will take full advantage of all The LORD has given us to share with you.

Wherever you are in the world, you can watch the *Believer's Voice of Victory* broadcast on television (check your local listings), kcm.org and digital streaming devices like Roku®. You can also watch the broadcast as well as programs from dozens of ministers you can trust on our 24/7 faith network—Victory Channel™. Visit govictory.com for show listings and all the ways to watch.

Our website, **kcm.org,** gives you access to every resource we've developed for your victory. And, you can find contact information for our international offices in Africa, Australia, Canada, Europe, Ukraine, Latin America and our headquarters in the United States.

Each office is staffed with devoted men and women, ready to serve and pray with you. You can contact the worldwide office nearest you for assistance, and you can call us for prayer at our U.S. number, +1-817-852-6000, every day of the week!

We encourage you to connect with us often and let us be part of your everyday walk of faith!

Jesus Is LORD!

Kenneth & Gloria Copeland

Kenneth and Gloria Copeland

Architectural rendering of The Ark in Canaanland, Ota, Nigeria, view A.

Architectural rendering of The Ark in Canaanland, Ota, Nigeria, view B.